Henry Elliot Malden

English Records

A Companion to the History of England

Henry Elliot Malden

English Records
A Companion to the History of England

ISBN/EAN: 9783337176808

Printed in Europe, USA, Canada, Australia, Japan

Cover: Foto ©ninafisch / pixelio.de

More available books at **www.hansebooks.com**

ENGLISH RECORDS

A COMPANION TO
THE HISTORY OF ENGLAND

BY

HENRY ELLIOT MALDEN

Methuen & Co.
36 ESSEX STREET, LONDON, W.C.
1894

PREFACE

THIS hand-book is intended to furnish the necessary basis of facts for those who are hearing historical lectures, or reading history apart from a teacher. It aims also at concentrating information upon dates, genealogies, historical geography, officials, wars, and constitutional documents, which is usually only to be found scattered in different volumes. References will be found to the places where acts and documents are to be seen in print, and references are also given to general histories and to special works, useful at various periods and for various subjects. Mention is also made of the small histories which deal with the several reigns. No attempt has been made to give a complete list of such books. Little reference has been made to the original narrative authorities for the earlier half of the history. The students who may use such a book as this do not all of them understand Anglo-Saxon, old French, nor Mediæval Latin. Such as do, and can avail themselves of the authorities, will find an excellent guide in *The Introduction to English History*, by Dr. Gardiner and Mr. Bass Mullinger.

No one can be more conscious than the author of the imperfections of such a work as this, and it is impossible to hope that no inaccuracies have crept into it. He trusts that they are neither numerous nor important. "'Tis not so deep as a well, nor so wide as a church door; but 'tis enough, 'twill serve."

Matters before the Norman Conquest are arranged under subjects. Subsequently they are arranged reign by reign, except when, as in the Reformation and some other times, the interest makes some departure from this plan advisable.

HENRY ELLIOT MALDEN.

Kitlands, Surrey, 1894.

CONTENTS

	PAGE
PREFACE	iii
BRITAIN BEFORE THE ENGLISH	1
AUTHORS	2
LOW GERMAN, OR ENGLISH, ATTACKS AND SETTLEMENTS IN BRITAIN	3
THE ENGLISH KINGDOMS	5
THE BRETWALDAS	7
THE WELSH KINGDOMS, ETC.	7
THE SCANDINAVIAN KINGDOMS IN BRITAIN	9
EARLY ENGLISH DIOCESES	11
DECISIVE BATTLES OF THE PERIOD BEFORE HASTINGS	13
ARCHBISHOPS OF CANTERBURY A.D. 597–1070	15
THE WITENAGEMOT	16
LOCAL GOVERNMENT AND AUTHORITIES ON IT	17
GENEALOGIES: *a.* WEST SAXON LINE OF KINGS	19
b. CONNEXION OF THE HOUSES OF ENGLAND, SCOTLAND, NORMANDY, FLANDERS, ORKNEY, ETC. ETC.	20
c. CONNEXION OF THE HOUSES OF DENMARK, GODWINE, BOULOGNE	21
d. ENGLISH KINGS AND EARLS IN BERNICIA; SCANDINAVIAN KINGS IN ENGLAND	22
ACTS AND DOCUMENTS BEFORE THE CONQUEST	24
AUTHORS	24

WILLIAM I.—
    Dominions. Wars. Officials. Government. Great Earldoms.
    Acts and Documents. Authors 25

Contents

WILLIAM II.—
Dominions. Wars. Officials. Acts and Documents. Authors — 28

HENRY I.—
Dominions. Wars. Officials. Acts and Documents. Authors — 29

STEPHEN—
Dominions. Wars. Officials. Acts and Documents. Authors — 31

HENRY II.—
Dominions. Wars. Officials. Henry the Young King. Acts and Documents. Authors — 33

RICHARD I.—
Dominions. Wars. Officials. Acts and Documents. Authors — 37

JOHN—
Dominions. Wars. Officials. Acts and Documents. Authors — 39

HENRY III.—
Dominions. Wars. Officials. Acts and Documents. Authors. The Baronage — 43

EDWARD I.—
Dominions. Wars. Officials. Acts and Documents. Cinque Ports. Parliament. Scotland, Ireland. Authors — 50

EDWARD II.—
Dominions. Wars. Officials. Acts and Documents. Authors — 59

EDWARD III.—
Dominions. Wars. Officials. Acts and Documents. Black Death and Lollards. The Baronage under Edward III. Authors — 61

RICHARD II.—
Dominions. Wars. Officials. Acts and Documents. Authors — 68

HENRY IV.—
Dominions. Wars. Officials. Acts and Documents. Authors. Genealogy of the House of Lancaster from Henry III. to Henry IV. — 71

HENRY V.—
Dominions. Wars. Officials. Acts and Documents. Authors — 74

HENRY VI.—
Dominions. Wars: Parties in Wars of the Roses. Genealogy: The Great Yorkist Family Connexion. Officials. Acts and Documents. Authors — 77

Contents   vii

EDWARD IV.—   PAGE
   Dominions. Wars. Officials. Acts and Documents. Authors   85
EDWARD V.—
   Officials 88
RICHARD III.—
   Dominions. Wars. Officials. Acts and Documents. Authors.
   Genealogy: Descendants of Richard Duke of York; Union of
   Spain, Burgundy, and Austria; Descendants of Henry VII. .   88
HENRY VII.—
   Dominions. Wars. Officials. Acts and Documents. Authors   92
HENRY VIII. (Part I.)—
   Dominions, Wars, and Officials for all the reign. Acts and
   Documents to 1529. Authors to 1529 96
HENRY VIII. (Part II.)—
   The Reformation. Parliaments of Henry VII. and Henry VIII.
   Acts and Documents, 1528-1546. The Will of Henry VIII.
   Authors 101
EDWARD VI.—
   Dominions. Wars. Officials. Acts and Documents. Will of
   Edward VI. Authors 109
MARY—
   Dominions. Wars. Officials. Acts and Documents. The
   Marian Persecution. Acts and Documents of 1558-1563.
   Changes in the Episcopate from Henry VIII. to Elizabeth.
   Authors 112
ELIZABETH—
   Dominions. Wars. Officials. Acts and Documents. Authors 120
JAMES I.—
   Dominions. Wars. Officials. Acts and Documents. The
   Gunpowder Plot. Authors 127
CHARLES I.—
   Dominions. Wars. The Civil Wars: Division of Parties in;
   Campaigns of. Officials. Acts and Documents. Authors . 132
COMMONWEALTH—
   Dominions. Wars. Officials. Acts and Documents . . 151
THE PROTECTORATE—
   Dominions. Wars. Officials. Parliaments of the Protectorate.
   Acts and Documents. Steps in the Restoration. Authors, on
   the Commonwealth and Protectorate. Genealogy of the House
   of Cromwell, &c. 153

Contents

CHARLES II.—
Dominions. Wars. Officials. Acts and Documents. Authors ... 161

JAMES II.—
Dominions. Wars. Officials. Acts and Documents. Authors. Genealogy of the House of Orange ... 169

WILLIAM III.—
Dominions. Wars. Officials. Acts and Documents. The Church and the Non-jurors. The Standing Army. Authors ... 172

ANNE—
Dominions. Wars. Ministers. Acts and Documents. Authors. Genealogy of the House of Hanover up to George II. ... 179

GEORGE I.—
Dominions. Wars. The '15. Ministers. Acts and Documents. Authors ... 187

GEORGE II.—
Dominions. Wars to 1748. The '45. Wars till 1762. The East Indian Wars. Ministers. Acts and Documents. Authors ... 192

GEORGE III.—
Dominions. Wars: Of American Independence; in India up to 1783; the French Revolutionary War; the Napoleonic War; the Peninsular War; the War in Flanders; the Second American War; in India. Administrations. Lords Lieutenant in Ireland. Governors General in India. Acts and Documents. Authors ... 201

POSSESSIONS ACQUIRED SINCE 1820 UP TO 1894 ... 236

POPULATION OF ENGLAND UP TO 1891 ... 237

PUBLIC REVENUE ... 238

NATIONAL DEBT UP TO 1892 ... 239

HISTORICAL GEOGRAPHY ... 239

ENGLISH RECORDS

BRITAIN BEFORE THE ENGLISH

WITHOUT entering upon the question as to how far the original British population was supplanted by the English conquerors, it may be taken for certain that the political and social history of England begins with the advent of the Low German tribes in the 5th century A.D. and subsequently.

Questions of the race, foreign communications, and material works of the Britons, belong rather to archæology than to history.

The Romans from A.D. 43 onwards reduced Britain to the state of a Roman province, till the Emperor Honorius abandoned the island in A.D. 410.

In the reign of Severus, A.D. 197, Roman Britain was divided into two districts—*Britannia Superior* and *Inferior*—each under a *Praeses*, with their respective capitals at *Eboracum* (York) and *Londinium*, afterwards *Augusta* (London). Under Diocletian the political divisions were *Maxima Caesariensis* and *Valentia*, under *Consulares*; *Britannia Prima*, *Britannia Secunda*, and *Flavia Caesariensis*, under *Praesides*; the whole being under the *Vicarius Britanniae*, who resided at York, the political capital, though London was probably the chief commercial town.

It is not certainly known to what parts of the country these provinces corresponded, except that Valentia was the district north of the wall of Hadrian and Severus, which ran between the Tyne and Solway, and south of the wall of Agricola and Lollius, between the Forth and Clyde, a district held only intermittently by the Romans. The name was given after the expedition of Theodosius, A.D. 368. The coast from the Wash to the Isle of Wight was specially administered, from the 3rd century onwards, under the name of the Saxon Shore—*Litus Saxonicum*—as a military frontier against the barbarians coming by sea. The Count of the Saxon Shore had a similar district and rule on the opposite side of the Channel. Under the Romans, probably in the century before Julius Caesar's invasion, and in the time from Edward the Confessor to John, the Channel was rather a connexion than a barrier between Britain and Gaul.

AUTHORS

On the Roman invasions and conquest of Britain the original narrative of Caesar, and Tacitus' account of the revolt of the Iceni and of the campaigns of Agricola, will be accessible to some in translations if not in the originals. Dean Merivale (*Romans under the Empire*, vols. i. and vi.) gives a good account of these events and of the conquest under Aulus Plautius.

Guest, *Origines Celticae*, deals in the form of essays with several interesting questions of early history—from the Belgic invasions before Julius Caesar down to the English conquests. Elton, *Origins of Early English History*, treats the earliest history in a more connected form.

Wright, *The Celt, the Roman, and the Saxon*, may be followed for an account of the material remains of British and Roman civilization.

Camden's *Britannia*, and Horsley's *Britannia Romana*, written under James I. and George II. respectively, are to some extent superseded by the discovery of coins and inscriptions since their date, but are great mines of information.

Mommsen, *Provinces of the Roman Empire*, has a not very satisfactory chapter on Britain.

All the authentic early information has been collected in the *Monumenta Historica Britannica*, ed. Petrie and Sharpe, which contains all the authorities down to the Norman Conquest.

There is no first-rate small history upon the earliest period. The first four chapters of Freeman's *Old English History* make an excellent summary for young readers.

Mr. York Powell's *English History down to 1509* is as good as any on a small scale—superior perhaps to Dr. Gardiner's *Students' History* in the earlier centuries; and more correct, though less picturesque, than Green's *Short History*.

LOW GERMAN, OR ENGLISH, ATTACKS AND SETTLEMENTS IN BRITAIN

A.D. 286. Franks and Saxons are before this date infesting the Channel and attacking the shores of Britain and Gaul.

363. Saxons harass Britain.

368. Theodosius delivers Britain from the Barbarians.

387. Maximus withdraws many soldiers from Britain to Gaul, who never return.

396. Stilicho the Roman general gives temporary help to Britain.

406. The Vandals, Suevi and Alani, "become formidable even to the armies in Britain" (*Zosimus*), who appoint emperors of their own.

409. The Britons defend themselves from the Barbarians.

410. The Emperor Honorius bids the Britons look to their own defence in future.

A.D. 418. The Roman Officials and upper classes finally abandon Britain.
430. Saxons fighting in Britain.
449. Landing of Hengist and Horsa in Kent.
455. Hengist and Æsc become kings of the Kentishmen.
477. Landing of Ælla and Cissa in Sussex.
491. Ælla called king of the South Saxons.
495. Landing of Cerdic and Cynric in Hampshire.
519. Cerdic and Cynric called kings of the West Saxons.
526. Æscwine first king of the East Saxons.
547. Ida first king of the Northumbrians in Bernicia.
560. Ælla first king of the Northumbrians in Deira.
571. Uffa first king of the East Angles.
584. Crida first king of the Mercians.

In these five latter kingdoms, to judge from what is told us of the southern kingdoms, settlements and conquests probably preceded the assumption of the title of king by a victorious leader (*alderman* or *heretoga*.)

Other accounts antedate the arrival of Hengist and Horsa by twenty years, and all the earlier dates of the conquest cannot of course be certainly accepted as accurate.

The student should observe the long space of time during which Britain had been exposed to piratical attack, before the era of Low German conquest and settlement began. It is probable that much of the coast outside the fortified towns had become depopulated, explaining its subsequent pure Teutonic character. Teutonic conquest, moreover, extended to both shores of the Channel, cutting the communications between the rest of Britain and the Roman world.

EARLY ENGLAND

THE ENGLISH KINGDOMS

Kent, including the modern county, perhaps sometimes divided into kingdoms of East and West Kent. Before the defeat of Ethelbert at Wibbandune, A.D. 568, by Ceawlin and the West Saxons, Kent included part of Surrey with an overlordship over the East and Middle Saxons, including London.

The South Saxons, including only the coast districts of the modern county of Sussex, from Chichester harbour to the great inlet of the sea where Romney marsh now is, reaching inland a few miles only. The centre of the county was filled with a nearly uninhabited forest, the Andredes Lea, which extended into southern Surrey and into much of Kent.

The West Saxons, including Hampshire, Berkshire, Dorsetshire, Wiltshire, Surrey (after 568), Oxfordshire, Buckinghamshire, and part of Bedfordshire (after 571), most of Gloucestershire and part of Somersetshire (after 577), some of the valley of the Severn and of the Warwickshire Avon (after 584), and gradually by successive conquests the rest of Somersetshire, Devonshire, and Cornwall. Sussex and ultimately Kent became subject to the West Saxon kings, and were ruled sometimes by under-kings appointed by them, either separately or conjointly with each other and with Surrey. The West Saxon lands north of the Thames were conquered by the Mercians, perhaps finally by Penda in 645. In 671 there was an under-king in Surrey dependent upon Mercia, and Mercian rule was for a time extended over Sussex and Kent.

East Saxons, including Essex, Middlesex, and Hertfordshire. They were early under the supremacy of Kent, afterwards of Mercia.

East Angles, divided into the subordinate peoples of the Northfolk and the Southfolk, including Norfolk and Suffolk, with part of Cambridgeshire. They retained kings of their own till the Danish invasions.

The Mercians, including many subordinate peoples, such as the Lindisfaras and Gainas, in Lincolnshire; the Magesaetas, in Herefordshire and Shropshire; the Hwiccas, in Worcestershire and Gloucestershire; the Pecsaetas, in Northern Derbyshire; the Snotingas, in Nottinghamshire; the Southumbrians, perhaps in part of the West Riding, Nottinghamshire,* and Lincolnshire; the Middle English, perhaps in Leicestershire, Warwickshire, and Northamptonshire. Mercian conquests extended south of the Thames, as mentioned above, and into South Lancashire. Under Offa they were supreme over all Southern Britain. The name Mercians, men of the *March* or boundary, must have been applied during the earlier conquests over the Welsh in Central England.

Offa, king of the Mercians, 757–796, fixed the boundaries of the Mercians and the North Welsh by Offa's dyke, which started from a point west of the estuary of the Dee, and went to a point on the Wye, some miles above Hereford, and thence the frontier ran to the mouth of the Wye. This boundary did not correspond to the present border-line of the English and Welsh counties, which is a purely artificial boundary fixed in Henry the Eighth's reign.

The Northumbrians of Deira, including generally Yorkshire and Durham, though a Welsh kingdom long existed in the West Riding about Leeds; and by conquest, if not by settlement, Nottinghamshire, Chester, parts of Lancashire and

---

* Nottinghamshire was ultimately included in Northumbria, in spite of being the home of the Southumbrians, a connexion attested by its inclusion in the diocese of York. (See below.)

Westmoreland, their western *March* with the Welsh of Cumberland. Anglesea was conquered for a time by Edwin of Deira, *circa* 620, and Lincoln from the Mercians in 677 by Ecgfrith.

The Northumbrians of Bernicia, including Northumberland and the south-east of Scotland. By conquest, from 756 for a short time, Strathclyde or South-west Scotland, but not for long. In the reign of Indulf, king of Scots, 954–962, the Scots occupied Edinburgh. In the reign of Eadgar, *circa* 966, the Scots perhaps received a grant of Lothian, which was certainly separated from Bernicia in or after 1018. It is impossible, however, to fix for certain the boundaries between the Northumbrian kingdoms and the Scots, and the Welsh of Strathclyde and Cumberland.

There were in all these kingdoms at different times kings reigning jointly or in subordination to an over-king.

THE BRETWALDAS

This title, meaning either Wide Ruler or Ruler of Britain, is given by Bede to seven kings; namely, Ælla of the South Saxons, Ceawlin of Wessex, Ethelbert of Kent, Redwald of the East Angles, Edwin, Oswald, and Oswy of the Northumbrians. Later writers add Egbert of Wessex. As, however, in the time of the three earlier kings the greater part of South Britain was not yet conquered by the English, and as none of the powerful Mercian kings, of whom Offa was probably more powerful than any of the seven named, are included, the title must be looked upon as more or less a fanciful appellation.

THE WELSH KINGDOMS

The West Welsh, under many kings in Somersetshire, Devonshire, and Cornwall.

The West Saxon victory at Deorham, followed by the fall

of Cirencester, Gloucester, and Bath in 577, separated them from the Welsh west of the Severn. In 652 the West Saxon victory at Bradford-on-Avon drove them from the strip of land between Frome and Cricklade. In 658 they were driven back to the Parrett. About 700 King Ine of Wessex conquered as far as the borders of Devonshire. In 926 Ethelstan drove the Welsh from Exeter, but in Egbert's time there had been Englishmen in Devonshire. Cornwall had submitted to Egbert, and in Edward the Confessor's reign the landowners of Cornwall had English names, but in all the south-western counties a large Welsh population remained after the English conquests, and are recognised in the West Saxon laws of Ine.

The dedication of parish churches to Celtic saints in Dorsetshire, Wiltshire, and Somersetshire helps to show where the West Welsh held their own, or were conquered but not expelled by the West Saxons.

The North Welsh, under many kings, in the modern Wales and the border counties.

There were four principal districts, Gwynnedd or North Wales, Dynevor or South Wales, Powys or the border-land, and Gwent or Monmouthshire. These were seldom united. Their kings submitted to Offa of Mercia, to Egbert and his successors. They were cut off from the West Welsh by Deorham (see above), from the Welsh of Strathclyde by Ethelfrith of Deira's victory at Chester in 607.

Strathclyde, the most obscure and difficult to define of the early kingdoms, reaching at one time from the Mersey to the Clyde, partly conquered on the south by the Mercians and broken into in the centre by Deira, which included at one time the land between the Ribble and Morecambe Bay. Danes or Norwegians conquered Cumberland, and in 945 Edmund granted it to the King of Scots to be held under him. From about 970 Northern Strathclyde also became subject to the kings of the Scots, under its own princes.

The Picts. Those of Galloway were included in the political fortunes of Strathclyde, though Bede describes Whiterne, the seat of their bishopric, as in Bernicia. Probably at the time they were subject to Bernicia.

The Northern Picts, in central Scotland, vindicated their independence of Bernicia by the battle of Nectansmere, 685, when Ecgfrith of Bernicia was defeated and killed.

The Scots. The Scots "that inhabit Britain"—that is not the Irish—were defeated by Ethelfrith of Northumbria, in 603, at Daegsastan, near the present English and Scottish border. In 842 they overthrew the Picts finally and established a kingdom north of Bernicia and Strathclyde.

THE SCANDINAVIAN KINGDOMS IN BRITAIN, AND THEIR CONQUEST BY THE WEST SAXONS

The invasions of the Danes or Norsemen in the ninth century overran and overthrew many of the kingdoms described above. When Alfred had defeated the Danes in 878, the boundary established between his kingdom and the Danes started from the Thames, went up the Lea to its source, thence straight to Bedford, thence up the Ouse to Watling Street (at Old Stratford), thence along Watling Street north-westward to Chester. Alfred thus at the greatest extent of his power reigned only in Wessex, and the other kingdoms south of the Thames, and in those early West Saxon conquests north of the Thames, which had afterwards become Mercian, and in London, with the adjacent districts of the East Saxons. Guthrum the Dane, baptized under the name of Ethelstan, was king in Essex, and perhaps East Anglia, but it is unknown what Scandinavian chiefs were ruling further north, and how far Alfred's power really extended over Western Mercia. The West Welsh and North Welsh admitted his overlordship or sought his protection from the Danes of Northumbria.

The son and daughter of Alfred, Edward and Ethelflaed, reconquered the Midland and Eastern Counties.

A.D. 905. Edward overran the Danish land north of the Ouse to the Fens.
907. Ethelflaed re-fortified Chester.
910. The Danes defeated in Staffordshire.
912. Bridgenorth fortified.
913. Hertford, Witham, Tamworth, and Stafford fortified, and part of Essex re-conquered.
917. Derby taken.
918. Leicester taken, Buckingham fortified.
919. Bedford fortified.
920. Maldon fortified.
921. Towcester and Wigmore fortified. Defeat of the Danes at Towcester, and conquest of all Essex and East Anglia.
922. Stamford fortified, South Lincolnshire conquered.
923. Manchester conquered.
924. Nottingham and Derby conquered, and all the Danes submit to Edward.

It was probably after this re-conquest that the Midland shires were made by Edward or Ethelstan. The southern shires answer to old kingdoms, or to tribes (such as Wilsaetas, Sumorsaetas, &c.). The midland shires seem to be named from the fortress-capitals which Edward built.

North of the Humber Danish and Norwegian kings continued to rule, many of them with a very uncertain succession till 954, when the last was expelled from York, and earls under the West-Saxon kings replaced them. Only in Bernicia English kings and earls seem always to have continued. They submitted to Ethelstan in 926.

The Danish wars, however, left a tendency to disunion between the North and South, Mercia sometimes inclining to the one, sometimes to the other.

NORTH AND SOUTH RULED SEPARATELY

A.D. 957. The Northumbrians and Mercians chose Eadgar for their king instead of Edwy.
959. Eadgar re-unites the kingdom.
1016. Edmund rules Wessex and Cnut Mercia.
1035. Harthacnut nominal king in Wessex, and Harold in the rest of England.
1037. Harthacnut re-unites the kingdom.
1066. William, king in South-East England.
1068. Conquest of the South-West, of the North-East Midlands and Yorkshire.
1069-70. Final conquest of the North, including Bernicia, and of the North-West Midlands. England finally united under one efficient central government; the greatest result of the Norman Conquest.

EARLY ENGLISH DIOCESES

When Christianity was restored in Britain by the Roman Mission of St. Augustine and his followers, and by the preaching of the Scots and other foreign missionaries, the ecclesiastical followed the political or tribal divisions of the people.

When Bede closed his history, A.D. 731, the diocesan divisions were as follows :—

Canterbury, the metropolitan see from the consecration of Theodore, 668, including in its diocese East Kent, with portions of West Kent, of Surrey, and of Sussex.

Rochester, including most of West Kent.

London, including the East Saxons.

Dunwich, including the southern East Angles.

Elmham, including the northern East Angles.

Winchester, including the eastern part of Wessex, Hampshire, Surrey, and the Isle of Wight.

Sherborne, including the rest of Wessex.

Lichfield, including North-West Mercia.

Hereford, including the Magesaetas.

Worcester, including the Hwiccas.

Sidnacester, including the people of Lindsey (Lincolnshire).

Dorchester (on the Thames), shortly after removed to Leicester, including South-East Mercia.

Selsey, including Sussex.

York, which became an archiepiscopal see in 735, including Deira and part of the Southumbrians.

Lindisfarne, including Northern Bernicia.

Hexham, including Southern Bernicia.

Whiterne, including the Picts of Galloway.

The name of one bishop of Ripon is preserved, and at the end of the seventh century Lincolnshire was attached to his diocese for a time.

The Welsh bishoprics in West Wales, North Wales, and Strathclyde are of uncertain extent.

In 787, during the reign of Offa, his power was marked by Lichfield, the chief Mercian bishopric becoming an archbishopric.

The Danish invasions swept away the ecclesiastical organization in much of the country.

Dunwich, Hexham, Sidnacester, Whiterne, disappear as separate sees.

In London, Elmham, Lichfield, and York the succession of the bishops becomes irregular.

Leicester is shifted back to Dorchester on the Thames; Lindisfarne first to Chester-le-street and finally to Durham.

Three new sees are founded by Alfred and Edward at Ramsbury or Sonning or Wilton, for Wiltshire and Berkshire, at Wells for Somersetshire, at Crediton for Devonshire.

The Cornish bishopric is at St. Germain's or St. Petroc's.

In A.D. 1050, according to the continental practice of placing the bishop's see in a large town, Exeter was made the see for the united dioceses of Crediton and Cornwall.

In 1075, the Council of London sanctioned a similar change in other sees. Consequently in the next few years—

The see at Sherborne, which had been reunited to Ramsbury after the Norman Conquest, was moved to Old Sarum, in 1221 to the modern Salisbury.

The see at Dorchester on the Thames was moved to Lincoln.

The see at Lichfield was moved first to Chester, then to Coventry.

The see at Wells was moved to Bath.

The see at Selsey was moved to Chichester.

The see at Elmham was moved to Thetford, and then to Norwich.

The see of Ely was founded in 1108, for a diocese taken out of Lincoln.

The see of Carlisle in 1133 for the country of Cumberland, which William Rufus conquered.

The number and position of the English sees remained unaltered from the reign of Henry I. to that of Henry VIII., with the exception of the migration from Old Sarum to Salisbury.

The Welsh dioceses of St. David's, Llandaff, Bangor, and St. Asaph, did not exactly correspond to any of the fluctuating political divisions of Wales. They finally acknowledged the metropolitan authority of Canterbury in the archiepiscopate of Anselm, 1093–1109.

DECISIVE BATTLES OF THE PERIOD BEFORE THE
NORMAN CONQUEST

A.D. 568. By the victory of Wibbandune Ceawlin of Wessex prevents the further extension of Kent.

571. By the taking of Bedford, Ceawlin prevents the further extension westward of the East Saxons.

A.D. 577. By the victory of Deorham Ceawlin separates the North and West Welsh.

603. Ethelfrith of Northumbria defeats the Scots at Daegsastan, in Southern Scotland.

607. Ethelfrith defeats the Welsh at Chester and separates the North Welsh and Strathclyde Welsh.

633. Penda of Mercia and Caedwalla of Strathclyde defeat Edwin of Northumbria at Heathfield. York recovered by the Britons for one year.

635. Oswald defeats Caedwalla of Strathclyde at Heavenfield, and checks the British reaction in the North.

642. Oswald killed by Penda at Maserfield.

655. Oswi of Northumbria defeats and kills Penda of Mercia at Winwidfield (near Leeds). Christian supremacy established under the political headship of Northumbria.

685. Ecgfrith of Northumbria killed by the Picts at Nectansmere (in Scotland). End of the greatness of Northumbria, and decisive check to the English conquest beyond the Forth.

825. Egbert of Wessex defeats the Mercians at Ellandune, and wins the supremacy of Britain.

878 Alfred defeats the Danes at Ethandune in Wiltshire, and by the Peace of Wedmore consolidates one kingdom south-west of Watling Street.

937. Ethelstan defeats the Danes, Norsemen of Ireland, and the Scots, at Brunanbuhr (site uncertain, but probably Brumby in Lincolnshire), and establishes West-Saxon supremacy over all the Danish and Northumbrian kingdoms.

A.D. 1016. Edmund Ironsides defeated at Assandun (near Rochford in Essex), by Cnut, and the kingdom divided.

1066. Harold Hardrada of Norway defeated and killed by Harold, son of Godwine, at Stamford Bridge in Yorkshire, and the era of Scandinavian invasions practically closed.

1066. Harold, son of Godwine, defeated and killed by William, Duke of the Normans, at Senlac near Hastings, and England brought into close political connexion with Western Europe.*

OFFICIALS

ARCHBISHOPS OF CANTERBURY FROM AUGUSTINE TO LANFRANC

Consecrated or translated.

A.D. 597. St. Augustine.
605. Laurence.
619. Mellitus, translated from London.
624. Justus, translated from Rochester.
631. Honorius, *ob.* 653.
655. Deusdedit, *ob.* 664, the first English archbishop.
668. Theodore of Tarsus, *ob.* 690.
693. Berthwald.
731. Tatwine, *ob.* 734.

* The removal of Britain from the sphere of Northern politics into the circle of Western European nations was further helped by the defeat of the Danes in Ireland at Clontarf, by Brian Boroihme in 1014; by the break-up of Cnut's northern empire after his death; by the defeat of the Scandinavian party in Scotland; by the Northumbrians and their Scotch allies under Siward in 1054, and by Tostig and Malcolm in 1058. The last actual invasion of Southern Britain by the Scandinavians was in 1098, when Magnus III. of Norway defeated Hugh de Montgomery and the Earl of Chester in Anglesea. After his death his island dominions acknowledged the ecclesiastical supremacy of England, and a bishop of Sodor and Man was consecrated by Thomas, Archbishop of York, 1109-1114.

Consecrated or translated.

A.D. 736. Nothelm.
  741. Cuthbert, translated from Hereford.
  759. Bregowin.
  763. Lambert or Iaenbert.
  790. Ethelard, translated from Winchester.
  803. Wulfred.
  829. Feologild.
  830. Ceolnoth.
  870. Ethelred, translated from Winchester, *ob.* 888.
  890. Plegmund.
  923. Ethelm, translated from Wells.
  925. Wulfhelm, translated from Wells.
  942. Odo, translated from Wilton, a Dane.
  958. Ælfsige, translated from Winchester.
  959. Dunstan, translated from London.
  988. Ethelgar, translated from Selsey.
  990. Siric, translated from Wilton.
  995. Elfric, translated from Wilton.
  1006. Ælfheah, translated from Winchester.
  1013. Living, translated from Wells.
  1020. Ethelnoth.
  1038. Eadsige.
  1050. Robert, translated from London, a Norman, left England 1052.
  1052. Stigand, translated from Winchester, deprived 1070.
  1070. Lanfranc, a Lombard, abbot of Bec, in Normandy.

THE WITENAGEMOT

A council of great men; ealdormen, bishops, king's thegns or personal followers, abbots, a queen and an abbess were known to attend; but it was never a large assembly, perhaps seldom reaching one hundred members. It gave the king counsel, and often originated measures and opposed or overruled the weaker kings. The Witan of the West-Saxons deposed king Sigeberht in 755, that of Deira, king Alchred in 774. The Witan was also the assembly in which the leading member of the royal house was nominated as king, on the death of his predecessor. But we must not conceive of it as exercising any distinctly defined constitutional powers.

THE LOCAL GOVERNMENT

There are probable indications and traces of self-government by freemen in the ancient townships, and the common agricultural interests of a township continued to be regulated by the inhabitants under a *reeve* or bailiff and other officers, sometimes popularly elected.

Later, the growth of manorial estates under a lord, with manorial courts, and with officers appointed by the lord, almost completely superseded the remains of free local government.

In the Hundred-Court the criminal business of a group of townships was transacted. The lords of the land and their stewards attended, and certain freemen, and from each township the reeve and four men, not freemen, with the parish priest.

The county business was transacted in the Shire Moot, or County Court, or Folk Moot. Here, as in the Hundred Court, the lords, their stewards, four men and the reeve from each township, and many freemen from the shire attended, perhaps once all freemen, but later on all freemen were not bound to attend the Shire Court.

The ealdorman, sheriff, and bishop presided. The first may be considered the chief officer in war, the second the chief civil officer, both appointed by the king, but sometimes with regard to hereditary pretensions.

After the beginning of the Danish dynasty the Scandinavian title earl began to supersede ealdorman, and many shires were grouped into earldoms such as Northumbria, Mercia, and

Wessex, under great earls who began to overshadow the crown.

This local government in townships, hundreds, and shires was not distinctly connected with the central government, and the Witenagemot was neither a general popular assembly nor a representative body gathered from the lesser courts.

On the social condition of the peasantry and local government during this early period and later, the student may consult Vinogradoff, *Villainage in England*, with the introductory chapter summing up the views of previous writers. The whole subject, however, one of great perplexity, may be further elucidated.

GENEALOGIES

A. The West Saxon Line from Egbert to Matilda, wife of Henry I.
B. Connexion of the houses of England, Scotland, Normandy, Orkney, &c.
C. Connexion of the houses of Denmark, Godwine, and Boulogne.
D. Danish kings in Northumbria, English kings and earls in Bernicia, &c.

A. WEST SAXON LINE

```
Ecgberht = Redburh.
   d. 836.
        |
   ┌────┴────────────────────────────────┐
(1) Osburh = Aethelwulf = Judith (2).    Athelstan, sub-king in Kent, Surrey, and Sussex.
              836-857.                   (Or son of Aethelwulf.)
   |
   ├──────────────┬─────────────┬──────────────────────────────────────┐
Aethelbald.   Aethelbyrht.   Aethelred.   Alfred = Ealswyth, dau. of Aethelred and Eadburh.
 d. 860.       d. 866.        d. 871.      d. 901.
                                             |
                                             ├────────────────────────────┬──────────────────┐
                              Aethelflaed = Aethelred,       Ecgwin = Edward = Eadgifu.   Aethelgifu.   Aethelfryth = Baldwin
Aethelwald,       Eadhelm.   "Lady of the                      d. 925.                                    of Flanders.
King in North-               Mercians."      |
umbria and                    d. 919.     Aelfwyn.
Essex 901–905.
(Or a son of Aethelred.)
                                                                |
         ┌────────────────┬──────────────┬─────────────┬──────────┬────────────┬──────────────────┬──────────────────┐
   Aethelstan.   Edmund = (1) Aelfgifu.   Edwine.   Aethelweard.   Eadgifu = Charles   Eadred.   Eadhild.   Eadgyth,   A daughter,
   d. 940.       d. 946.  (2) Aethelflaed. d. 933.     d. 924.              the Simple. d. 955 s.p. m. Hugh   m. Otto I.,   m. Sihtric,
                                                                                                   of Paris.  the Emperor.  King in
                                                                                                                            Northumbria.
                    |
                    ├────────┐
                 ? 1.     Eadwig.
                          d. 958.
                               |
                          ? 2.
                          Eadgar = Aelfthryth (2) = Wulfthryth (a nun)
                          d. 975.       |                  |
                                        |             St. Eadgyth.
                               ┌────────┴────────┬───────────────────────┐
                            Edward.        (1) Aethelflaed = Aethelred the Unready = Emma (2).   Aelfgifu,   m. Lewis
                            d. 979 s.p.                              d. 1016.                              of Arles.
                                        |                                    |
              ┌─────────────┬───────────┴─────┬──────────────┐               ├──────────────────┬──────────────────┐
          Eadwig,     Eadgyth,        Aelfgifu,    Ulfhild,       Alfred.          Edward.       Edmund.   Godgifu = Eustace
          d. 1017.    m. Edric Streona. m. Uchtred.  m. Ulfcytel.   o.s.p. 1036.   o.s.p. 1066.    o.s.p. 971.  (1) Drogo =   of Boulogne (2).
                                                                                                                of Mantes.
          Edmund = Eadgyth.
           d. 1016.                           Edmund = dau. of Stephen of Hungary.    Edward = Agatha.        Count Ralf.
                                                                                       d. 1057.                d. 1057.
                                                               |
                                                  ┌────────────┼────────────────┐
                                               Eadgar.   Margaret = Malcolm, King of Scots.   Christina.
                                                                |
                                                         Eadgyth = Henry I.
```

19

B. CONNEXION OF THE HOUSES OF ENGLAND, SCOTLAND, NORMANDY, ORKNEY, ETC.

[Kings and Dukes of Normandy printed in heavier type.]

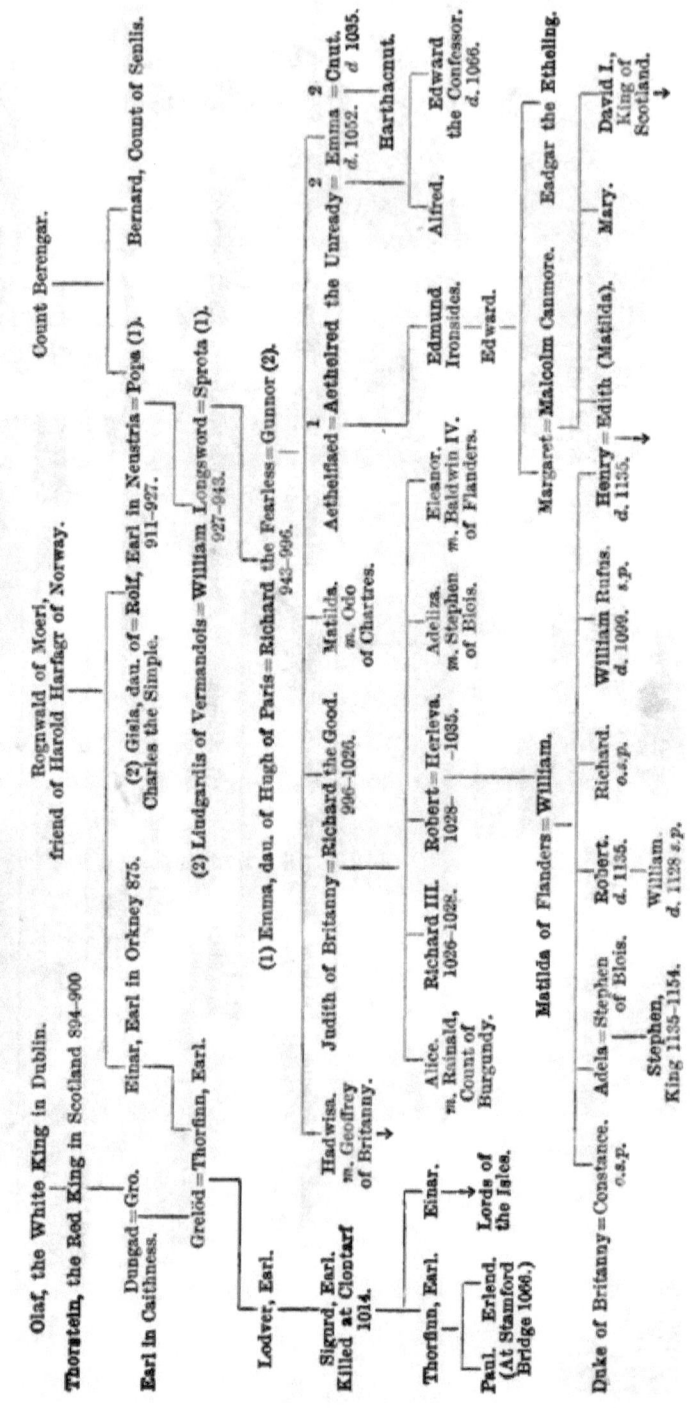

C. CONNEXION OF THE HOUSES OF DENMARK, GODWINE, AND BOULOGNE

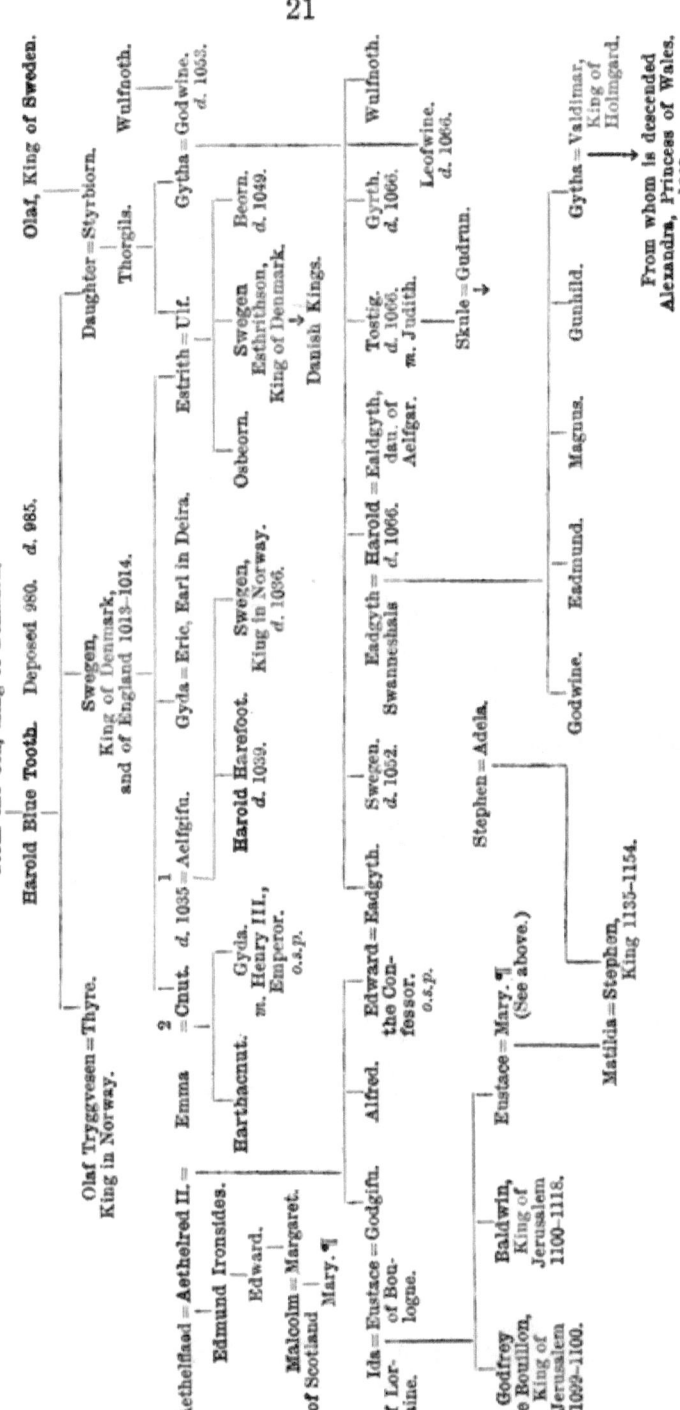

D. ENGLISH KINGS IN BERNICIA

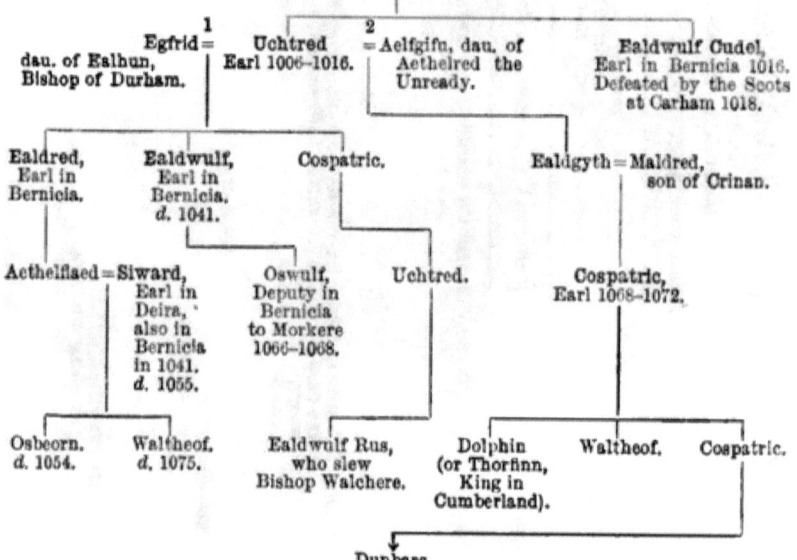

DANISH AND NORWEGIAN KINGS IN DEIRA

Halfdane and Ecwils. *d.* 911.

- Njal or Nigel. *d.* 921.
- Sihtric = 925 dau. of Edward the Elder. King 921–926.
  - Olaf, 941. Baptized 943. Expelled 944.
    - Ragnald. "Got York" 923. Expelled 944.
  - Guthfrith. Expelled 927.
    - Olaf, 939–941 *d.*

Harald the Fair-haired of Norway, King 872.

Eric Blood Axe, King in Deira 948. Expelled 950. Restored 952. Expelled 954. Killed at Stanemore.

? Olaf Cuaran, King in York 949–952, unless he is the same as Olaf, son of Sihtric.

DANISH EARLS IN DEIRA

Thored (father-in-law to Aethelred the Unready), Earl in Deira 979–993.

Aelfhelm, in Deira 993–1006. (? English).

Eric = Gyda, sister to Cnut. Earl in Deira 1016–1023. Banished.

DANISH KINGS IN EAST ANGLIA AND ESSEX

Guthrum (Aethelstan), 878–890.

Eohric, 890–905. Killed in battle.

Guthrum, 905–921. Killed in battle, and the kingdom incorporated with England.

ACTS AND DOCUMENTS

The laws of the Early English, West Saxon, Danish, and Norman kings; the Peace of Wedmore between Alfred and Guthrum; the agreement between Edward, son of Alfred, and Guthrum; ecclesiastical documents, &c.—are to be found in Thorpe's *Ancient Laws and Institutes of England*. Some of the more important of the same are given, with introductory remarks, in Bishop Stubbs' *Select Charters*, and are further illustrated in the same author's *Constitutional History*.

AUTHORS

For the general history, up to the end of William the Conqueror's reign, Freeman's *Norman Conquest* is the safest modern authority; though the author makes perhaps an exaggerated estimate of the efficiency of the early English government, and of its permanent results on later constitutional developments.

Green's *Making of England*, and *History of the English People*, may be read for picturesque narrative.

For young readers Freeman's *Old English History* is the best *résumé* of the period.

Though some of the conclusions of Bishop Stubbs and Professor Freeman are questionable, and being questioned, yet the student must follow them rather than modern writers of an earlier time; and must use such books as Kemble's *Saxons in England*, Palgrave's *History of the English Commonwealth*, Pearson's *History of England in the Early and the Middle Ages*, Wright's *The Celt, the Roman, and the Saxon*, Lappenberg's *History of the Anglo-Saxons*, cautiously, in the light of what he has learned from Stubbs and Freeman. Thierry's *Norman Conquest* should not be used at all, and Sharon Turner's *History of the Anglo-Saxons* is out of date.

Such a caution extends of course more strongly to the use of compilations and small histories based upon any except the two great authorities.

WILLIAM I. 1066-1087

Married Matilda of Flanders.

DOMINIONS

Before the conquest of England William added Ponthieu, 1056, and Maine, 1063, to the Duchy of Normandy, which also included a titular supremacy over Britanny. In 1066 he was acknowledged and crowned king at Westminster. In the spring of 1068 he took Exeter, and really conquered the South-West; in the summer of the same year he first conquered the North, except Bernicia. In 1069-70 he again conquered the North, including Bernicia, and by the conquest of Chester conquered the North-West Midlands. In 1072 he received the nominal submission of Scotland; in 1081 he invaded Wales, and received homage. Most of modern Cumberland and Westmoreland were not in his dominions, but were ruled by a Scandinavian chief. His county of Cheshire included the lower parts of Flint and Denbigh as far as the Conway; Shropshire included parts of Montgomeryshire; Herefordshire parts of Radnor and Brecknock; Gloucestershire parts of Monmouthshire.

WARS

With Anjou, 1073-74. With the Baronage and Robert, 1075-80. With France, 1087.

OFFICIALS

Archbishops.—Stigand, deprived 1070; Lanfranc.

Justiciars.—Odo Bishop of Bayeux and Earl of Kent, the King's half-brother, and William Fitz-Osbern, 1067; William de Warenne and Richard Fitz-Gilbert, 1073; Archbishop Lanfranc, Geoffrey Bishop of Coutances, and Robert of Mortain, Earl of Cornwall, the King's half-brother, 1078.

Chancellors.—Herfast, afterwards Bishop of Elmham and Thetford, 1068; Osbern, afterwards Bishop of Exeter, 1070-74; Osmund, afterwards Bishop of Salisbury, 1074-78; Maurice, afterwards Bishop of London, 1078-83; William de Beaufeu, afterwards Bishop of Thetford, 1083-85; William Giffard, afterwards Bishop of Winchester, 1086-1087.

Of these officials the Archbishop was *ex-officio* the spiritual and constitutional adviser of the king—a place which he retained, though with waning influence latterly, unless the office of Chancellor was conferred upon him, down to the Reformation. Even after that, Cranmer, Pole (Chancellor), and Laud may be said to have retained something like this position.

The Justiciar was an official created by the necessities of the Norman kings. He was Lieutenant-General to the king, whose continental dominions necessitated the appointment of some representative of the crown in England during his absence abroad, and Prime Minister, though with varying power, according to the character of the king. He was supreme administrator of law and finance under the king, and had a body of Justiciaries, who may be considered as a permanent committee of the king's vassals and servants for superintending judicial and financial business of all kinds, and who received the name of Curia Regis, or, when dealing with financial affairs, Barones Scaccarii.

The Chancellor, an ecclesiastic, was the head of the king's clerks, who formed a secretarial body to the Curia Regis and to the king.

GOVERNMENT

The Commune Concilium, or, as English writers continue to call it, the Witenagemot, consisted after the Conquest of the king's feudal tenants-in-chief—ecclesiastical and lay—thereby differing from the Norman Council, in which apparently ecclesiastics were not as a rule present. The lesser tenants-in-chief probably seldom attended, and asking the counsel and consent of the Council to their measures was a form only with the Norman kings.

The local administration of the counties, hundreds, and towns was as far as possible unaltered by the Norman kings, who discouraged the extension of the influence of the great barons. The Sheriff of the county is, however, brought more closely under the control of the central government. The organization of the central government, and its extension so as to touch the whole of the affairs in the country, is the great constitutional effect of the conquest.

GREAT EARLDOMS

Four only were created by William, on the frontiers; Chester, in the hands of Hugh Lupus; Shrewsbury, in the hands of Roger de Montgomery; Kent, in the hands of Odo, Bishop of Bayeux; and Durham, in the hands of the Bishop. Kent was suppressed by William himself, 1082; Shrewsbury by Henry I., 1102. Chester continued till it lapsed to the Crown in Henry III.'s time, in 1245, and retained its separate organization much later, returning no members to Parliament till Henry VIII.'s reign. Durham, in the hands of the bishops, returned no members to Parliament till 1675, and retained some features of its palatine jurisdiction till the present reign. By palatine earldom is meant an earldom, in which the earl, though under the king, exercised regal power. Writs ran in his name, and offences were against the peace of the earl, not of the king. Chester, for instance, had not only its own courts and judges, but its own parliament. Lancashire was created a Palatine Earldom in 1351, but, like Chester, speedily became (in 1399) an appanage of the Crown.

ACTS AND DOCUMENTS

The laws ascribed to William the Conqueror are to be found in Thorpe's *Ancient Laws and Institutes of England*, and extracts from them in Stubbs' *Select Charters*, whose *Consti-*

tutional *History* forms the best guide to that side of the Norman Conquest and its effects. His conclusions, however, should be compared with those of Gneist in the *History of the English Constitution*.

For the *Domesday* Survey the student may consult Sir H. Ellis's *Introduction to Domesday*, and the Appendices on *Domesday* in Freeman's *Norman Conquest*, vol. v.

AUTHORS

For the general history of the reign Freeman's *The Norman Conquest*, vol. iv., supersedes all others.

WILLIAM II. 1087–1100

DOMINIONS

William succeeded, according to his father's disposition, and by the general consent of people in England, to the kingdom of England, and his elder brother Robert to the Duchy of Normandy, separating England again for the time from any foreign dominion. In 1090 by conquest, and in 1091 by treaty, William acquired many places in Normandy from Robert, and in 1095 Robert mortgaged the whole Duchy to him to obtain money for the Crusade. In 1092 William conquered Cumberland, and planted colonists from Southern England in the neighbourhood of Carlisle. In 1090 he gave license to his barons to make conquests in Wales. Most of the lower and coast country of South Wales round to Cardigan Bay, the eastern frontiers, the northern coast and Anglesey, were conquered in consequence; and though the Welsh partly recovered these conquests in 1092, and subsequently, the hold of the Norman adventurers was never completely shaken off.

WARS

With the party of Robert, 1087–1090 and 1094–5. With Maine and Anjou, 1096–99.

OFFICIALS

Archbishops.— Lanfranc, d. 1089—see vacant four years. Anselm, 1093.

Justiciars.—Odo of Bayeux, 1087-1088; William de St. Carileph, Bishop of Durham, 1088; Ranulf Flambard, afterwards, in 1099, Bishop of Durham, 1094-1100.

Chancellors.—William Giffard, 1087; Robert Bloett, 1090; Waldric, 1093; William Giffard, 1094-1100.

ACTS AND DOCUMENTS

There are no constitutional acts of William's reign.

AUTHORS

Freeman's *Norman Conquest*, vol. v., and, more in detail, Freeman's *The Reign of William Rufus*, are the best authorities to follow.

Church's *Life of Anselm* will also be found useful for the important ecclesiastical side of the history, which may be generally studied, for other reigns of course also, in Milman's *Latin Christianity*.

HENRY I. 1100-1135

Married first Eadgyth, called Matilda of Scotland; secondly, Adela of Louvain.

DOMINIONS

Henry was elected king of the English at Winchester, and crowned in London with the national consent, though many of the Norman barons favoured his elder brother Robert's claims. In the same year Robert returned to Normandy from the East, and took possession of the duchy, with the exception of a few places held by King Henry's men. In 1106 Henry conquered Normandy, and afterwards called himself Duke of the Normans, though his possession of the duchy and of the county of Maine was continually disputed by his brother's partisans, his nephew William the son of Robert, the French king, and the Count of Anjou.

In 1105 Henry secured his possession of Pembrokeshire by settling some Flemings in the country.

In 1107 Gilbert de Clare conquered Cardigan.

WARS

1101-2. Henry was at war with his brother Robert, and in the latter year defeated Robert of Belesme, his leading partisan in England.

1104. Henry went to war with his brother, and in 1106 at Tenchbrai defeated and captured Robert of Normandy, Normandy being thus conquered by England.

1116-20. Henry at war with the French king and the partisans of Robert and his son in Normandy. Petty warfare went on almost continually in Normandy and in the Welsh Marches.

OFFICIALS

Archbishops.—Anselm, d. 1109—see vacant five years; Ralph d'Escures, trans. from Rochester 1114-1122; William de Corbeil, 1123.

Justiciars.—Robert Bloett, Bishop of London, 1100-1107; Roger le Poor, Bishop of Salisbury, 1107-1135.

Chancellors.—William Giffard 1100-1101; Roger le Poor 1101-1103; William Giffard 1103-1104; Waldric 1104-1107; Ranulf 1108-1123; Geoffrey Rufus 1124-1135.

ACTS AND DOCUMENTS

The Charter of Henry I., issued on his accession, and probably again during the struggle with the Norman barons who supported Robert, is printed in Thorpe, *Ancient Laws and Institutes*, vol. i., and in Stubbs, *Select Charters*.

The Laws ascribed to Henry I. are printed in the former also, but are probably a compilation of perhaps Henry the Second's reign.

The Charter to the City of London, granted probably in the latter part of the reign, is printed in Rymer's *Foedera*,* i. 11, in *Ancient Laws and Institutes*, and in *Select Charters*.

AUTHORS

The student may still follow the general history in Freeman's *Norman Conquest*, vol. v., the constitutional history in Stubbs' *Constitutional History*.

STEPHEN. 1135–1154

Married Matilda of Flanders.

DOMINIONS

Stephen was elected king in England with little difficulty, in spite of the homage done to Henry's daughter Maud before the king's death, and in spite of the claims of Stephen's own elder brother Theobald, to whom the Normans in Normandy offered the crown and duchy. David king of Scots, however, received Cumberland, that is Cumberland and probably most of Westmoreland and Furness in Lancashire, in 1136 as a fief for his son Henry, and in 1139 he occupied the present county of Northumberland also. These were practically annexed to Scotland till 1157.

In Normandy Stephen was at first acknowledged, but the Duchy was gradually conquered by the partisans of Maud between 1138 and 1145.

During a great part of the reign Maud's partisans were also in possession of much of England.

---

* Rymer's *Foedera* is a collection of treaties, alliances, capitulations, and many domestic documents, issued by English kings from A.D. 1134 to 1654. It was compiled from 1683 onwards. A *Syllabus* to the *Foedera* was published by Sir T. D. Hardy, and will be found nearly indispensable to its consultation. The references given are to the original edition of the *Foedera*, unless otherwise stated. The more complete and orderly Record Edition only extends to 1383.

WARS

The whole of England was convulsed by the great civil war of Stephen and Matilda, and the private wars accompanying it.

1138. At Northallerton, or the battle of the Standard, David of Scotland was defeated by the northern barons, and confined to his own kingdom, Northumberland and Cumberland.

1141. At Lincoln, Stephen was defeated and captured by Robert of Gloucester, natural son of Henry I., but exchanged the same year for Robert, who had himself been captured near Winchester.

OFFICIALS

Archbishops.—William de Corbeil, d. 1136—see vacant three years; Theobald 1139.

Justiciars.—Roger, Bishop of Salisbury, 1135-1139. On the arrest of Roger and his nephews by Stephen in 1139 the whole administration was thrown into disorder. One first-rate writer, Roger Hoveden, states that Henry, afterwards king, was appointed Justiciar in 1153 by the treaty of Wallingford.

Chancellors.—Roger le Poor, son of the Bishop of Salisbury, 1135-1139; Philip, 1139; Theobald, the Archbishop, acted for the Empress Maud in 1142.

ACTS AND DOCUMENTS

The Treaty of Wallingford, 1153, putting an end to the civil war and securing the present possession of Stephen and the accession after him of Henry son of the Empress Maud. Negotiated through the influence of Theobald the Archbishop and of Henry de Blois, Bishop of Winchester and Papal Legate, brother to Stephen. Printed in substance, as a charter of King Stephen's, in Rymer's *Foedera*, 1-13.

None other of any validity or importance.

AUTHORS

The same authorities may be followed as before, with *Geoffrey de Mandeville, A Study of the Anarchy*, J. Horace Round.

HENRY II. 1154–1189

Married Eleanor of Acquitaine and Poictou, divorced wife of Louis VII. of France.

DOMINIONS

By the treaty of Wallingford Henry succeeded to the kingdom of England, being already in possession of most of Normandy, Maine, and Anjou with Touraine, the latter through his father Geoffrey Count of Anjou. Died 1151. In 1157 he reclaimed Cumberland and Northumberland from the Scotch king, who, like his predecessors, acknowledged in general terms the overlordship of the English king. In Wales the hold of the Norman *Lords Marchers* on the southern part of the country was strengthened during the reign. In 1169 the same families of adventurers who had become powerful in South Wales extended their enterprises to Ireland, and in 1171 the supremacy of Henry was acknowledged by the Irish kings, but there is no charter or seal extant in which the title of Lord of Ireland (Dominus Hiberniae) borne by his son John and by his successors appears. The rule of Henry's Norman subjects in Ireland extended over the east and south of the island.

In 1174 William the Lion did full feudal homage to Henry for the kingdom of Scotland, and gave up the chief castles of the south of Scotland into Henry's hands. See Rymer's *Foedera*, i. 39.

In 1151 Henry married Eleanor, the heiress of Acquitaine and Poictou, including Guienne, Gascony, Saintogne, Angoumois, Marche, Limousin, Poictou, with some rights over Auvergne and Toulouse.

In 1156 he deprived his brother Geoffrey of some castles which he held in Anjou; in 1158 he took possession of Nantes; in 1159 he fully annexed Querci. In 1161 he obtained full possession of the Vexin, on the borders of France and

D

Normandy. In 1182 the marriage of his son Geoffrey to Constance, the heiress of Britanny, secured that important but uncertain dependency of Normandy, which Henry had already conquered when he defeated the Earl of Chester and the Bretons at Dol, 1173, during the great revolt of his sons and the feudal party against him.

WARS

The campaigns of Henry II. against the French, his rebellious vassals and his sons, were not generally marked by great pitched battles. The most important years of warfare in the reign were 1173–74, when the King of France, the sons of Henry, the King of Scots, the Counts of Flanders and Champagne, and the party of the greater feudal nobility who disliked Henry's reforming and centralizing policy, the Earls of Chester, Leicester, Norfolk, and Derby, the Bretons and the Poitevins, all combined against him, and were defeated. The French were defeated by Henry at Conches, 1173, the Earl of Chester and the Bretons at Dol, 1173, the King of Scots taken prisoner in a skirmish at Alnwick, 1174, the Earls of Leicester and Norfolk defeated at Farnham St. Genevieve, in Suffolk, by Henry's officers, with a great slaughter of their Flemish mercenaries.

The art of building defensible stone castles was probably in advance of the art of attacking such fortifications, and castles and fortified towns played a great part in warfare. The square Norman keep, like Rochester or London, and the shell keep encircling an artificial earthern mound, like Lewes, were the great types of castle in England. The exceedingly numerous castles, the 375 or the 1115, which Henry is said to have destroyed at his accession, for instance, were not all of masonry. Many were earthworks crowned with palisades, or mere moated houses. See "On Castles," Clark, *Mediæval Military Architecture in England*.

The armies of the reign of Henry II. and his sons were

largely composed of mercenaries, Brabanters and Flemings in particular.

OFFICIALS

Archbishops.—Theobald, d. 1161; Thomas Becket, 1162-1170; Richard, 1174-84; Baldwin, trans. from Worcester 1185.

Justiciars.—Robert, Earl of Leicester, 1154-1167; Richard de Lucy, 1154-1179; Ranulf Glanvil, 1180-89.

In 1170 the king removed all the sheriffs from office, and replaced them by officials of his own immediate court and surroundings; and in 1178 he in like manner cut down the numbers of the Curia (see on William I.'s reign) to five, chosen "de privata familia sua."

Chancellors.—Thomas Becket, afterwards Archbishop, 1154-1162; Ralph de Warneville, 1173-1181; Geoffrey, the king's natural son, Bishop of Lincoln, and afterwards Archbishop of York, 1181-89.

The Chancellorship was in abeyance, or in commission, from the resignation of Becket, the year of which is not quite certain, till after the defeat of the great rebellion in 1173. Ralph de Warneville resided in Normandy, and his duties in England were performed by a deputy, Walter de Coutances, afterwards Bishop of Lincoln.

Henry, the second son of Henry II., William the eldest dying as a child, was crowned king in his father's lifetime, 1170, but died in 1183. He was styled the Young King or even Henry III. He had a chancellor of his own, and exercised the functions of royalty in his father's absence.

ACTS AND DOCUMENTS

On the Constitutional side the reign of Henry II. is most important, for he succeeded in re-organizing the administration, while his dynastic schemes for a great Angevin confederacy under his family failed, through the bad conduct of his wife and sons.

The Charter of Henry II. promises the good government of

Henry I. in general terms. It is printed in Stubbs, *Select Charters*.

The Constitutions of Clarendon, 1164, attempted to bring the Church Courts immediately under the control of the King's Court, and to make ecclesiastical persons amenable to punishment from the latter, after degradation had been inflicted in the former, thereby modifying the separate jurisdiction of the royal and ecclesiastical courts, which had been the result of the action of William I. and Lanfranc, to increase the royal control over the appointment to clerical dignities, to restrain the ordination of villeins without the consent of their lords.

Printed in Stubbs, *Select Charters*, and in Littelton's *Life of Henry II.*

The Assize of Clarendon, 1166, regulated the police of the country, and provided for circuits by the king's justices, a practice which had existed under Henry I.

Printed in Stubbs, *Select Charters*.

The Assize of Northampton, 1176, is a repetition of the Assize of Clarendon of additional strictness, with clauses requiring a general oath of allegiance, and providing for the custody of castles in the hands of the king. These clauses pointing to the rebellion just suppressed, 1173–74.

Printed in Stubbs, *Select Charters*.

The Assize of Arms, 1181, is for the organisation of a national militia.

Printed in Stubbs, *Select Charters*.

The latter three are noticeable for the constant use directed of the evidence on oath of men in each district concerning offences, valuations, and so on, involving the germ of the Jury-system and training the people themselves in the business of Government.

The *Dialogus de Scaccario* is a treatise on the Exchequer, and incidentally on much of the Government, written by Richard Bishop of London, Treasurer, son of Nigel Bishop of

Ely, also Treasurer, and great nephew of Roger Bishop of Salisbury, Justiciar and Treasurer.

Printed in Stubbs, *Select Charters*, and in Madox, *History of the Exchequer*.

Glanvil, the Justiciar, wrote a Treatise on the Laws of England, an English translation of which, by Beames, was published in London, 1812.

AUTHORS

The student may still follow Freeman, *Norman Conquest*, vol. v., for an outline of the history. For the constitutional side Stubbs, *Constitutional History*. The little volume by the same author, *The Early Plantagenets*, in Longmans' *Epochs Series*, is a first-rate *compendium* of the history from Stephen to Edward II. inclusive. The essay on Thomas Becket in Freeman's *Historical Essays*, second series, and the account of his murder in Dean Stanley's *Memorials of Canterbury*, are strongly recommended.

Miss Norgate, *England under the Angevin Kings*, is trustworthy, and particularly useful for foreign affairs.

RICHARD I. 1189-1199
Married Berengaria of Navarre.

DOMINIONS

Richard succeeded to all his father's dominions, but in the first year of his reign he gave up the castles in Scotland, and released the Scotch king, William, from the precise feudal homage for his kingdom, extorted by Henry II. in return for money for the Crusade. During his crusade and captivity the French took possession of parts of his dominions, which he recovered on regaining his freedom. In 1193 he received from the Emperor Henry VI. the crown of Burgundy, that is, roughly the country from Franche Comté southward to the

Mediterranean, bounded on the west by the Saône and Rhone and on the east by the Alps. This was a nominal kingdom only, but might easily have become more real had Richard, lord of Aquitaine and overlord of Auvergne, lived to put the alliance of his nephew Otto, the Emperor-elect, the Flemish and Low Country Germans, and the Count of Champagne, into action against the French king. The family quarrels of Henry II.'s reign, the absence and captivity, and finally the premature death of Richard, destroyed the great Angevin dominion and hastened the separate development of both France and England.

WARS

Richard on his return from captivity was engaged in incessant war with the French king and rebellious vassals abroad. Decisive battles there were none, for the whole course of the war was decided in a contrary direction to that indicated for the moment by Richard's victories over the French king at Fretteval, 1194, and at the bridge of Gisors, 1198.

The warfare of the Crusades hardly belongs to English history, but Richard distinguished himself in them as a general as well as a soldier. Students may refer for this to the *Itinerarium Regis Ricardi*, attributed to Geoffrey de Vinsauf, trans. in Bohn's Series.

OFFICIALS

Archbishops.—Baldwin, d. 1190; Reginald Fitz-Joscelin, trans. from Wells, 1191; see vacant two years; Hubert Walter, trans. from Salisbury, 1193.

Justiciars.—Hugh Bishop of Durham, and William de Mandeville, Earl of Essex, 1189; Hugh Bishop of Durham, and William Longchamp, Bishop of Ely, 1190; William Longchamp alone, 1190; Walter of Coutances, Archbishop of Rouen, 1191–1193; Hubert Walter, Archbishop of Canterbury, 1194–1198; Geoffrey Fitz-Peter, Earl of Essex, 1198–1199.

Chancellors.—William Longchamp, Bishop of Ely, 1189–1197; Eustace, Bishop of Ely, 1197–1199.

Constitutionally the officials of Richard's reign are interesting as the first example of really supreme ministers, owing to the king's absence on the crusade and in captivity. Their rivalry is the first instance of ministerial struggles, and their comparatively orderly government and legal procedure are a strong testimony to the efficacy of the government established by Henry II.

ACTS AND DOCUMENTS

The constitutional monuments of the realm are interesting as shewing the continued working of this government. In 1198 one of the earliest occasions of successful opposition to a demand on the part of the king by the great council is found —Hugh, Bishop of Lincoln, refusing to furnish the king with knights for the French war to be maintained for a year at the expense of the English tenants in chief, and taking the council with him. The earliest accounts of the debate are printed in Stubbs, *Select Charters*.

AUTHORS

Stubbs, *Constitutional History*, and Miss Norgate, *England under the Angevin Kings*, may still be followed. Stubbs, *Early Plantagenets*, for a short view; Sir G. W. Cox, *The Crusades*, in Longmans' *Epochs Series*, give a brief and fairly good history of the crusades in this and other reigns.

JOHN.   1199–1216

Married (1) Hawisia, or Isabella, of Gloucester.
(2) Isabella of Angoulême.

DOMINIONS

John was received as duke in Normandy and elected king in England with peculiar solemnity, swearing to govern well. In Anjou, Maine, and Touraine his nephew Arthur was generally acknowledged, but old Queen Eleanor kept Poictou and Aquitaine steady on the whole to John, though he had personal enemies among the barons there. In 1201 the Poitevins revolted from him, aided by Hugh de Lusignan, Count de la Marche, but were defeated in 1202. In 1203 John's paternal inheritance abroad, but not Eleanor's inheritance in Poictou and Aquitaine, was declared forfeited to the French crown, owing to the death of Arthur. In 1204 Eleanor died, and Normandy, Anjou, Maine, Touraine, and most of Poictou, were conquered or submitted to the French. In 1205 all the north-eastern part of Aquitaine was lost, in 1206 Poictou and Saintogne followed, John retaining only Gascony, the half of Guienne and the Channel Islands, out of all the French possessions. In 1214 John recovered much of Poictou, and the Poitevin barons continued to acknowledge a king in France or England, but to obey neither, as they chose.

In Great Britain John extorted the customary acknowledgement of his supremacy from the Scotch king and the Welsh princes, and invading Ireland received the homage of the native chiefs. He bore the title *Dominus Hiberniae*, granted to him in his father's reign, which was assumed by all English kings after him till Henry VIII. exchanged it for *Rex Hiberniae*.

WARS

John was at once engaged in war with the supporters of his nephew and with the French king.

At Mirabeau, or Mirabel, in 1202 John defeated Hugh de la Marche, the Poitevin, Angevin, and Breton rebels, and captured Arthur.

In 1211–12 John invaded and ravaged Wales. In 1212 the French prepared to invade England, but the Earl of Salisbury burnt their fleet in the harbour of Damme in Flanders. In 1214 John fruitlessly invaded Poictou.

At Bouvines in 1214 the French defeated John's half-brother the Earl of Salisbury, his nephew the Emperor Otto, and the Count of Flanders. A decisive victory, leaving

John

John helpless in the hands of his barons for the time, and permanently establishing the supremacy of the French king in northern France. The defeat of Pedro of Aragon at Muret in 1213 by De Montfort, similarly established French supremacy in Languedoc on the borders of Gascony.

In 1215–16 John was engaged in civil war with his barons and Louis of France, whom they invited to their assistance.

OFFICIALS

Archbishops.—Hubert Walter, d. 1205; Stephen Langton, 1207–1216.

Justiciars.—Geoffrey Fitz-Peter, 1199–1213; Peter des Roches, Bishop of Winchester, 1214–1215; Hubert de Burgh, Seneschal of Poitou, afterwards Earl of Kent, 1215–1216.

Chancellors.— Hubert Walter, Archbishop, 1199–1205; Walter Grey, afterwards Bishop of Worcester and Archbishop of York, 1205–1213; Peter des Roches, Bishop of Winchester, 1213–1214; Walter Grey, 1214; Richard de Marisco, afterwards Bishop of Durham, 1214–1216.

ACTS AND DOCUMENTS

Submission of John to the Pope, Innocent III., and cession of his kingdom, an act which had the greatest consequence in the subsequent struggle between John and his barons and the French prince Louis, and in the reign of Henry III. Printed in Stubbs, *Select Charters*, and in Rymer's *Foedera*, i. 176.

The Great Charter (Magna Carta), a treaty in fact between John and the nation, with the object of restraining some special forms of tyranny of John's, and of restoring the legal and orderly government of Henry the Second's reign, with certain features modified, which clergy, barons, or people had found oppressive, and with the whole made to depend upon a joint agreement, under the sanction of the Church, and not, as in Henry's reign, upon the pleasure of the king.

The method of enforcing the observance of the Charter, the

license to twenty-five barons to make war upon the king, if remonstrances against a breach of the Charter fail, is an instance of the backwardness, as the clauses of the Charter are of the advance of the constitutional and legal spirit of the age.

The Charter of King John is printed in the original Latin in Stubbs, *Select Charters*; in English, with notes, in Sir E. Creasy, *Rise and Progress of the Constitution*; in Latin and in English, with notes, the clauses summarized and arranged according to subject-matter, in Taswell Langmead, *Constitutional History*.

The form in which it is printed at the beginning of the Statutes is as made in the ninth year of Henry III., and confirmed in the twenty-eighth year of Edward I.

AUTHORS

Stubbs, *Constitutional History*, Miss Norgate, *England under the Angevin Kings*. More briefly the summary in Freeman, *Norman Conquest*, vol. v., and in Green, *History of the English People*. This last writer is specially at home in the twelfth and thirteenth centuries. Hallam, *Middle Ages*, gives a learned and moderate review of the principal points of English and French history during this period, and down to the fifteenth century, but is generally considered to be insufficiently appreciative of Edward I., and of the favourable influence of the Church in the twelfth and thirteenth centuries.

Hook, *Lives of the Archbishops of Canterbury*, gives a useful view of an important side of the history from Stephen Langton's time to Robert of Winchelsey, *temp.* Edward I. Milman, *Latin Christianity*, gives a wider view of the same subject.

HENRY III. 1216–1272

Married Eleanor of Provence.

DOMINIONS

Henry succeeded John in so much of the kingdom of England as was not in the hands of the barons supporting Louis of France, and did homage to the Papal Legate for the kingdom of England and for Ireland. In 1217 the French withdrew, agreeing, it was said, to surrender the continental dominions which they had conquered, which was not done.

In 1224 the French took La Rochelle, completing the conquest of Poictou and its dependencies, and were proceeding to the reduction of Guienne and Gascony, but were checked by Richard the king's brother, and the Earl Marshall, and diverted to the conquest of Toulouse.

In 1230 Henry tried in vain to recover the provinces, marching from Britanny through Anjou and Poictou. In 1242 another attempt was followed by disastrous defeat and a five years' truce, by which Poictou was practically resigned. It was probably owing to the good faith and moderation of St. Louis of France, that the remaining possessions of Henry were not lost also.

In 1259 a peace was signed between Henry and the French king, by which Henry surrendered all claim to Normandy, Maine, Anjou, Touraine, and Poictou, receiving from the French an acknowledgment of his rights in the whole of Guienne and Gascony, in Limousin, Perigord, Cahors, and the part of Saintogne beyond the Charente, with an annual payment on account of the English king's rights in Agenois. This treaty was concluded when the domestic troubles of Henry rendered him quite incapable of successfully asserting any claims. (Rymer, i. 675.)

In Great Britain the customary acknowledgment of supremacy was made by the King of Scots, and the usual border contests carried on with the Welsh. The princes of North Wales, however, were taking more part in English political struggles, siding with De Montfort against Edward Earl of Chester, the king's son, and the Mortimers, and becoming more like turbulent barons on the outskirts of the country, sure to be conquered when the royal authority was generally vindicated.

WARS

The war with the Barons supporting Louis of France continued. At the Fair of Lincoln, 1217, the Earl of Pembroke won a decisive victory over the party of the French and the Barons. Hubert de Burgh defeated their fleet near Sandwich in the same year.

In 1242 Henry was nearly taken at Taillebourg in Santoigne by the French, and his troops defeated at Saintes two days later. These defeats were followed by the practical surrender of Poictou. In 1264 De Montfort and De Clare defeated Henry, his brother Richard, and his son Edward at Lewes, establishing the temporary supremacy of the baronial party. In 1265 Edward, the Mortimers, and the De Clares defeated De Montfort and the Welsh at Evesham, killing De Montfort, and restoring the royal power. The reduction of Kenilworth and Winchelsea, 1266, of Ely, 1267, and the defeat of the Earl of Derby by Edmund, the king's son at Chesterfield in 1266, concluded the war.

OFFICIALS

Archbishops.—Stephen Langton d. 1228; Richard le Grand, 1229-1231; Edmund Rich, 1234-1240; Boniface of Savoy, uncle to the queen, 1245-1270.

Justiciars.—Hubert de Burgh, Earl of Kent, 1216-1232; Stephen Segrave, 1232-1234; Hugh Bigod, 1258-1260; Hugh le Despencer, 1260, of the party of the Barons; Philip Bassett, 1261, of the party of the king. Hugh le Despencer seems to have been re-appointed as Justiciar after Lewes, but in 1265 De Montfort was Justiciar himself. He was perhaps the last to bear the style of *Justiciarius Angliae*. In 1268 Robert de Bruce was appointed *Capitalis Justiciarius ad placita coram rege tenenda*, or, as we should say, Chief Justice of the King's Bench. The great ministerial position of the Justiciar here formally ends.

Chancellors.—Richard De Marisco, Bishop of Durham, 1216–1226; Ralph Neville 1226–1244; Walter de Merton, Bishop of Rochester, 1261; Nicholas de Ely, afterwards Bishop of Winchester and Worcester, 1263; Thomas of Cantilupe, afterwards Bishop of Hereford, 1265, of the party of the barons; Walter Giffard, Bishop of Bath and Wells, afterwards Archbishop of York, 1265; Godfrey Giffard, afterwards Bishop of Worcester, 1267; Richard Middleton, 1269–1272. In the middle period of Henry's reign he ruled without the usual ministerial machinery.

In 1258 the Barons at Oxford imposed upon the king a complicated series of ministerial councils for the management of the different branches of public business, but the arrangements were not permanent, and were probably unworkable.

In 1264, after the battle of Lewes, the baronage nominated three Electors, who were on their part to nominate nine ministers, who were to advise the king and his son for some years of his reign. The three Electors were Simon de Montfort, Earl of Leicester, Gilbert de Clare, Earl of Gloucester, and Stephen Berkstead, Bishop of Chichester. Successors to the Electors were to be appointed by the king prelates and barons in Parliament; vacancies among the ministers were to be filled up by the Electors. The scheme never had time to work, but is interesting as anticipating in some respects modern ministerial government. The three Electors answer practically to the modern Premier, the nine ministers to the rest of the Cabinet.

ACTS AND DOCUMENTS

In 1216 the Charter was re-issued with alterations, especially the clause forbidding the levying of scutage or aid without consent, except the three accustomed feudal aids, was omitted. This form of the Charter is printed in Stubbs, *Select Charters*. The Charter was again re-issued with alterations in 1217, and this edition is printed also in Stubbs, *Select Charters*. The original idea of the Charter, a treaty between king and people, is lost sight of, owing to the adherence of many of the original supporters of the Charter to Louis of France, and the Charter in these issues is an act of grace on the part of those governing in the king's name, resting on an agreement with Louis of France, if on any, not on any pact with the church and barons. This especially appears in the third re-issue in 1225, which is declared by the king to be *spontanea et bona voluntate nostra* in return for the grant of a fifteenth for the war in Gascony. In 1217 a treaty was concluded for the evacuation of the country by Louis of France, including clauses for the maintenance of the provisions of the Charter and for the future restitution of the lost French provinces.

In 1243 the truce with France, entered upon after the disasters at Taillebourg and Saintes in the preceding year, was confirmed. Rymer's *Foedera*, i. 4, 16.

In 1258 the Provisions of Oxford, for the reform of the government and for the establishment of ministerial committees with that end, were made. They are printed with the documents relating to them in Stubbs, *Select Charters*.

In 1264 the award of St. Louis in the contest between the king and the barons was made. It provided for the annulling of the Provisions of Oxford, but for the keeping of the charters. It was found impossible to enforce it. It is printed in Stubbs, *Select Charters*, and in Rymer's *Foedera*, i. 776.

In 1264 the Mise of Lewes was made after the defeat of the king. The text is not preserved, but an agreement for a reform of the constitution made in Parliament is printed, as *Forma regiminis domini regis et regni*, in Stubbs, *Select Charters*, and in Rymer's *Foedera*, i. 793.

In 1266 the award of Kenilworth was made, to settle the

terms of peace and to provide for the future government. Printed in the Statutes i. 12–17, and in Stubbs, *Select Charters*.

In 1267 Statutes were passed at Marlborough with the same object. Printed in the Statutes 52, Henry III.

Throughout the reign instances occur of the summons of the knights of the shire to Parliament. The writs are, some of them, printed in Stubbs, *Select Charters*, as also the writs issued under the government of De Montfort to the cities and boroughs to send representatives to Parliament in 1265.

AUTHORS

As on the reign of John, see above; but Prothero, *Simon de Montfort*, and Blaauw, *The Barons' War*, should be consulted also.

THE BARONAGE

The greater men who had accompanied the Conqueror looked upon themselves more as his allies than as his subjects, and resenting his determination and that of his sons to rule as national sovereigns, were from the first in opposition to the Crown, trying to establish that feudal independence which triumphed for a time under Stephen. They were from the beginning weakened by a distribution of their manors about England, and were steadily depressed in the course of the next two hundred years.

In 1075 William I. began the confiscation of the lands of Norman barons, when he put down the insurrection called the Bridal of Norwich. In 1082 he seized the estates of his brother Odo. In 1088 William Rufus confiscated the estates of the nobles who supported Robert, but they were some of them restored in 1091. In 1102 Henry I. confiscated the great possessions of Robert of Belesme. In 1176 Henry II. destroyed some of the castles of the greater disaffected barons and took others into royal keeping. In 1206 the Beaumonts, Earls of Leicester, became extinct in the male line. In 1228 the Mandevilles, Earls of Essex, became extinct in the male line. In 1242 William Longue Epée, grandson of Henry II., to whose family the earldom of Salisbury had passed by marriage with the heiress of D'Evreux, died without heirs. In 1242 the De Newburghs, Earls of Warwick, became extinct in the male line. In 1243 the D'Albinis, Earls of Arundel, became extinct in the male line. In 1245 the earldom of Chester lapsed to the crown. In 1245 the Marshalls, Earls of Pembroke, became extinct. In 1260 the line of the Earls of Albemarle and Holderness became extinct.

The De Quincys, Earls of Winchester in 1207, became extinct in the male line in 1264.

In 1267 the earldom of Ferrers, Earl of Derby, was granted to Edmund, son of Henry III., in whose favour the new earldom of Lancaster was erected.

The heiress of the Beaumonts of Leicester had married the elder Simon de Montfort, who became Earl of Leicester, and after the battle of Evesham, the earldom of Leicester also was bestowed upon Edmund, son of the king.

The more important baronage existing in Henry III.'s reign, who continued to hold their earldoms or lordships later, were as follows:

De Warennes, Earls of Surrey, till 1347.

De Bohuns, Earls of Hereford, Essex, and later of Northampton, till 1371.

De Clares, Earls of Gloucester and Hertford, till 1314.

Lacys, Earls of Lincoln, till 1312.

By the marriage of Thomas, second Earl of Lancaster, with the heiress of the Lacys, this earldom was also merged in the great earldom of Lancaster.

*De Dreux, Earls of Richmond, till 1235, again from 1268 till 1330.

* The earldom of Richmond was bestowed upon the Duke of Britanny by William I. It was held by the successive husbands of Constance, was forfeited in 1235 and restored in 1268, and was held by two De Montforts after the extinction of the house of De Dreux, from 1341

Henry III.

De Valences, Earls of Pembroke, till 1323.
Bigods, Earls of Norfolk till 1305.
De Veres, Earls of Oxford, till 1703.
Beauchamps, Earls of Warwick, till 1449.
De Vescis, Lords of Alnwick, till 1297.
Fitzwalters, till 1432.
De Ros, fell into abeyance in 1508.
Mortimers, Lords of Chirk and Wigmore, Earls of March in 1327 till 1424.
Baliols, Lords of Biwell in Northumberland, and of many other lordships in England, and Lords of Galloway in Scotland, till 1363.
Bruces, Lords of Skelton and Gisburn, and Earls of Carrick in Scotland. Merged in the Scotch Royal Family.
Hastings, Lords of Abergavenny, Earls of Pembroke in 1339 till 1390.
In the reign of Edward I., and in the next century, the Fitz-Alans became Earls of Arundel from 1289–1579.
Montacutes, Earls of Salisbury, 1333–1428.
Courtenays, Earls of Devon, 1335–1556.
Staffords, Earls of Stafford, 1351–1521, and Dukes of Buckingham, 1444–1521.
Hollands, Earls of Kent, 1353–1407.
Percys, Earls of Northumberland, 1377.
Mowbrays, Earls of Nottingham, 1377, and Dukes of Norfolk, 1397–1475.
De la Poles, Earls, afterwards Dukes of Suffolk, 1385–1513.
Hollands, Earls of Huntingdon, afterwards Dukes of Exeter, 1388–1461.
Beauforts, Earls, afterwards Dukes of Somerset, 1396–1471.
Nevilles, Earls of Westmoreland, 1398–1569.
Beaufort, Earl of Dorset and Duke of Exeter, 1412–1417.

to 1345 and 1372 to 1384, when it was forfeited. The second De Montfort was restored in 1398, but died 1399, when the earldom passed first to the Earl of Westmoreland, and on his death to the royal family.

To these may be added as being almost as closely connected with English history—

Dunbars, Earls of March and Dunbar, 1068-1434.

Douglasses, Earls of Douglas, 1356-1455, and, a younger branch, Earls of Angus, 1389-1761.

The manors and castles of an earl are not by any means to be certainly found in the county from which his title is taken, though this is more generally the case the earlier the date of his title.

Two great groups of territorial distribution, however, may be noticed, the northern Barons, Mowbray, Lacy, De Vesci, De Ros, Percy, Neville, Baliol, Bruce; the Lords on the Welsh Marches, Chester, De Clare, Marshall, De Bohun, Mortimer, Hastings.

Many Barons in the North held land in England and Scotland, and it was almost accidental that Bruce, Baliol, Douglas, Dunbar, became names connected specially with Scotland, while Percy and De Vesci became English entirely.

EDWARD I. 1272-1307

Married, first, Eleanor of Castile; second, Margaret of France.

DOMINIONS

On his father's death he was acknowledged king in his absence; his regnal years are dated from four days after his father's death. In 1277 he annexed all Wales, except the district of Snowdon and Anglesea, directly to the Crown; and in 1283 he completely annexed the whole country. Wales, however, was not divided into counties, nor completely incorporated with England. Sheriffs were appointed to certain districts, but the jurisdiction of the Lords Marchers was continued in others, though the numerous royal castles erected in Wales served as a check upon their power, as well as upon the disaffection of the Welsh. In 1301 the principality of

Edward I.

Wales was granted to the king's eldest son.* In 1292 Baliol did full feudal homage to Edward for the kingdom of Scotland, in accordance with the submission made by the principal nobility in the previous year; in 1296 Baliol surrendered his throne to Edward; in 1305 regulations were made for the practical union of Scotland with England, but while the capture of Wallace in that year closed the movement for local independence, the coronation of Robert Bruce, in 1306, opened a new contest of baronial and local opposition combined, which gathered strength till, in league with the baronial opposition in England, it resulted in the complete independence of Scotland, in 1328, under Edward III.

In 1279 Edward obtained possession of Ponthieu in right of his wife Eleanor, whose mother was Jeanne de Ponthieu, and in the same year he formally renounced all claim to Normandy.

In 1294 the French seized Guienne and Gascony, but in 1296 Bordeaux was recovered, and in 1303 Edward by treaty resumed possession of the provinces as they were at his accession.

WARS

In 1277 and 1282 Edward was employed in warfare in Wales. In 1287 a rising in Wales was put down. In 1293 disputes began with France, and a naval victory was won by the men of the Cinque Ports over the Norman sailors off St. Mahé, in Brittany. It was the chief incident in a quarrel which may be said to have begun the great wars between England and France, which lasted 160 years, with intervals. In 1294–95 there were renewed troubles in Wales, and the Scotch baronage in alliance with France began to refuse obedience to Edward, and hostilities commenced, which lasted for the rest of this reign and the next. In 1296 the Scots were defeated by Earl de Warenne near Dunbar, and the

* Except on two occasions under Edward II. Wales was not represented in Parliament till Henry VIII.'s reign.

monarchy of Baliol brought to an end. In 1297 Wallace defeated the Earl de Warenne at Stirling, but in 1298 the king completely defeated Wallace at Falkirk, and ruined his influence. In 1306 the Earl of Pembroke defeated Bruce at Methven.

OFFICIALS

Archbishops. — Robert Kilwardby, 1273, resigned 1278; John Peckham, 1279–1292; Robert Winchelsey, 1294.

Chancellors. — Walter de Merton, Bishop of Rochester, 1272; Robert Burnell, afterwards Bishop of Bath and Wells, 1273–1292; John Langton, afterwards Bishop of Chichester, 1292–1302; William Greenfield, afterwards Archbishop of York, 1302–1304; William of Hamilton, 1304–1307; Ralph Baldock, Bishop of London, 1307.

With the resolution of the King's Court into the three judicial branches, the King's Bench, Common Pleas, and Exchequer, a division dating from Edward's reign, the political importance of the justices ceases. Hubert de Burgh had been, in fact, the last great political Justiciar, with the exception of De Montfort in 1265, who was powerful for other reasons, not because he was Justiciar. Though the Chancellor about this same time began to preside over a court of equity, he became generally from this period the nearest approach to a Prime Minister. Robert Burnell is, perhaps, the first great political Chancellor. After his death Walter Langton, Bishop of Lichfield, the Treasurer, 1295–1307, was one of Edward's chief ministers. Such ministers are recorded here henceforward for their personal importance, not necessarily for their office, various offices being held at different times by the most influential men.

ACTS AND DOCUMENTS

In the time of Edward, Parliament, Convocation, the Law Courts, assumed the definite forms in which they have existed, with slight modification ever since; and his reign may be considered as marking the actual, as opposed to the historical or antiquarian, beginning of the English law and government.

The first statute of Westminster, 1275, granted a Customs duty on wool, wool-fells, and leather exported. Printed in Stubbs, *Select Charters*.

Statute of Mortmain, or *De Viris Religiosis*, 1279, restrained the withdrawing of estates from liability to public service by bestowing them upon the Church. Printed in Stubbs, *Select Charters*, and in the Statutes, 7 Edward I. c. 2.

Quia Emptores, 1290, aimed at stopping subinfeudation, with the same object as Mortmain, but allowing the division of estates. Printed in Stubbs, *Select Charters*, and in the Statutes, 18 Edward I. c. 1.

The statute of Wales, 12 Edward I., 1283, regulated the newly-conquered Wales. Printed in the Statutes.

By the statute of Westminster, 13 Edward I., c. 30, 1285, the circuits of the judges and the legal business of the assizes were regulated. Printed in the Statutes.

By the statute of Winchester, 13 Edward I., 1285, the whole police of the country was organized, and provision made for the equipment of a national militia. [Compare with the Assize of arms of Henry II.] Printed in Stubbs, *Select Charters*, and in the Statutes.

In 1297 the confirmation of the Charters was passed, with the additional clauses limiting the royal powers of raising money by "aids, tasks, or prises," to the "ancient aids and prises due and accustomed," save with the common assent of all the realm (*tut le roiaume*). Printed in Stubbs, *Select Charters*, and in the Statutes, 25 Edward I. c. 1.

De Tallagio non concedendo, though quoted as a statute in the preamble to the Petition of Right, 1628, is an abstract only of the confirmation of the preceding statute by the king's son, acting as Regent, and of the pardon of the two Earls Bigod and Bohun, who had withstood the king in the matter of arbitrary taxation.

THE CINQUE PORTS

In 1278 the king issued a charter to the Cinque Ports, with an *inspeximus* of charters since Edward the Confessor's reign. The Cinque Ports, Hastings, Sandwich, Dover, Romney, and Hythe, with the two ancient towns, Winchelsea and Rye, and the subordinate members of the Ports, held certain liberties and rights on condition of finding a navy for the king's service, and specially for the defence of the Channel seas and shores. They were, in fact, a military and naval frontier, organized as a separate county from Kent and Sussex. They had their origin in the policy of Edward the Confessor, allied with Normandy, and guarding against attacks from the Danes and exiles in Flanders. They were further favoured by the Norman kings as guardians of the Channel and connecting links with Normandy, and finally became the first line of defence against the French, whose basis of attack was chiefly in the Norman ports.

The Cinque Ports had favoured the baronial party in the late reign, and Edward had only reduced Winchelsea after an obstinate defence in 1266. After he became king he built a new town of Winchelsea, and the remains of the old town were destroyed by a high tide and storm. The prosperity of the Ports began to decay rapidly after the disastrous termination of the French wars, and their harbours became more and more silted up and insufficient for large ships. The French ports opposite to them fortunately suffered from the same cause. They were, however, the principal naval defence of the country down to the end of the fifteenth century. The decay of the Ports however had caused Henry V. to build an independent Royal Navy with its headquarters at Southampton. Their practical extinction as a fighting force led to the permanent establishment of a navy by Henry VII. and Henry VIII. (See Yonge, *History of the Navy*.)

The Charter of the Ports is printed in Rymer's *Foedera*, i. 558, Record Edition. Professor Montagu Burrows, *Cinque Ports*, in the *Historic Towns' Series*, gives a full account of the Ports.

PARLIAMENT

In the reign of Edward I. Parliament assumed a fixed and regular form.

Knights had been summoned from the shires to attend the Common Council of the Realm in the struggle for the Charter at the end of John's reign, and at intervals in that of Henry III. In 1265 De Montfort had caused citizens and burgesses to be summoned. Both De Montfort and Edward had been governors of Gascony, and in the South of France Parliaments, including representatives from the towns, had existed since the early part of the thirteenth century. In 1283 Edward summoned two assemblies at York and Northampton, at which four knights from each shire and four citizens or burgesses from many cities and boroughs, and elected proctors for the clergy, attended, but no barons were present. In 1283 the barons, representatives from the counties and from twenty towns, met at Shrewsbury. In 1290 knights of the shires met with the baronage. In 1294 representatives of the clergy met in August, and of the shires in October.

In 1295 a complete Parliament of prelates, baronage, knights of the shires, members from the towns, and proctors of the clergy was assembled, and from this time onward Parliament so constituted may be looked upon as continuous, except that the clergy, steadily refusing to tax themselves except in their own convocation, gradually lost their right of Parliamentary summons.* The bishops and greater abbots continued to sit with the baronage as holding land of the king in barony. The elections of knights of the shires, citizens, and burgesses, were in every case in the hands of the local governing bodies, the county courts and towns' meetings.

The *Modus Tenendi Parliamentum* may be taken as a

* The convocations of the clergy, existing in some form at a very early period, were organized in this same reign. The Convocation of York in 1279, that of Canterbury in 1283.

description of Parliament as it existed early in the fourteenth century. It is printed in Stubbs, *Select Charters*.

SCOTLAND

In 1290 Edward negotiated a marriage treaty at Brigham between his son Edward and Margaret, Queen of Scotland, then in Norway, reserving to Scotland certain marks of independence, which the king refused to allow when Baliol had been appointed to the Crown. Printed in Rymer's *Foedera*, ii. 482.

In 1305 Edward drew up regulations for the government of Scotland, in a Council at London attended by English and Scotch deputies, by which Scotland was divided into four districts, each under an English and a Scotch justice, and by which the Scotch Parliament was to send up commissioners to the English Parliament. The scheme of union failed owing to the inherent feeling of baronial opposition to the crown, and the love of local independence in the Lowlands of Scotland.

The war of Edward I. resulted in the complete separation of Scotland, and the almost complete separation of Ireland for a time from the English crown. The kingdom of the Scots, north of the Firth of Forth and Clyde, had played somewhat the same part in the north of Britain, which Wessex had played in the south, offering a centre round which gathered all who opposed the Scandinavian invasions.

In the tenth century the Scottish kings were established as overlords of Strathclyde, including Cumberland, Furness, and perhaps Westmoreland. From 954–1018 A.D. they became masters of Northern Bernicia. The Scottish kings, however, acknowledged the overlordship of the more powerful English kings, such as Edgar and Cnut, certainly for these southern dominions, probably for all their kingdom, the distinct ties of feudal homage being not yet existent. Malcolm Canmore, 1058–1093, acknowledged the superiority of William the Conqueror in general terms. He conquered the Scandinavians in the north of the island. The existing English population in the south and on the east coast was reinforced in his reign by many English exiles, and his marriage with Margaret, the sister of Edgar the Etheling, resulted in English manners and ecclesiastical influence being introduced. In the time of David I. 1124–1153, there was a great influx of Norman adventurers, and feudal tenures were probably introduced. For the next 130 years the various elements of the kingdom, Celtic Scots, Strathclyde Welsh, Scandinavians, English, and Normans were being gradually moulded into a nation under the Anglicized kings, in more or less dependence upon England. The attempt of Edward I. to make this dependence complete resulted in the final shaping of a Scottish nation, which in alliance with France was a perpetual trouble to the kingdom of England. For authors *vide infra*—Professor Freeman takes the extreme English, Robertson the Scottish, view of the relations of the crowns.

IRELAND

The conquest of part of Ireland in the reign of Henry II. had been carried out by baronial not royal forces. John, created *Dominus Hibernia* by his father, had made the royal authority more of a reality. He established the counties of Dublin, Kildare, Meath, including West Meath, Louth, Carlow, Wexford, Kilkenny, Waterford, Cork, Tipperary, Kerry, and Limerick. The De Courcis ruled most of Ulster, the De Burghs most of Connaught. The Great Charter was extended to the rulers in Ireland, the native Irish law being confined to the native Irish, and efforts being continually made upon their part and upon the part of the kings to bring them also within the pale of the English law. The baronage withstood these efforts, preferring to keep the Irish in a position of a foreign enemy, whom they could despoil at pleasure. Under the Regency of William Marshall, Earl of Pembroke, who possessed large Irish estates, *temp.* Henry III., the royal authority was extended over most of Ireland. The baronage, however, exercising quasi-royal powers in their palatine jurisdictions, became practically independent during the reign of Henry III. Edward I. took steps to strengthen the royal power, but was too much occupied with the Scotch war to carry out his aims. The invasion of Edward Bruce, *vide infra*, springing from the same wars, though defeated, completely upset the civilization and royal authority, such as they were, in the island. Most of the Anglo-Norman barons adopted native customs and even names. In the fifteenth century the name of the English Pale was given to the district including about Dublin, Louth, Kildare, and Meath, with a few seaport towns, to which the royal authority and the English law were confined. This district, being Yorkist in sympathies, was practically separated from the English crown during part of Henry VI.'s and the beginning of Henry VII.'s reign.

For a brief impartial account of the early history and constitution of Ireland the student may consult Hallam, *Constitutional History*, chapter xviii.

AUTHORS

In addition to works on the history of the thirteenth century mentioned at the end of John's reign, the student may consult for Scotland, Robertson, *Scotland under her Early Kings*; Burton, *History of Scotland*; Freeman, *The Relations of the Crowns of England and Scotland*, in Historical Essays, 1st series. For the constitutional history, Stubbs, *Constitutional History*, is indispensable; Gneist, *History of the English Parliament*, is very valuable; Hallam, *Middle Ages*, is useful, but is too severe upon Edward I.; and Stubbs, *Early Plantagenets*, still supplies the best *compendium* of the whole story down to the end of Edward II. *Edward I.*, by Professor Tout, in the *English Statesmen* Series, is very good.

EDWARD II. 1307–1327

Married Isabella of France.

DOMINIONS

Edward nominally succeeded to all his father held in France and Great Britain, but came near to losing most of it. Scotland, mostly in the hands of his officers and partisans in 1307, was gradually recovered by Bruce, till the battle of Bannockburn extinguished English dominion, and Bruce took Berwick in 1318. The Welsh were in revolt in 1316. The Scots invaded Ireland in 1315 and nearly overthrew the English power, but the Irish were defeated and the Scots expelled in 1318 by the Anglo-Irish nobles, but the royal authority in Ireland was reduced to a shadow. In 1325 Gascony and Ponthieu were made over to the king's son. In 1313 the Isle of Man was conquered by the Scots, and remained in their hands till 1343.

WARS

The Scotch war continued, generally to the advantage of the Scots. At Bannockburn, 1314, Robert Bruce completely defeated Edward, with the Earls of Pembroke and Gloucester, the barons of the party of Lancaster not being present.

In 1316 some of the danger of the Scotch invasion of Ireland was averted by the defeat of the O'Connors with great loss at Athunree by the De Burghs.

In 1318 Edward Bruce was defeated and killed at Dundalk by John de Bermingham.

In 1319 the Scots won a victory in Yorkshire called the Chapter of Mytton.

In 1322 the Earl of Lancaster, openly in alliance with Bruce, was defeated by the king's forces at Boroughbridge, and he himself taken and executed. In the same year the Scots defeated and nearly captured the king, near Byland Abbey in Yorkshire.

OFFICIALS

Archbishops.—Robert Winchelsey, d. 1313; Walter Reynolds, trans. from Worcester, 1313–1327. He was the king's tutor and friend, but turned against him in 1327, and is said to have died of shame at the result.

Chancellors.—Ralph Baldock, 1307; John Langton, Bishop of Chichester, 1307–1310; Walter Reynolds, Bishop of Worcester, afterwards Archbishop, 1310–1311; Adam de Osgodebey, Keeper of the Seal, 1311; Walter Reynolds, Keeper of the Seal, 1312–1314; John de Sandall, afterwards Bishop of Winchester, 1314–1318; John de Hotham, Bishop of Ely, 1318–1320; John Salmon, Bishop of Norwich, 1320–1323; Robert Baldock, afterwards Bishop of Norwich, 1323–1327.

Walter Reynolds, afterwards Chancellor and Archbishop, was Treasurer from 1307–1310.

Walter Langton, Edward the First's minister, was made Treasurer in 1312 in spite of the opposition of Lancaster's party, but was removed altogether from the royal council in 1315.

Thomas, Earl of Lancaster, was made President of the Royal Council in 1316.

Hugh le Despenser, the younger, was made Chamberlain in 1318.

Hugh le Despenser, the elder, Justice of the forests south of Trent, in 1324.

ACTS AND DOCUMENTS

In 1311 the Lords Ordainers, appointed in Parliament by the influence of Lancaster's party, made a reform of the government, providing that the royal ministers should be appointed by the advice of the baronage, and should be sworn in parliament, that the king should not go to war without the consent of the baronage, that parliament should be called once or twice every year. The ordinances are distinctly baronial in tendency, not popular. Printed in *Rolls of Parliament*, i. 281–286.*

The substance of the ordinances is given in Stubbs, *Constitutional History*.

AUTHORS

As on the reign of Edward I.

EDWARD III. 1327–1377

Married Philippa of Hainault.

DOMINIONS

Edward III., under the tutelage of Mortimer, concluded the treaty of Northampton with Bruce, 1328, by which the English claim to supremacy over Scotland was formally abandoned. In 1332 Edward, the son of John Baliol, having acquired the Scottish crown by the aid of the disinherited lords—that is, those who, having held land in England and Scotland, had lost the latter by adhering to the English interest—again subjected it to that of England. In 1334 Baliol ceded the Lowlands to England, but was himself driven from the country, and the English partisans and garrisons were expelled by 1342, Berwick only being permanently retained by England. Roxburgh Castle too was held by an English garrison till 1460. In 1356 Baliol ceded his nominal sovereignty to Edward, but in 1357 David Bruce was released from captivity without doing homage.

In France Edward at first appeared likely to lose the remaining possessions of his throne. He assumed the title of King of France in 1337, but Ponthieu was immediately lost, and the French gained ground in Guienne and Gascony till 1345, when the Earl of Derby defeated them, and in the course

* The *Rolls of Parliament*, from Edward I. to Henry VII., were published in the last century, in six vols. folio. An index has been added since.

of two years extended the English rule further than it had reached since Henry III.'s reign. In 1347 Edward took Calais, which became an English town. In 1360 the treaty of Bretigni ceded to him in full sovereignty all Guienne and Gascony. The old county of Poictou, with Angoulême, Santoigne, Perigord, and Limousin, but excluding La Marche, and Ponthieu and Calais were also ceded. In 1369, on the renewal of the war the French re-conquest began. Ponthieu was immediately re-conquered, and by the end of the reign the English held only Bordeaux, Bayonne, and a narrow strip of country on the Garonne. The nominal rule, however, of the English and French kings varied with the disposition of the nobility, and in Richard II.'s reign there were castles in Auvergne still nominally held for the King of England.

WARS

The Scotch war, inherited from the late reign, was concluded in 1328, but in 1332 the private enterprise of the disinherited lords renewed it. In 1333 the defeat of the Scots at Halidon Hill, near Berwick, appeared to establish the throne of Edward Baliol, but after two years of warfare the English were only in possession of Berwick, and Baliol was living in England.

In 1337 war began with France. The old maritime jealousy, rival interest in Flanders, where the commercial towns favoured an English alliance, while the count who quarrelled with the townsmen sought French help, help given by the French to the Scots, and the natural policy of the French to expel English influence from Guienne, all combined to produce war, as they had done earlier under Edward I. The claim to the French crown by Edward III. was a consequence of hostility, not a cause of it. The war began on the sea, and continued in Flanders and Guienne with unsuccessful results to Edward at first.

In 1340 the king won the great naval victory over the French fleet in Sluys Haven. In 1345 the Earl of Derby defeated the French at Bergerac, in Guienne. In 1346 the English and Gascons made the famous defence of Aiguillon, in Guienne, from April till August. In 1346 David of Scotland was defeated and taken at Neville's Cross, in Durham, but the battle was of no lasting effect beyond prolonging disorder in Scotland. In 1346 the king and the Black Prince defeated the French at Cressy. In 1347 Edward took Calais. In 1350 the king won the naval victory called Les Espagnols-sur-Mer over a Biscayan fleet off Winchelsea. In 1356 the Black Prince with a far inferior English and Gascon army defeated and captured King John of France at Poitiers, a victory which led ultimately to the Treaty of Bretigni.

In 1364 Charles of Blois, the claimant supported by the French in Britanny, was defeated and killed at Auray by the English ally De Montfort.

In 1367 the Black Prince defeated Henry of Trastamare, King of Castile, and Du Guesclin, at Navaretta, on the Ebro. The war, after its renewal in 1369, was mainly one of sieges and minor operations, the French avoiding pitched battles. In 1372, however, the Spaniards completely defeated the Earl of Pembroke in a naval battle off La Rochelle. This was really the most decisive battle of the war, and fatal to the English supremacy in Aquitaine.

The real objects of Edward, the safety of Guienne and Gascony, and free intercourse for English trade with these countries, Britanny, and Flanders, had been secured by the previous naval victories, and by the taking of Calais, but were rendered impossible by this defeat. The whole commercial policy of England was modified in consequence of it in the succeeding reign.

OFFICIALS

Archbishops.—Simon Mepeham, 1327–1333; John Stratford, translated from Winchester, 1333–1348; Thomas Bredwardine, 1349; Simon Islip, 1349–1366; Simon Langham, translated from Ely, 1366–1369, resigned; William Whittlesey, translated from Worcester, 1369-1375; Simon of Sudbury, translated from London, 1375.

Chancellors.—John de Hotham, Bishop of Ely, January to March, 1327; Henry de Burgersh, Bishop of Lincoln, 1327-30; John Stratford, Bishop of Winchester, afterwards Archbishop, 1330-1334; Richard de Bury, Bishop of Durham, 1334-1335; John Stratford, Archbishop, 1335-1337; Robert Stratford, brother to the preceding, 1337-1338; John Wentworth, Bishop of London, 1338. No Chancellor appointed for nearly two years. The Great Seal in commission. John Stratford, Archbishop, 1340; Robert Stratford, Bishop of Chichester, July to December, 1340; Sir Robert Bourchier, the first Lay Chancellor, 1340-1341; Sir Robert Parnyng, 1341-1343; Robert de Sadyngton, 1343-1345; John Ufford, 1345-1349; John de Thorseby, Bishop of St. David's, 1349-1356; William de Edington, Bishop of Winchester, 1356-1363; Simon Langham, Bishop of Ely, afterwards Archbishop, 1363-67; William of Wykeham, Bishop of Winchester, 1367-1371; Sir Robert de Thorpe, 1371-1372; Sir John Knyvet, 1372-1377; Adam de Houghton, Bishop of St. David's, 1377.

ACTS AND DOCUMENTS

In 1328 the treaty of Northampton recognized the full independence of Scotland, and English enterprises against Scotland henceforward are pure aggression, not as before attempts to strain to the utmost certain undefined rights. See Rymer's *Foedera, II.,* p. ii. 734, 741. Record edition.

In 1341, by an act 14 Edward III. c. 7, sheriffs were to be appointed annually. Printed in the Statutes.

In 1342, by an act 15 Edward III. c. 2, peers of the realm were to be tried for offences only before their peers in parliament. An act springing out of the attack by the king upon his minister Stratford the archbishop. Printed in the Statutes.

In 1349 the first statute of labourers was passed, 23 Edward III. c. 1, amplified later, regulating the wages of labourers, and compelling them to work for the wages formerly accustomed to be paid, and confining them to their own counties. This was passed owing to the great Pestilence, the Black Death, which had reduced the number of labourers by perhaps one half, and naturally raised the rate of wages. It was, of course, inoperative, and the cause of intense dissatisfaction among the lower classes. Printed in the Statutes.

In 1351 the statute of Provisors was passed, 25 Edward III., c. 6, to hinder papal appointments to English benefices. The first so-called statute of Praemunire was a royal ordinance of 1353, supplementing this by punishing with outlawry and forfeiture all who sued in foreign, *i.e.*, papal, courts for matters cognisable in the king's courts. These acts defined and strengthened the ancient royal supremacy over persons and cases ecclesiastical. Printed in the Statutes.

In 1352 the statute of Treasons, 25 Edward III., s. 5, c. 2, limited treason to well-defined acts against the person and authority of the king, and the persons of his queen and eldest son. Printed in the Statutes.

In 1360, by 34 Edward III., c. 1, Justices of the Peace had their powers confirmed and defined. Their sessions gradually supplanted the old police jurisdiction of the Courts of the Hundreds. Printed in the Statutes.

In 1360 the treaty of Bretigni put a temporary end to the French war, ceding to Edward the full sovereignty of Gascony, Guienne, Agenois, Santoigne, Angoulême, Perigord, Limousin, Bigorre, Rovergue, Gaure, Caoursin, Poictou, Calais, and Ponthieu, in return for a renunciation of his claim to the French crown. Britanny and Flanders were to be free from the suzerainty of either sovereign. The non-fulfilment of this treaty gave a handle to the claims of Henry V. against France, as the lawful representative of Edward III. in the throne of England, though not his heir by blood. Printed in Rymer's *Foedera*, vi. 178.

In 1366 the statute of Kilkenny in Ireland passed in a

Parliament held under Lionel Duke of Clarence, attempted to suppress the native Irish laws and customs, and to prevent the Hibernizing of the English colonists. Printed in Davis, *Irish Statutes*, 202.

In 1376 the Good Parliament gave the first example of an attack by impeachment upon the royal ministers, the attack being countenanced by the Black Prince and the Mortimers, heirs to Lionel Duke of Clarence, and directed against the partisans of the Duke of Lancaster. Sir Peter de la Mare, spokesman (*prolocutor*) of the House of Commons on this occasion, is commonly called the first Speaker, but the title does not seem to have been used till 1377.

The Proceedings are printed in the *Rolls of Parliament*, ii. 323, &c.

The whole reign of Edward III. is distinguished by copious acts of social, commercial, and sumptuary legislation, and it forms one of the greatest eras of our earlier commercial history. The student may pursue this whole subject in Cunningham, *Growth of English Industry and Commerce*.

THE BLACK DEATH

The Black Death, the great pestilence which first visited England in 1349, was the most important influence in social change; it perhaps destroyed half the population. The three principal visitations were used sometimes as eras from which to date events or deeds, and were thus computed:

The first or great pestilence, from May 31st to September 29th, 1349.

The second pestilence, from August 15th, 1361, to May 3rd, 1362.

The third pestilence, from July 2nd to September 29th, 1369.

The student may consult Mr. Seebohm, Essays on the Black Death, in the *Fortnightly Review*, 1865, and Creighton, *History of Epidemics in Britain*.

THE LOLLARDS

The reign of Edward III. saw also the commencement of the Lollard movement, summarised in Milman, *Latin Christianity*, vol. vi. See also Shirley, Introduction to *Fasciculi Zizaniorum*, in the Rolls Series; and, briefly, The Lollards, in Gairdner and Spedding, *Studies in English History*, a reprint of magazine articles.

THE BARONAGE UNDER EDWARD III.

The character of the baronage in Edward's reign was largely modified by the marriages of the royal family to heiresses in England. The great earldom of Lancaster had already been created in the royal family, and endowed with the confiscated estates of De Montfort and Ferrers. (See after the reign of Henry III.) The second Earl of Lancaster had married the heiress of the Lacys, and the heiress of Lancaster daughter of the first duke who as Earl of Derby had defended Guienne in 1345, was married to John of Gaunt, the king's son. The son of this marriage, Henry of Bolingbroke, married one of the co-heiresses of the De Bohuns, of Hereford, Essex, and Northampton.

The earldom of Kent had been created for Edmund, third son of Edward I., whose heiress Joanna married first Sir Thomas Holland, who was created Earl of Kent; secondly Edward the Black Prince. Lionel, second surviving son of Edward III., married the heiress of the De Burghs, earls of Ulster, who was also one of the co-heiresses of the De Clares of Gloucester and Hertford. The daughter of Lionel was married to the head of the house of Mortimer, whose ultimate heiress married the son of the Duke of York, Edward's fourth son who reached manhood. Thomas, youngest son of Edward III., married a co-heiress of the De Bohuns. His daughter married the head of the Staffords.

Thomas, the second son of Edward I., had been created Earl of Norfolk, and his heiress was the mother of Thomas Mowbray, Earl of Nottingham and first Duke of Norfolk.

The throne was thus surrounded by a powerful baronage, related to the crown and wielding great local influence, whose dissensions helped to produce the civil wars of Richard II. and the Lancastrian reigns.

AUTHORS

Stubbs, *Constitutional History*; Hallam, *Middle Ages*, for the constitutional and general history; Green, *History of the English People;* Longman, *Life and Times of Edward III.* The picturesque, though one-sided and incomplete, *Chronicle* of Froissart is accessible in English translations.

RICHARD II. 1377–1399

Married first Anne of Bohemia, secondly Isabella of France.

DOMINIONS

Richard succeeded to the kingdom of England and to the diminished French possessions of his grandfather, but the internal dissensions of his reign led to no serious diminution of what remained, though French fleets ravaged the shores of England. In 1378 Charles the Bad of Navarre and Evreux put certain Norman fortresses into English hands, and Cherbourg was held till 1396. Brest was put into the hands of the English in 1378 by the Duke of Britanny, and restored in 1397.

WARS

Though there was continuous warfare with the French and in Britanny, in Flanders, and in Spain, where the Duke of Lancaster long prosecuted a claim to the crown of Castile through his second wife, daughter to Pedro the Cruel, there were no great battles. In 1387 the Earl of Arundel captured a French fleet in the Flemish harbours near Sluys, and in 1388 the most famous of the border battles was fought at Otterbourn, where Henry Percy, called Hotspur, was defeated and taken, but the Scotch leader, the Earl of Douglas, slain. In 1396

Richard II.

Richard made peace with France for thirty years on marrying the child Isabella, daughter to Charles VI., and withdrew the English garrisons from Cherbourg and Britanny.

OFFICIALS

Archbishops.—Simon of Sudbury, beheaded by Wat Tyler's rioters, 1381; William Courtenay, translated from London, 1381-1395; Thomas Fitz-Alan, translated from York, brother to the Earl of Arundel, 1395-1398; in 1398 Fitz-Alan, often called Arundel, was translated to St. Andrews on the king's request, being at the time in exile, and Roger Walden was consecrated his successor, but Fitz-Alan returned in 1399 and Walden was deposed.

Chancellors.—Adam de Houghton 1377-1378; Lord Scrope, 1378-79; Simon, the Archbishop, 1379-1381; William Courteney, Archbishop, 1381; Lord Scrope, 1381-1382; Robert de Braybrooke, Bishop of London, 1382-1383; Michael de la Pole, 1383-1386; Thomas Fitz-Alan, Bishop of Ely, 1386-1389; William of Wykeham, 1389-1391; Thomas Fitz-Alan, Archbishop of York, 1391-1396; Edmund Stafford, Bishop of Exeter, 1396-1399; in 1399, after the landing of Henry of Bolingbroke, Fitz-Alan returned and began at once to act as chancellor and archbishop.

In 1386 a Council of Regency superseded the king. They were Courtenay the Archbishop, Neville, Archbishop of York, William of Wykeham, Bishop of Winchester, Thomas Brentingham, Bishop of Exeter and Treasurer, the Abbot of Waltham, the Dukes of Gloucester and York, the king's uncles, the Earl of Arundel, Lord Scrope, Lord Cobham, and Sir John Devereux.

In 1388 the following five Lords Appellant appealed the king's favourites of treason, the Duke of Gloucester, the Earl of Derby, afterwards King Henry IV., the Earl of Nottingham, afterwards Duke of Norfolk, the Earl of Arundel, the Earl of Warwick.

ACTS AND DOCUMENTS

In 1393, the Act of Praemunire, 16 Rich. II. c. 5, was passed, inflicting very heavy penalties upon all who tried to evade Edward III.'s acts against Papal Provisions, making the Papal authority in fact only valid in England, or between Englishmen, with the royal consent, and confirming a real royal supremacy. Printed in the Statutes. In 1395 the bill of the Lollards, against religious and social abuses, was delivered in Parliament. The decay of charity, the sinfulness of war, denunciation of useless trades, the doctrine that "dominion is founded in grace," the principle upon which the saints claimed to rule in 1653, appear side by side with Protestant views. Printed in Wilkins and Spelman, *Councils*, ed. Haddan and Stubbs, iii. 225.

In 1397 Richard seized absolute power, and by Act of Parliament in 1398, 21 Rich. II. c. 1–13, annulled the Council of Regency of 1386 and all the Acts of the Parliament of 1388, punished those engaged with the Lords Appellant in those years, and made it treason to attempt the repeal of the acts of the present Parliament. By 21 Rich. II. c. 16, the powers of Parliament were delegated to eighteen commissioners who were supposed to be in the king's interest. Printed in the Statutes.

The same Parliament voted the subsidy on wool, woolfells, and leather to the king for life. (*Rolls of Parliament*, iii. 368.)

In 1399 thirty-three articles of accusation were exhibited in Parliament, and were voted sufficient ground for the deposition of the king. (*Rolls of Parliament*, iii. 416–422.)

AUTHORS

Stubbs, *Constitutional History*, remains not only the best for its special subject, but most useful for a general view. Green, *History of the English People*, is very interesting for its view of the Lollard movement and the Peasant revolt of 1381, and the whole social history in connexion with the latter may be studied in Cunningham, *Growth of English Industry and Commerce*, or in Thorold Rogers, *The History of Prices*.

On Richard II. and the subsequent reigns to Henry VII. the student has again the advantage of a small handbook by a first-rate historian, Gairdner, *The Houses of Lancaster and York*, Longmans, *Epoch Series*.

HENRY IV. 1399-1413

Married first Mary de Bohun ; secondly, Joan of Navarre.

DOMINIONS

Henry claimed the crown as the representative of Henry III., by the Lancastrian line, the realm being "in point to be undone by default of governance and undoing of the good laws." He was, in fact, king by choice of Parliament upon this account, to reverse the policy of Richard II., but the nation as a whole was not quite prepared to accept a Parliamentary title only. The French, with whom Richard was allied, invited Bordeaux and the other towns of Guienne and Gascony to come over to them from the usurper. But though it was said that Richard of Bordeaux was popular in his native place, the inhabitants valued the English trade and the civic rights they enjoyed, and remained faithful to the house of Lancaster. Not so Wales, where as there was no Parliamentary representation, the attempt at despotism by Richard was not resented. Henry IV. cannot be said to have ruled in a great part of Wales from 1400, when Owen of Glyndwrdy or Glendower first rose in arms, till 1409, when the defeat of a Welsh raid into Shropshire was followed by the gradual submission of much of the country.

WARS

The Chronic Scotch Wars continued.

In 1402 Henry Percy defeated the Scots at Homildon ; but the expenses of the war helped to provoke the rebellion of the Percys, which was happily crippled in 1403 at Shrewsbury, where the king defeated and killed Henry Percy, and took and executed Thomas Percy, Earl of Worcester, and crushed in 1408, at Bramham Moor, where the Earl of Northumberland was killed by Sir Thomas Rokeby. All through the reign there were rebellions in England, war in Wales, war with Scotland, troubles in Ireland, where the Mortimers had estates and influence, and hostilities with France, whose fleets burnt English towns and landed troops in Wales. In 1411 Henry's troops in France helped the Burgundians to defeat the Orleans party at St. Cloud.

OFFICIALS

Archbishop.—Thomas Fitz-Alan, restored 1399–1413.

Chancellors—John de Searle, 1399–1401; Edmund Stafford, Bishop of Exeter, 1401–1403; Henry Beaufort, Bishop of Lincoln, afterwards Bishop of Lincoln and Cardinal, the king's half-brother, 1403–1405; Thomas Longley, afterwards Bishop of Durham, Keeper of the Privy Seal, 1405–7; Thomas the Archbishop, 1407–1410; Sir Thomas Beaufort, the king's half-brother, afterwards Earl of Dorset and Duke of Exeter, 1410–12; Thomas the Archbishop, 1412–1413.

Henry, Prince of Wales, was Lieutenant of Wales and the Marches, 1403, a commission repeated in different terms, 1405–1406–1407. A Privy Councillor from 1406–1411, Warden of the Cinque Ports, 1409, Captain of Calais, 1410.

ACTS AND DOCUMENTS

The House of Lancaster were to reign as strictly Parliamentary sovereigns, and by 1 Henry IV., c. 3, the whole of the legislation of the Parliament of 21 Richard II., and the powers conferred by it, were repealed. Printed in the Statutes.

In 1402, by 2 Henry iv., c. 15, an act was passed against the Lollards, the first great persecuting act in England. It was considered that Richard had not been severe enough against them, and the Earl of Salisbury, the chief leader of the

DESCENT OF THE HOUSE OF LANCASTER FROM HENRY III.

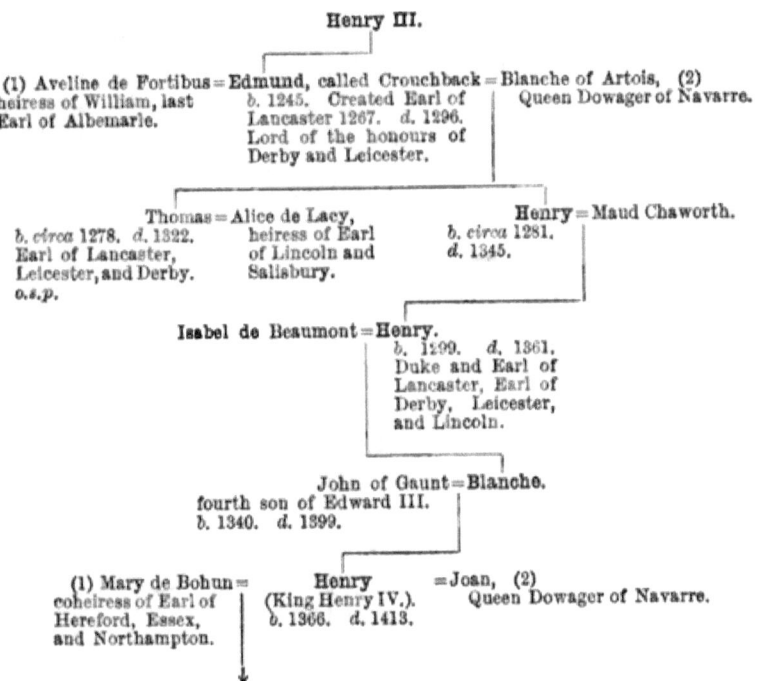

Lollards, had been a partisan of Richard's. But the same Parliament urged the strict enforcement of the Statute of Provisors. Printed in the Statutes.

In 1406 the Parliament passed a vote of confidence in the ministers, but insisted on an audit of public accounts, and on freedom of election for knights of the shires. (*Rolls of Parliament*, iii. 567–589.)

In 1407 the Commons succeeded in establishing their right of declaring all grants of money by the mouth of their Speaker. (*Rolls of Parliament*, iii. 611.)

In 1410 the Lollard party in Parliament proposed the conconfiscation of all the temporalities of the Church for the permanent endowment of 15 earls, 1500 knights, 6000 esquires, and 100 hospitals, leaving £20,000 over for the king. The scheme, which was probably impracticable, was rejected. See Stubbs, *Constitutional History*, vol. iii., § 640.

AUTHORS

Stubbs, *Constitutional History;* Hook, *Lives of the Archbishops,* Thomas Arundell (Fitz-Alan); Mr. Wylie, *History of the Reign of Henry IV.;* Halle's *Chronicle,* though not a first-rate authority, is valuable to the English reader, from the fall of Richard II. onward. A handy modern edition of it is greatly to be desired.

Briefly, Gairdner, *Lancaster and York.*

HENRY V. 1413–1422

Married Catherine of France.

DOMINIONS

He succeeded to a more united dominion than his father; feuds in England were at least quiescent, and Wales was mostly in obedience to the crown. His great enterprise against France was suggested partly by a desire to keep occupied the turbulent nobility and the turbulent lower classes, whose attempted revolt, instigated by the Lollard party, he nipped in the bud in 1414; partly to revenge the persistent hostility of the French to his dynasty; partly to secure the command of the Channel; partly because England was vitally interested in supporting Burgundy, the ruler of Flanders, our great market, against the French; but chiefly, no doubt, to establish his dynasty by means of brilliant success abroad. Wider schemes of pacifying France, healing the Papal schism, and heading a crusade against the Turks were entertained by him, but the second only was accomplished partly by his aid. Though he laid aside the title of king for that of heir and regent of France after the treaty of Troyes, he really ruled more of France than any English king since Henry II.

WARS

In 1415 Henry took Harfleur, in Normandy, and marching to Calais purposely provoked the French to a pitched battle at Agincourt, October 25th, 1415, which resulted in a great victory and terrible slaughter of the French nobility. In 1416 the French attempted to retake Harfleur, but were defeated by sea and land. In August 1417 Henry invaded Normandy for the second time, and began a systematic conquest. A week before his arrival a Genoese fleet, which was blockading Harfleur, was beaten. In 1417 Caen and Bayeux fell. In 1418 the whole of the Cotentin, Cherbourg, and other strong places, were taken, and Rouen besieged; early in 1419 Rouen surrendered, and Picardy and places in Maine and the Isle of France were conquered. In 1421 the Scottish auxiliaries of the French defeated and killed Henry's brother Thomas, Duke of Clarence, at Beaugé, in Anjou; but in the same year Henry captured Dreux, in 1422 Meaux, and forced the Dauphin to abandon the siege of the Burgundian town of Cosne on the Loire.

OFFICIALS

Archbishops.—Thomas Fitz-Alan, d. 1414; Henry Chichele, translated from St. Davids, 1414–1422.

Chancellors.—Henry Beaufort, Bishop of Winchester, afterwards Cardinal, 1413-1417; Thomas Longley, Bishop of Durham, 1417-22.

Thomas Fitz-Alan, Earl of Arundel, was made Treasurer in 1413, when his uncle was removed from the chancellorship, so as not to break entirely with the powerful Arundel interest.

Sir William Gascoigne, Chief Justice of the king's bench since 1401, was removed in 1413.

ACTS AND DOCUMENTS

In 1413, by 1 Henry V. c. 1, it was enacted that knights, citizens, and burgesses, chosen to represent shires, cities, and boroughs, should be resident in the said shires, cities, and boroughs. Printed in the Statutes.

In 1414, on the petition of the Commons, the Alien Priories in England were finally suppressed, and their revenues taken into the king's hands. (*Rolls of Parliament,* iv. 22; Rymer's *Foedera,* ix., 280, 281, &c.)

The property of the Alien Priories, that is, Priories in England attached to foreign monasteries, had been confiscated at times since Edward the First's reign: they were looked upon as a source of profit to foreigners and of injury to England, especially in time of war. They were 110 in number, and their revenues were employed partly in the public service, partly in the new foundations, partly in grants to private persons.

In 1416 the Duke of Burgundy undertook to do homage to the king of England, and to aid him in gaining his rights in France. (Rymer's *Foedera,* ix. 394.)

Burgundy before this had some secret understanding with Henry, who in his father's reign had consistently upheld the Burgundian alliance, but even after 1416 the duke intrigued also with the Dauphin and the Queen. He was murdered by the Dauphin's attendants in 1419, and his son immediately made a close alliance with England.

In 1420 the Treaty of Troyes arranged that Henry should

marry the French king's daughter Catherine, and be acknowledged as Regent of France during the life of the imbecile Charles VI., and king after his death. Coins, however, struck at Rouen after the negociation had begun, but before it was concluded, still bear the legend Henricus, Rex Francorum. (Rymer's *Foedera*, ix. 895.)

AUTHORS

Stubbs, *Constitutional History*. Freeman, Essays, first series, *The Wars of Edward III. and Henry V. in France*. Sir Harris Nicholas, *Agincourt*.

For a brief account, Gairdner, *Lancaster and York*. Halle's *Chronicle* and Monstrelet's *Chronicle* (a Burgundian partisan) translated into English, will be interesting and valuable to those who can avail themselves of them.

Sir James Ramsay's *History of England in the Fifteenth Century*, is particularly good upon the French wars.

HENRY VI. 1422–1461
Married Margaret of Anjou.

DOMINIONS

Henry succeeded to the throne and claims of his father, and within less than two months to the throne of France by the death of Charles VI. The countries actually in possession of the English were the Duchy of Normandy, Calais, Ponthieu, Picardy, the Isle of France, Champagne, most of Anjou and Touraine north of the Loire, part of the Orleannais, Gascony, Guienne, including Perigord, Limousin, Angoulême, and part of Santoigne. In Guienne, however, the allegiance of the feudal nobility fluctuated considerably, and the Count d'Armagnac, the head of the party opposed to Burgundy, whose estates lay in that province, was strongly against the English. The Duke of Burgundy, who acknowledged Henry VI.

as king, was not only generally influential in Northern France, but ruled over Flanders and Artois, the Duchy of Burgundy, including the Nivernois, and over the county of Burgundy, Franche Comté, which was outside the limits of France. The Duke of Britanny acknowledged Henry in 1423. Towns, castles, or small tracts of land were held for one side or the other within the limits generally assigned to its rival.

The national distinction between the English and the French side was not so decided as might appear to us likely. The Count d' Armagnac, who had principally upheld the party of Orleans and the Dauphin against the Burgundians, had flooded the North of France with Gascon soldiers, speaking a language different from that of Paris. The armies of the Dauphin were full of Scots, speaking Northumbrian-English, and of Italians. The armies of Henry V., and much more those of the Duke of Bedford and his captains, were full of Normans and Picards, though these ultimately went over to the French side.

The significance of the appearance of Joan of Arc is, that a peasant girl in the duchy of Bar, on the extreme frontier of France, should have any national French feeling at all, and that she had it shows that the French had at last begun to rise to a consciousness that it was a national struggle in which they were engaged, and not a contest between English, Burgundian, Gascon, and French rulers, of whom the first were not the worst masters for the townsfolk and peasantry. When once the struggle became national its termination was assured.

In 1429 the English were driven from the Orleannais, Rheims, Troyes, Chalons-sur-Marne, and part of the Isle of France.

In 1430 they lost nearly all Champagne.

In 1431 the French made conquests in Normandy, though they failed to retain them all continuously.

In 1435 the Burgundians abandoned the English alliance.

In 1436 the French retook Paris.

In 1448 Anjou and Maine were handed over, according to

the marriage treaty of the king, to the French, though Anjou was not for the most part in English hands before the transfer.

In 1449 most of Normandy was lost, and in 1450 the whole except the islands, by the capture of Cherbourg.

In 1451 Bordeaux and Bayonne were reduced, and though Bordeaux declared for the English again in 1452, it was finally taken by the French in 1453, Calais and the Norman Islands alone remaining of the French possessions.

The wars in which the kings of England had been engaged —first, to protect their continental dominions; secondly, to regain them or to conquer France—had been one great stimulus to the growth of a constitutional government, causing a need of money, and leading to public interest in questions concerning the raising and spending of money, and of administration generally. Above all, the wars encouraged a national pride and sense of unity, which resented and combined against abuses at home as readily as against a foreign enemy. Ultimately, from their exhausting effects and disastrous termination, and from the ferocity and rapacity which they engendered, the wars became fatal to the constitutional rule of England, which disappeared in the Wars of the Roses, which began in Henry's reign.

Roxburgh Castle, which had been held by the English since Edward III.'s reign, was recovered and demolished by the Scots in 1460.

WARS

In 1423 the Earl of Salisbury and the Burgundians defeated the French and Scots with great loss at Crévant on the Yonne. In 1424 the Dauphin's troops attempted to penetrate Normandy, and were defeated with great loss by the Duke of Bedford at Verneuil, the Scottish auxiliaries suffering especially, and the Earls of Douglas and Buchan being killed. In 1428 the siege of Orleans was begun; in 1429 Sir John Fastolfe defeated the French, who attacked his convoy of provisions for the besiegers at Rouvray, called also the Battle of the Herrings. In 1429 the siege of Orleans was raised, the Earl of Suffolk was defeated at Jargeau and Sir John Talbot at Patay. The war henceforward was not marked by battles on a large scale, and the French regular soldiers, aided by an improved artillery and by the sympathy of the inhabitants, recovered towns and castles rapidly. The Duke of York did all that was possible for the defence of Normandy in 1435-1437 and in 1442-44, but in that year he was superseded by the Duke of Somerset, a truce was concluded, and the defences of Normandy were neglected. In 1449 war was resumed, and Rouen and most of Normandy was conquered. In 1450 Sir Thomas Kyriel was defeated at Fourmigny in Normandy, and Cherbourg was taken. In 1451 Bordeaux and Bayonne surrendered, the latter after a long defence. In 1453 Talbot was defeated and killed at Castillon; and Bordeaux, which had again declared for England, was finally surrendered.

BATTLES OF THE CIVIL WARS

The quarrels among the nobility culminated in that between the Duke of York and the Duke of Somerset, who, closely connected with the royal family, were rivals for power both in Normandy and England.

In the first phase of the war York was not ostensibly fighting against King Henry, but against the government in his name by the Beauforts and the Queen.

The battles of this stage were: St. Albans, 1455, when York and his brother-in-law Salisbury defeated and killed the Duke of Somerset and the Earl of Northumberland. In 1459 the Earl of Salisbury defeated and killed Lord Audley at Blore Heath. In 1460 the Earl of Salisbury and the Earl of Warwick his son, and Edward Earl of March, son of the Duke of York, defeated and killed the Queen's general, the Duke of Buckingham, at Northampton. York then formally claimed the crown, and a compromise was effected, by which he was to succeed Henry.

Henry VI.

This agreement was broken by the Queen, and the second era of the wars begins—a struggle of rival dynasties. In reality a struggle for a firm, central government or the contrary, in which the disorderly nobility and the disorderly Borderers support the Lancastrians, and the towns and the more stable southern counties support York and Warwick his nephew.

At Wakefield the Queen and the Borderers defeated and killed the Duke of York and the Earl of Salisbury, December 30th, 1460. On February 2nd, 1461, the son of the Duke of York defeated the Earl of Pembroke at Mortimer's Cross, and assumed the crown in London, March 3rd. The Queen, with an army of Borderers and Yorkshiremen, defeated the Earl of Warwick at St. Albans, second battle, February 17th, 1461, but was shut out of London and retired to the North, whither King Edward IV. followed her, and won a crowning victory for York against Lancaster, for the South against the North, for the Crown against the nobility, after three days' fighting and pursuit, March 28-30, at Ferrybridge and Towton.

THE PARTIES IN THE WARS OF THE ROSES

The greater nobility, who controlled parliament, were for the most part Lancastrian. The families of Beaufort, Holland, Courtenay, Talbot, Butler, Stafford, De Vere, Percy, the elder branch of Neville, Tudor, Grey, Clifford, Dacre, were Lancastrians, with the more disorderly elements of society, the Borderers, the Welsh. The more violent Lancastrians intrigued with France and Scotland for help. The younger branch of Neville, that is Salisbury, the brother-in-law to the Duke of York, with his son the Earl of Warwick, John Mowbray Duke of Norfolk, an hereditary enemy of the house of Lancaster, who married a sister of the Earl of Essex, and Henry Bourchier Earl of Essex, who married a sister of the Duke of York, were the principal Yorkist nobility at first. The party was strong in London and all the greater towns of the South and Midlands, in the Eastern Counties, Kent, Sussex, and in the Welsh

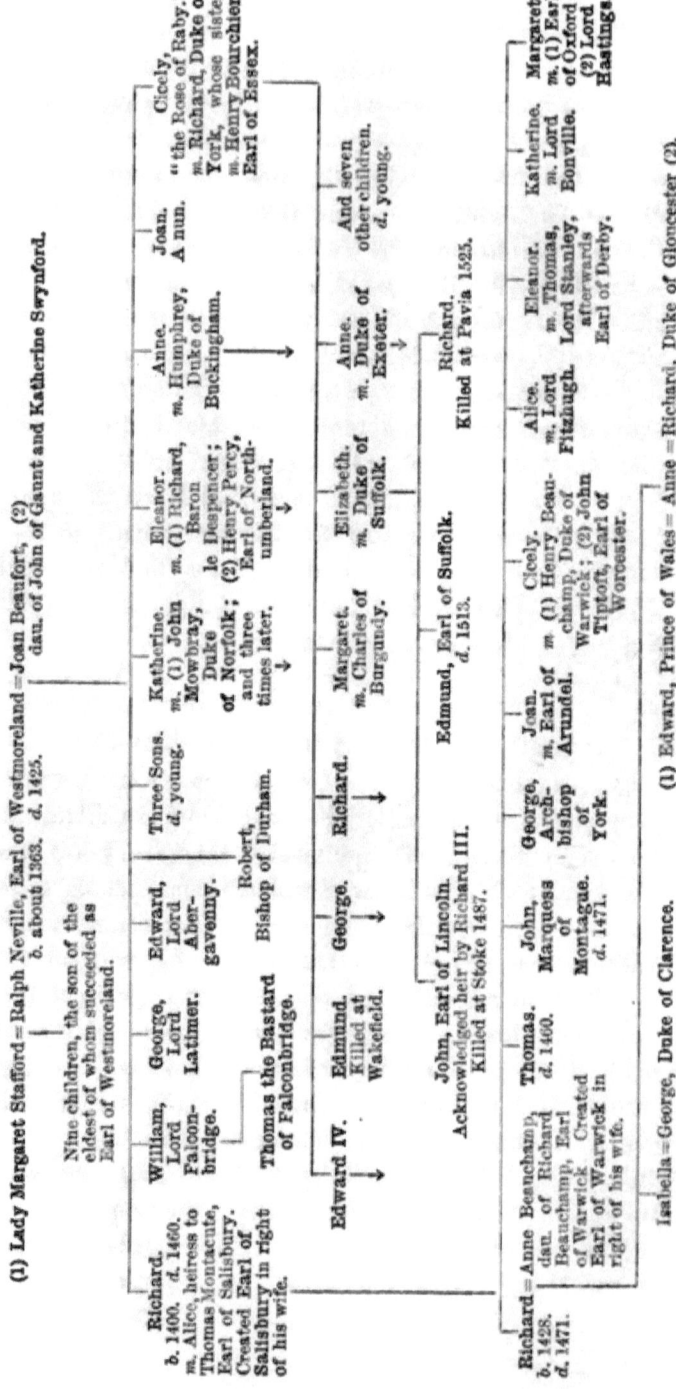

Marches where the Mortimer estates had been. They possessed Calais, and had the sympathy of the English Pale in Ireland. In 1470-1 the French support of Lancaster was met by Burgundian support to York. The support of the Cinque Ports, however, and to some extent of London also, was given rather to the Earl of Warwick than to the House of York, and in 1470-71 their sympathies were consequently divided.

OFFICIALS

Archbishops.— Henry Chichele, d. 1443; John Stafford, Cardinal, translated from Bath and Wells, 1443-1452; John Kempe, Cardinal, translated from York, 1452-1454; Thomas Bourchier, Cardinal, translated from Ely, 1454-1461.

Chancellors.—Simon Gaunstede, Keeper of the Seal, 1422-1424; Henry Beaufort, Bishop of Winchester, 1424-1426; John Kempe, Bishop of London, 1426-1454; Richard Neville, Earl of Salisbury, of the party of the Duke of York, 1454-1455; Thomas Bourchier, Archbishop, 1455-1456; William Waynflete, Bishop of Winchester, 1456-1460; Thomas Bourchier, Archbishop, Keeper, 1460; George Neville, Bishop of Exeter, brother to the Earl of Warwick, 1460-1461.

On Henry's accession the Duke of Bedford was made Regent of France, the Duke of Gloucester, Protector of England. On the death of Bedford, in 1435, the Duke of York was made Lieutenant and Governor-General of France, 1436-1437. Richard Beauchamp, Earl of Warwick, succeeded him, 1437-39. York succeeded again from 1440-1447, when the Duke of Somerset succeeded.

York was "Protector and Defender of the Realm and Church of England," 1454, and in 1455-1456. He was Lieutenant of Ireland, 1447-1453, and 1457-1459.

Richard Neville, Earl of Warwick, was Captain of Calais, 1455-1459, when he was attainted, but he never surrendered Calais. He was Captain again in 1461, Lord Warden of the Cinque Ports, and Great Chamberlain of England.

Sir John Fortescue was Chief Justice of the King's Bench, 1442–1462. He wrote *De Laudibus Legum Angliæ*, which is an exposition of the Constitutional Theory of the English Government under the Lancastrians.

ACTS AND DOCUMENTS

In 1429, by 8 Henry VI. c. 7, it was enacted, that owing to the disorder consequent upon the presence of men of small substance at the election of knights of the shire, the franchise should henceforth be confined to residents owning lands or houses of forty shillings a year and upwards. By 10 Henry VI. c. 2, it was explained that this meant Freeholders of forty shillings a year value and upwards. This distinctly altered the theoretical basis of the representation, for the suitors at the County Court, the reeve and four men from each township, had not been freeholders, but in practice it is doubtful if the character of the representatives was changed; the House of Commons was evidently becoming a mere complement to the parties and feuds of the nobility, but the same families furnish knights of the shires before and after the act, of which too much has been made as an oligarchic statute. See Stubbs, *Constitutional History*, ch. xx., § 403; xxi. §§ 800–6. The Acts are printed in the Statutes.

In 1435 a general congress of European ambassadors was held at Arras to try and mediate in the matter of the French war. It resulted in the defection of Burgundy from the English side, with the certain loss of France. War followed between England and Burgundy, interrupted by frequent truces, and presently suspended altogether, owing to the natural ties of common interest between England and Flanders.

The Treaty of Arras is printed in Dumont, vol. ii., part 2, p. 309. Dumont, 19 vols. folio, contains the complete text of many European treaties from Charlemagne down to the middle of the eighteenth century. See also Monstrelet, vol. ii., folio 108.

In 1444 a marriage treaty was concluded between the king

and Margaret of Anjou, daughter of the titular king of Naples, Sicily, and Jerusalem, by which Maine and Anjou were surrendered to him and a truce made with France.

Printed in Rymer's *Foedera*, xi. 59.

In 1460 the Duke of York claimed the crown in Parliament, but the lords drew up objections that they were bound by oath to the House of Lancaster, that the succession was settled by acts of Parliament in that House, that they were the heirs male of Edward III., that York did not bear the arms of Lionel Duke of Clarence, the ancestor through whom he claimed, that Henry IV. had been the true heir to Henry III. A compromise was agreed upon, that Henry should keep the crown for his lifetime, and that York should succeed him. *Rolls of Parliament*, v. 375–381.

AUTHORS

Stubbs, *Constitutional History*. Hallam, *Middle Ages*, which gives succinctly the arguments for the rival parties, York and Lancaster.

The Introduction to the *Paston Letters*, by Mr. Gairdner, will throw much light for the general reader upon the true meaning of both Henry VI.'s and Edward IV.'s reigns.

The *Lancaster and York*, of the same author, is still available for a *résumé*.

EDWARD IV. 1461–1483

Married Elizabeth Woodville, though possibly he was pre-contracted to the Lady Eleanor Butler, and if so the legitimacy of the children of Elizabeth was fairly disputable, according to the ecclesiastical law of the time.

DOMINIONS

England, Ireland, and Calais.

WARS

The victory of Towton, 1461, properly belongs to his reign. In 1462 Queen Margaret obtained some help from France, and in 1463 from Scotland, and resumed the war in the North.

In 1464 her troops were defeated at Hedgeley Moor and Hexham. In 1469 the jealousy of the old nobility, and specially of the Earl of Warwick, for the Queen's Lancastrian relatives, the general discontent at the continuance of heavy taxes and oppression, and the desire of Warwick to free himself from a king who had escaped from his control, produced a combination of the Warwick and Lancastrian parties, which began what was in effect a struggle of the nobility against the Crown. A popular insurrection was prepared, which defeated the king's troops at Edgecote, and captured and executed the father and brother of the queen. In 1470 Edward defeated a similar insurrection at Loosecoat Field, near Stamford, and forced Warwick to fly the country, but the latter returning with Edward's brother Clarence, Edward fled in turn to Holland. In 1471 he returned, and with his brother Richard defeated and killed Warwick at Barnet, and ruined the remaining strength of the confederacy at Tewkesbury.

The bastard of Falconbridge made an invasion of Kent, and an abortive attempt on London, while Edward was in the West. Henceforward the power of the Crown was established as it had not been for long, and a peace policy abroad saved the king from the necessity of asking for frequent supplies. The immense confiscations which came into his hands helping to render him independent of Parliament.

The baronage, however, were not exterminated by these wars. Only the families of Beaufort, Holland, Tiptoft, Lovel, and Bonneville were exterminated in the male line; but of the older important nobility Beauchamp, Montacute, Mowbray, had all merged in other lines by female descent, and many great families were nearly ruined.

OFFICIALS

Archbishop.—Thomas Bourchier, 1461-1483.

Chancellors.—George Neville, Bishop of Exeter, afterwards Archbishop of York, brother to the Earl of Warwick, 1461–

1467; Robert Stillington, Bishop of Bath and Wells, 1467–1473; John Morton, afterwards Bishop of Ely, Archbishop and Cardinal, and Henry Bourchier, Earl of Essex, were Keepers in 1473; Lawrence Booth, Bishop of Durham, 1473–1475; Thomas Rotherham, Bishop of Lincoln, afterwards Archbishop of York, 1475–1483, except for a short time in 1475, when John Alcock, Bishop of Rochester, was Chancellor; Thomas Bourchier, the Archbishop, was Treasurer, 1461–1462; Richard, Earl Rivers, the Queen's father, was Treasurer, 1466–1469; Henry Bourchier, Earl of Essex, brother to the Archbishop, was Treasurer, 1471–1483. He married the sister of Richard Duke of York.

ACTS AND DOCUMENTS

In 1461, by 1 Ed. iv. c. 1 the acts of the Lancastrian kings were confirmed, except with regard to such persons as the king might consider his enemies, an exception allowing of extensive forfeiture. Printed in the Statutes. To this first Parliament 44 peers were summoned, and 14, already dead or in exile, were attainted by it.

In 1465 tunnage and poundage and the subsidy on wool were granted to the king for life. This became the practice in the case of tunnage and poundage down to the accession of Charles I. (*Rolls of Parl.* v. 508.)

In 1474 Edward made a treaty with Charles the Bold, the Duke of Burgundy, for the recovery of France, ceding, in anticipation to the duke, Bar, Champagne, the Nivernois, and other possessions. (Rymer's *Foedera*, xi. 804–810.)

In 1475, when in France, he informed the French king that he was willing to return on receipt of a sum of money, and a treaty was accordingly concluded at Amiens. (Rymer's *Foedera*, xii. 14, xii. 20.)

AUTHORS

As above on the reign of Henry VI. The Memoirs of Philippe de Comines are interesting from their many references to English affairs and persons, and are available in English. Halle's *Chronicle* becomes of greater value for this period.

EDWARD V. April 9th to June 26th, 1483

OFFICIALS

Archbishop.—Thomas Bourchier.
Chancellor.—John Russell, Bishop of Lincoln.
Richard, Duke of Gloucester, Protector of the kingdom, May 14th, 1483.

RICHARD III. 1483-1485

Married Anne Neville, Co-heiress of Richard Neville, Earl of Warwick.

DOMINIONS

England, Ireland, and Calais.

WARS

After an abortive insurrection by the Duke of Buckingham, the Earl of Richmond was brought over by a combination of Yorkists and Lancastrians.

At Bosworth, on August 22nd, 1485, Richard was betrayed by Lord Stanley and the Earl of Northumberland, and defeated and killed in consequence by the troops of Henry Tudor, Earl of Richmond, and Sir William Stanley. As the leader of the House of York, the Lancastrians were of course hostile to him, as the supplanter and probable murderer of the children of Edward IV.; the Yorkist party was not warmly in favour of him; and as a resolute king and strong ruler the French feared him and the nobility distrusted him. The latter hoped by a coalition to set up a king who should be in their hands. This calculation the statesmanship of Henry VII., using the means which the state of popular feeling and European policy afforded him, completely foiled.

OFFICIALS

Archbishop.—Thomas Bourchier, 1483-1485.
Chancellor.—John Russell, Bishop of Lincoln, 1483-1485. Thomas Barowe, Keeper, 1485; Henry Stafford, Duke of

YORKIST FAMILIES OF POLE, DE LA POLE, AND COURTENAY

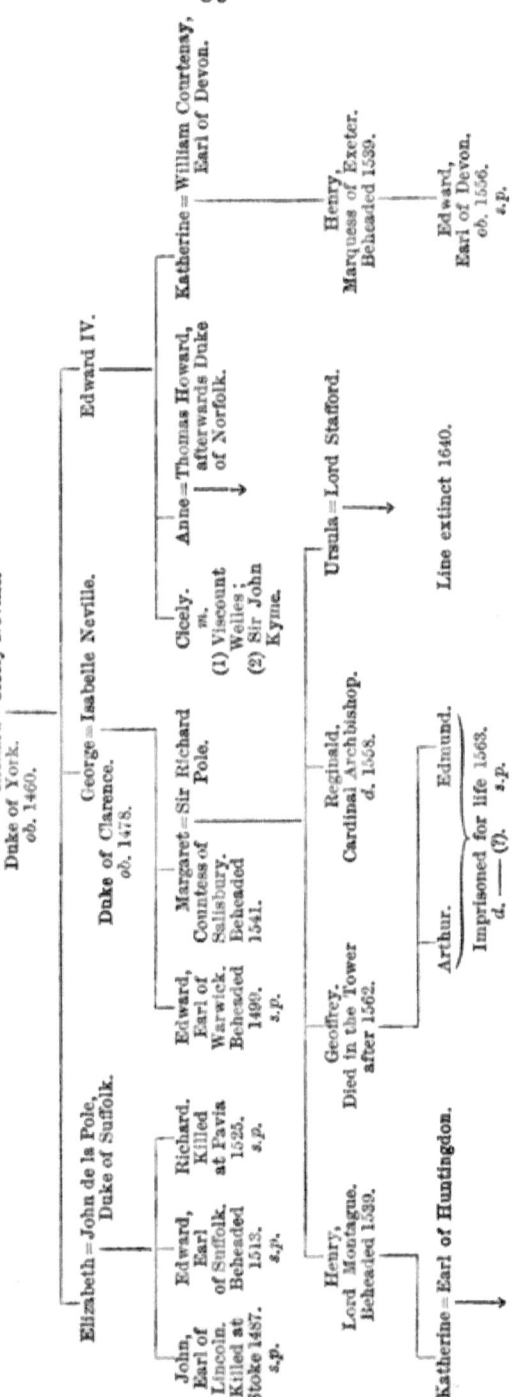

GENEALOGY TO ILLUSTRATE THE UNION OF SPAIN, BURGUNDY, AND AUSTRIA

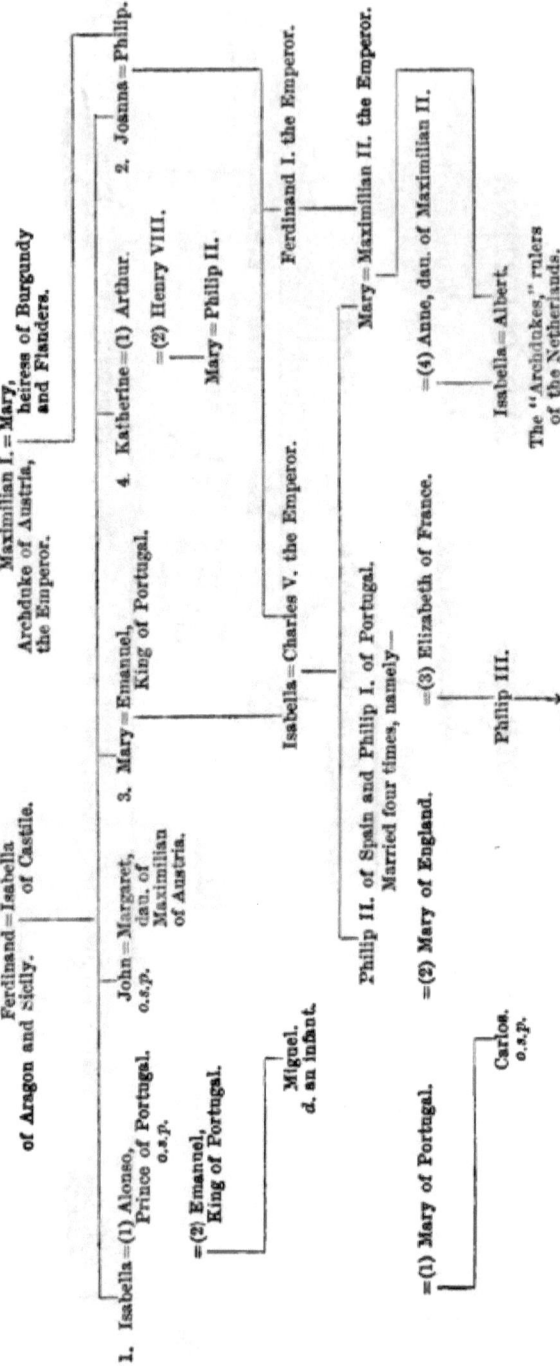

DESCENDANTS OF HENRY VII.

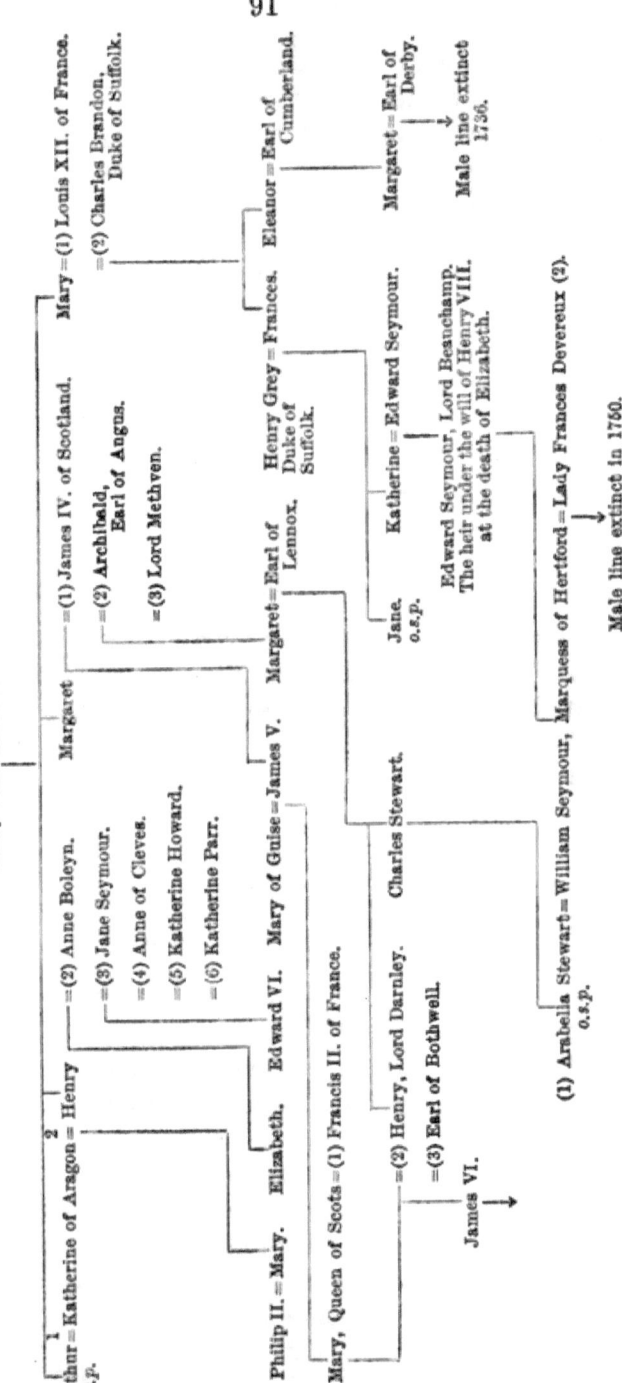

Buckingham, Lord High Constable; John Lord Howard, Duke of Norfolk, and Earl Marshall; Henry Percy, Earl of Northumberland, Warden of the Scottish Marches, and Great Chamberlain of England; Thomas Lord Stanley, Lord High Constable, December, 1483.

ACTS AND DOCUMENTS

In 1484 by 1 Richard III. c. 2, benevolences were abolished. According to Sir Thomas More Richard himself levied them afterwards, and they were commonly levied under Henry VII. Printed in the Statutes.

The Statutes of Richard III. were the first in the English language, and the first printed.

AUTHORS

As above; but in addition Gairdner, *Life of Richard III.*, is most excellent. *The Lives of Edward V. and Richard III.*, by Sir Thomas More, are accessible in the English version, and though certainly a partisan view, are written with much first-hand information, available very shortly after the events recorded.

HENRY VII. 1485-1509

Married Elizabeth of York.

DOMINIONS

England, Ireland, and Calais.

Henry succeeded as the nominee of the coalition of Yorkists and Lancastrians which had won Bosworth, on condition of marrying the eldest daughter of Edward IV. Descended from the illegitimate line of Lancaster, the Beauforts, he had no claim by birth to the throne, and the birth of his wife had been declared to be illegitimate by Parliament under Richard III., on the ground of Edward's pre-contract with Lady Eleanor Butler, before marrying Elizabeth Woodville. The strength of the monarchy notwithstanding rested upon the ruin of so many great houses; the great possessions in the hands of the crown; the desire of the middle classes to support a strong executive for the sake of peace and order; the similar attitude of the clergy; the changes in the method of warfare, the use of cannon and professional soldiers, which gave a great advantage to the possessor of money; the growth of strong monarchies abroad, the aid of which would be indispensable to English parties, and made the support of the king an act of patriotism; the decay of the sentiment in favour of Constitutional government, owing to its breakdown under Henry VI.; and the growth of feeling in favour of monarchical power.

WARS

Henry's policy was to keep the peace, and to free England from the dependence upon foreign powers, which had become marked during the late wars. Nevertheless, he was involved in both civil war and foreign war.

In 1487 the Earl of Lincoln, nephew and adopted heir to Richard III., was defeated and killed at Stoke, near Newark, with a force of Yorkists, Irish, and mercenaries from the Burgundian dominions.

In 1488 some English troops under the Earl Rivers were in the battle of St. Aubin, when Henry's ally, the Duke of Britanny, was defeated by the French. In 1497 the Cornishmen rose against a subsidy voted by Parliament, and were defeated at Blackheath by the king's artillery and trained soldiers.

OFFICIALS

Archbishops.—Thomas Bourchier, 1485-1486; John Morton, translated from Ely, afterwards Cardinal, 1486-1500; Henry Deane, translated from Salisbury, 1501-1504; William Warham, translated from London, 1504-1509.

Chancellors.—John Alcock, Bishop of Worcester, afterwards Bishop of Ely, 1485-1487; John Morton, Archbishop, 1487-

1500; Richard Nikke, Keeper, 1500; Henry Deane, Bishop of Salisbury, afterwards Archbishop, Keeper, 1500-1502; William Barons, Keeper, 1502; William Warham, Bishop of London, afterwards Archbishop, Keeper, 1502-1504, Chancellor, 1504-1509.

Thomas Howard, Earl of Surrey, afterwards Duke of Norfolk, son to the Duke of Norfolk killed at Bosworth, and himself attainted for the part he took in supporting Richard III., was Lord High Treasurer in 1501, and continued under Henry VIII. to 1522, when he retired at the age of seventy-nine.

ACTS AND DOCUMENTS

In 1485, by 1 Henry VII. c. 6, the attainder under which many members of the Parliament lay was reversed, in the absence of those members. The case of the king himself, attainted in Richard III.'s time was raised, but the Judges decided that the possession of the crown removed all taint of blood, and that from the day that the king assumed the crown he was freed from all such disability. The possession of the crown became the starting-point for the re-organization of government.

The parliament also settled the crown upon Henry and his heirs, and the Papal Bull granting a dispensation for the marriage of the King with Elizabeth of York confirmed the king's title. Printed in the Statutes, *Rolls of Parliament*, vi., 270, and Rymer's *Foedera*, xii. 294-297.

In 1487, by 3 Henry VII. 1, the irregular jurisdiction of the council was put into legal form, and the chancellor, treasurer, privy seal, or any two of them, with a bishop and temporal lord of the council, and the chief justices of the king's bench and common pleas, or in their absence two other justices, were given summary and arbitrary power to proceed in cases of riots, combinations, intimidations, untrue returns, the bribing of juries and other cases. This act legalized what was afterwards done without parliamentary sanction by the Star Chamber

—a name which does not appear in the act, but is used earlier. (Printed in the Statutes.)

In 1495, by 11 Henry VII. c. 1., service of obedience to the king *de facto* was declared not to be punishable by parliament or any other court as treason, notwithstanding any acts made to the contrary. It is significant that this act was passed when Perkin Warbeck was in Scotland. Though an impostor, his appearance indicated a Yorkist movement, which might result in another change of dynasty. (Printed in the Statutes.)

Ireland, so far as it was English at all, had been in favour of the Yorkist party, and had supported all but unanimously the attempt of 1487.

In 1495 Sir Edward Poynings, Lord Deputy in Ireland to Henry's, the king's son, procured the passing of Poynings' Act, by which English laws passed before that time were to be in force in Ireland, and no legislation could be proposed in the Irish Parliament without the permission of the English Council. (Printed in Leland, *Irish Statutes*, ii. 102.)

In 1496 the Great Intercourse, a treaty of peace and commerce, was made with Philip Archduke of Austria and Duke of Burgundy, the ruler of the Netherlands. The Yorkist sympathy of Burgundy being overruled by the commercial necessities of Flanders. (Rymer's *Foedera*, xii. 578.)

In 1506 another treaty, called by the Flemings *Malus Intercursus*, because it limited their right of fishery on the English coasts, was made during the accidental detention of Philip in England owing to bad weather. It provided for the surrender of the Earl of Suffolk, Edmund de la Pole, a grandson of Richard Duke of York. (Rymer's *Foedera*, xiii. 123.)

In 1504, by 19 Henry VII. 14, the giving of liveries was further forbidden. It had been continually forbidden since Richard II., but had been continually the practice. Henry VII. had already severely punished infractions of the former statutes. Liveried retainers, personal followers, must be distinguished from feudal tenants, who as landholders had a certain weight and position of respectability. (Printed in the Statutes.)

AUTHORS

Hallam, *Constitutional History of England*, begins with the reign of Henry VII., and is always learned and impartial. The reign of Henry VII. is among the more obscure periods of our later history, and is not the subject of any considerable recent work.

Bacon's *Life of Henry VII.* is the chief authority followed by many writers, but is of doubtful weight on some points. Halle's *Chronicle* is still useful. Stubbs, *Lectures on the Study of Mediaeval and Modern History*, has thrown light on the reign, and Ranke at the beginning of his *History of England, principally in the Seventeenth Century*, has in Book II. ch. 1, 2, reviewed the position of England with regard to European politics under Henry VII., and under Henry VIII. in his earlier years.

Henceforward down to the reign of George I. the history of England as one of the European family of nations is nowhere treated with such learning and thoroughness as by Ranke. His history is translated from the German, and published by the Clarendon Press. For the social condition of England in this and the following reign Thorold Rogers, *History of Prices*, may be consulted.

HENRY VIII. 1509–1547

Married (1) Katharine of Aragon ; (2) Anne Boleyn — (the marriage certainly took place, but the exact date is uncertain ; it was at all events before any competent court had declared the king's previous marriage null and void); (3) Jane Seymour ; (4) Anne of Cleves ; (5) Katharine Howard ; (6) Katharine Parr.

DOMINIONS

England, Ireland, Calais. The royal government of Ireland was made much more complete than had been the case. The supremacy of the Earls of Kildare within the English Pale was broken down, and the Irish chieftains were encouraged to send their children to England for education, to accept English titles, and by degrees it was hoped English laws and customs. The spoliation instead of the reform of the church, and the religious quarrel fomented by foreign powers, prevented the favourable progress of this policy. Henry took the title of King instead of Lord of Ireland. In 1536 Wales was incorporated with England by act of Parliament, and Welsh counties and boroughs were directed to return members to the English Parliament. In 1543 the County Palatine of Chester was directed to return members to Parliament.

From 1513 to 1519 Tournay, and some small places in the neighbourhood, were in the hands of the English.

In 1544 Henry's officers took Boulogne, which remained in English hands till the end of the reign.

WARS

In 1511 Henry formed a league with Ferdinand of Aragon against France and Scotland, and in 1513 the Emperor Maximilian became a party to it.

In 1513, during a campaign in alliance with the Emperor against France, a cavalry skirmish near Terouenne was dignified by the name of the Battle of the Spurs. In the same year the Earl of Surrey, who had fought at Barnet for the house of York, and been made prisoner at Bosworth, defeated and killed James IV. of Scotland in an obstinate battle at Flodden in Northumberland. There was continued desultory warfare on the Scotch border, and Scotland, which had held a really independent position since the return of James I. from his English captivity in 1424, became alternately dependent upon England, a connexion usually supported by the Douglasses, or upon France, whose alliance was chiefly upheld by the Chancellors James Betoun from 1513-1526, and David Betoun, Privy Seal 1528-1543, Chancellor 1543-1546, uncle and nephew, both Archbishops of St. Andrews.

In 1542 war again broke out with Scotland, and in 1543

Henry and the Emperor declared war against France. In 1544 the English took Boulogne. Peace was concluded with France and Scotland in 1546.

In 1536 a dangerous insurrection, called the Pilgrimage of Grace, broke out in the Northern Counties and Lincolnshire against the king's ecclesiastical policy—the insurgents were cajoled into dispersing. The insurrection was renewed and put down in the following year. The older nobility and the remains of the Yorkist party were concerned in it, or at least wished it well.

OFFICIALS

Archbishops.—William Warham, d. 1533; Thomas Cranmer, 1533–1547.

Chancellors.—William Warham, Archbishop, 1509–1515; Thomas Wolsey, Archbishop of York and Cardinal, 1515–29; Thomas Howard Duke of Norfolk, and Charles Brandon Duke of Suffolk, the king's brother-in-law, Keepers, 1529; Sir Thomas More, 1529–1532; Sir Thomas Audley, Keeper, 1532–1533, Chancellor, 1533–1544; Thomas Lord Wriothesley, 1544–1547.

Thomas Howard Earl of Surrey, afterwards Duke of Norfolk, was Treasurer, 1509–1522. He was succeeded by his son, Thomas Earl of Surrey, afterwards Duke of Norfolk, 1522–1546. Thomas Cromwell, afterwards Earl of Essex, was Chancellor of the Exchequer, 1533–1540; Principal Secretary to the king, 1534–1536; Vicar-General and Vice-Regent to the king *in Spiritualibus*, 1536–1540. Stephen Gardiner, afterwards Bishop of Winchester, was Secretary to the king, 1528–1533. Thomas Wriothesley, afterwards Chancellor, was Secretary, 1536–1546.

ACTS AND DOCUMENTS
Up to 1529.

In 1511 Henry made an alliance with Aragon, the Pope Julius II., Venice, and in 1513 with the Emperor Maximilian against France. (Rymer's *Foedera*, xiii. 305, 311.)

By this alliance Henry entered upon the adventurous foreign policy, which Wolsey afterwards directed with a view to the maintenance of a balance of power in Europe. Though the immediate cost was great, with small results to show, there is no doubt that England was thereby replaced in a leading position in Europe, and made ready for her share in the colonial and commercial expansion which were to come from the discovery of the New World and of the maritime route to India, a place which could only be won and kept by a nation recognized as a great power. Indirectly, too, this foreign policy probably resulted in a modification of the exclusively monarchical rule which had been prevailing since Edward IV.'s reign, and which a continuance of Henry VII.'s policy might have made perpetual.

In 1512, by 4 Henry VIII. sess. 2, c. 2, Benefit of clergy was taken from murderers and felons. One of the first indications of the approaching control of the royal over the ecclesiastical courts. (Printed in the Statutes.)

Another sign of the future course of the reign was that in 1524 the royal assent was given to the suppression of the Monastery of St. Frideswide at Oxford; a bull of Clement VII. was issued extending Wolsey's legatine powers for the visitation of monasteries; and another provided for the suppression of all monasteries with less annual income than 3000 ducats. (Rymer's *Foedera*, xiv. 15, 18, 23.)

In 1514 Henry concluded peace with France, and a marriage treaty was made between Louis XII. and the king's sister Mary. (Rymer's *Foedera*, xiii. 412, 423.)

In 1515, however, Louis died, and Francis I., his successor, renewing the French claims on Milan, won the great victory of Marignano over the Swiss, who garrisoned the Milanese, and so threatened the balance of European power that England formed a new league with the Pope, the Emperor, the prince of Castile (Charles, afterwards Emperor), and the Swiss. (Rymer's *Foedera*, xiii. 555.)

This league, however, came to little, owing to the poverty and perhaps insincerity of the Emperor, and Charles, now king of Spain, having concluded a treaty with France at Noyon, to which the Emperor became a party, England made a peace with France, surrendering to France, and not to Charles as he had hoped, Tournay and its surroundings, and including all the European powers in the pacification, 1518. (Rymer's *Foedera*, xiii. 624, 656.)

In 1522, war having broken out between Charles, now Emperor, and Francis, England joined the former. But the ill success of the Duke of Suffolk in 1523, the great success of Charles at Pavia, February 24th, 1525, and the sack of Rome, 1526, inclined England to the French side. Peace had been made with France on August 30th, 1525 (Rymer's *Foedera*, xiv. 48), and a treaty was made by Cardinal Wolsey with Francis at Amiens, 1527, to force the Emperor to reasonable terms of peace, England receiving money and a promise of Boulogne and Ardres. (Rymer's *Foedera*, xiv. 203.)

This change of side left the king free to consider further the question of the annullment of his marriage with Katharine, the Emperor's aunt.

In 1529, on August 5th, the general peace of Cambrai was concluded, modifying very much the terms extorted by the Emperor from Francis, when the latter was a prisoner at Madrid, after Pavia. (Rymer's *Foedera*, xiv. 326; *Previous Treaty of Madrid*, xiv. 308.)

Though Wolsey was no longer the directing spirit of European affairs—he was deprived of the seal on October 17th, 1529 —yet the peace of Cambrai was a triumph for the policy which he had pursued. It left the power of France and of Charles fairly balanced, and the importance of England to one side or the other well established.

AUTHORS

For the earlier twenty years of Henry VIII.

Brewer's *History of Henry the Eighth's Reign* is the standard work on the subject. The constitutional features are not marked, and Hallam's *Constitutional History*, though interesting in his account of attempts by Wolsey to overawe the Parliament, and to raise money by extraparliamentary means, is silent on the more important points of the history.

For a brief sketch *Cardinal Wolsey*, by Bishop Creighton, in the *English Statesmen Series*, is useful as the work of a first-rate historian.

HENRY VIII. PART II.

THE BEGINNING OF THE REFORMATION

The series of events which led to the separation of the Church in England from Rome, and to the completion of the royal supremacy over the Church, began with Henry's attempts to annul his marriage with his brother's widow Katharine, on the ground that the marriage was against the law of the Church, and that no Papal dispensation could make it valid. The Pope, not unnaturally, was slow to countenance such a doctrine.

Henry's subsequent measures greatly increased the royal power by adding to it authority in spiritual things. His policy, leading to hostility with the Pope and Emperor, caused a yet further increase of his power on the ground of public safety, as all the elements of opposition to the Crown, the relations of the Yorkist House, the older nobility, and the discontented poor, found a rallying point in the ecclesiastical discontent.

The king, though practically despotic, conducted his government by the aid of Parliament during this latter half of his reign. The turning out of the mitred abbots from the House of Lords, the dependence of the bishops upon the Crown, the creation of new peers, the summoning of members from small boroughs, and the distribution of monastic property among commoners, giving the Crown a strong hold over both Houses of Parliament. This revival of Parliamentary activity, however, was pregnant of results in the future. The increasing frequency of Parliamentary sessions is illustrated by the following table:

Henry VIII.

PARLIAMENTS OF HENRY VII. AND VIII.

Henry VII. Parliament met in 1485, 1487, 1489, 1491, 1495, 1497, 1504.

Henry VIII. Parliament met in 1510, February, 1512, November, 1512, 1513, 1514, 1515, 1523, 1529, 1530, 1531, 1532, 1533, 1534, 1535, 1536, 1539, 1540, 1542, 1543, 1544, 1545.

The same Parliament sat from November 3rd, 1529, till July 18th, 1536, and passed the most important of the anti-Papal Acts.

ACTS AND DOCUMENTS

The suppression of some of the smaller monasteries, and the application of their revenues to the foundation of colleges, had been already begun by Wolsey. (See too A.D. 1414.)

In 1528 a Bull of Pope Clement VII. gave the king leave to suppress very small monasteries for the benefit of his colleges at Windsor and Cambridge (*hodie* the chapter of Windsor, and Trinity College, Cambridge). (Rymer, xiv. 270.)

In the same year another Bull provided for the suppression of monasteries with less than twelve inmates, and their amalgamation with larger houses. (Rymer, xiv. 272.)

Another Bull to the same effect was issued in 1529. (Rymer, xiv. 345.)

Yet another sanctioned the suppression of small monasteries for the sake of providing funds to build new cathedrals. (Rymer, xiv. 273.)

The subsequent entire suppression of the monasteries was therefore the completion of a policy which had already been entered upon by degrees, both with and without Papal concurrence.

The larger houses whose abbots and priors were summoned to the Parliament of 1529 were the following: St. John's Colchester, St. Edmund's Bury, Abingdon, the Holy Cross of Waltham, Shrewsbury, Cirencester, Gloucester, Westminster, Bardney, Selby, Hulme, Thorney, Evesham, Ramsey, Hide,

Glastonbury, Malmesbury, Croyland, Battle, Winchcombe, Reading, St. Augustine's Canterbury, St. Mary's York, Tewkesbury, Tavistock, Coventry. The Prior of St. John of Jerusalem, in England, the head of the English Knights Hospitallers, was also summoned.

Henry VIII. 21, c. 24. The king released from his debts by Act of Parliament, on the ground that he had expended his treasure in securing the peace of Europe. (Printed in the Statutes.)

Henry VIII. 22, c. 15. The clergy of the province of Canterbury acknowledging that they are liable to the penalties of *Praemunire* for obeying the Legatine authority of Wolsey, pardoned on payment of £100,000 in five years.

Henry VIII. 23, c. 19. The clergy of the province of York similarly pardoned on payment of £18,840 0s. 10d. The royal supremacy practically vindicated thereby. (Printed in the Statutes.)

1532. Henry made with Francis of France a defensive alliance against the possible hostility of the Emperor, on account of his meditated repudiation of the Emperor's aunt. (Rymer, xiv. 434.)

Henry VIII. 24, c. 12. An Act forbidding any appeals to Rome.

"Whereas . . . this realm of England is an Empire, and so hath been accepted in the world, governed by one Supreme Head and King . . . he being institute and furnished . . . with plenary, whole and entire power . . . to render and yield justice and final determination to all manner of folk . . . and that part of the body politick called the spirituality, now being usually called the English Church . . . hath been always thought and is at this hour sufficient and meet of itself . . . to declare and determine all such doubts, and to administer all such duties and offices as to their rooms spiritual doth appertain," &c. (Printed in the Statutes.)

It is noticeable that the King in Parliament asserts the

separation of England from the Holy Roman Empire, of which the Bishop of Rome was naturally the chief bishop. Reference is made to the statutes of Edward I., Edward III., Richard II., and Henry IV., and appeals to Rome, or to any foreign power, are made punishable by the penalties of *Praemunire*, the old Act under which a Royal Supremacy over spiritual persons and causes had been vindicated. The Act of *Praemunire* itself being based on more ancient precedents.

In 1533 the Convocation of the Province of Canterbury determined that the king's marriage with his brother's widow was null and void from the beginning, and that no Papal dispensation could render it valid. In accordance with which decision the Archbishop's Court dissolved the marriage. (Rymer, xiv. 454.)

Henry VIII. 25, c. 19. Convocation was only to assemble by the king's writ, and was only to enact constitutions by the king's leave. Appeals from the Archbishops' Courts were to be to the Court of Chancery.

Henry VIII. 25, c. 20. The payment of Annates and First-fruits to Rome forbidden. Persons elected to bishoprics not to be presented to the See of Rome, and if election by the chapter is delayed, the king empowered to present to a bishopric by letters patent under the Great Seal.

Henry VIII. 26, c. 3. First-fruits and Annates granted to the crown.

Henry VIII. 25, c. 21. All payments to the See of Rome, and all laws, dispensations, indulgences, licenses, and visitations by the See of Rome abolished in England.

Henry VIII. 26, 1. "The King our Sovereign Lord . . . shall be taken, accepted, and reputed the only Supreme Head in earth of the Church of England, called *Anglicana Ecclesia*."

This Act was confirmatory of what had been already determined. In February, 1531, the Convocation of Canterbury, and in May, 1531, the Convocation of York, had admitted the Supreme Headship of the king "so far as the law of Christ allows." On June 15, 1535, the king formally took the title *In terra supremum caput Anglicanae Ecclesiae.* Rymer, xiv. 549. The title was adopted on their succession by Edward VI. and Mary. The above act was repealed by 1 and 2 Philip and Mary, c. 8. The title was never afterwards assumed.

Henry VIII. 26, c. 13. The penalties of treason extended to cover wishing or desiring by words or writing any bodily harm to the king, queen, or their heirs apparent, depriving them of any dignity, style, or name, or publishing that the king is an heretic, schismatic, infidel, or usurper. An act which the spies employed by Thomas Cromwell turned into a frightful engine of tyranny, men being made traitors for hasty words.

Henry VIII. 27, c. 10. The Statute of Uses, providing that the possession of land shall be in him or them who hath the use. The effect of the law was to hinder the power of landholders to make provision for younger sons by a charge upon their land, and it was one of the grievances of those gentlemen who joined the "Pilgrimage of Grace."

The Acts, Henry VIII. 32, c. 1, and Henry VIII. 34–5, c. 5, allowed the owners of real estate (land) to devise it by will.

Henry VIII. 27, c. 28. All monasteries with lands, if not above £200 a year value, given into the king's hands.

Henry VIII. 28, c. 17. The king's successor empowered to repeal any statutes made in his reign before he reaches the age of twenty-four.

Henry VIII. 31, c. 8. The king's proclamations given the force of law. An act which if carried to its possible extent would have entirely abrogated the Parliamentary constitution. Repealed Edward VI. 1, c. 12.

Henry VIII. 31, c. 13. Suppression of all remaining monasteries, reciting that many have been already surrendered, and confirming such surrenders to the king.

Henry VIII. 31, c. 14. The Statute called the Six Articles.

By this denial of Transubstantiation was punished as heresy, with death by burning, and forfeiture of all goods to the crown. Affirmation of the necessity of Communion in both kinds for the laity; of the lawfulness of the marriage of priests; of the lawfulness of marriage by persons who have professed chastity or widowhood; that private masses are not lawful, laudable, and agreeable to the law of God; or that auricular confession is not expedient and to be used; to be punished by death, as felony, with forfeiture of goods. If a priest, or other man or woman who has vowed chastity or widowhood marry or commit unchastity, both parties to be adjudged felons.

The excessive severity of the act may have tended to make it a dead letter, or it may have been intended rather to terrify the extreme Reforming party and satisfy the Ecclesiastical Conservatives than to be strictly enforced. Though certainly a large number, and such as the archbishop himself who was married, must have been liable to its penalties, Foxe has only collected the names of twenty-eight persons who suffered under it, and they cannot all be certainly included.

Henry VIII. 34–35, c. 26. (Extending and completing the act, Henry VIII. 27, c. 26.) Dividing Wales into counties, establishing a President and Council for Wales, and Justices of the Peace as in England. Members were returned to Parliament from Welsh counties and boroughs, and the later boundaries not only of Wales, but of the English counties bordering upon Wales were fixed. The present geographical Wales dates only from these acts.

Henry VIII. 35, c. 3. An Act confirming an Irish Act of Henry VIII. 33, c. 1, giving Henry the title of king (*Rex*) of Ireland, instead of lord (*Dominus*). The creation of a kingdom had been in mediaeval Europe the prerogative of the pope or emperor, and by this act Henry continued to assert the imperial independence of the crown of England.

Henry VIII. 35, c. 12. The king's debts incurred since the

thirty-third year of his reign remitted, and sums repaid by him to be returned. The lands and revenues of the monastic houses had been expended in erecting new bishoprics, in building castles for coast defence, in small pensions to former inmates, and chiefly in extravagant grants to nobility and gentry. Moreover the total revenue of the abbey lands had apparently not been so large as was expected.

Henry VIII. 37, c. 4. Divers Colleges, Free Chapels, Chantries, Hospitals, Guilds, &c., suppressed. The terms of the act seemed to include the Colleges in the Universities, but the King promised that they should be unmolested. The above are all printed in the Statutes.

1546, June 7. A peace concluded with France to terminate the war undertaken in conjunction with the Emperor in 1543, stipulating for the return of Boulogne to the French on the payment of certain sums of money, neither party to erect new fortifications in the *Boulonnais* till after Michaelmas, 1554. (Rymer, xv. 93.)

THE WILL OF HENRY VIII.

The succession to the crown, the uncertainty concerning which had been a principal reason for the avoidance of the king's first marriage, had been three times regulated by Act of Parliament. By Henry VIII. 25, c. 22 the marriage with Katherine had been declared void, and the crown settled upon Elizabeth or other male issue of the marriage with Anne Boleyn. By Henry VIII. 28, c. 7 Elizabeth had been declared illegitimate, and the crown settled on the children of Jane Seymour. By Henry VIII. 35, c. 1 the crown was settled upon the king's son, and, should he die without heirs, upon Mary and her heirs, and upon Elizabeth and her heirs in succession. The king reserving to himself the right to impose conditions upon their succession, as being heirs only by favour, not right, and further reserving power to dispose of the crown entirely by will.

His will was accordingly made, dated December 30th,

1546. By it he left the crown to his son Edward and his heirs, failing these to Mary and her heirs, failing these to Elizabeth and her heirs. Failing all issue of his body to the daughters of his younger sister Mary and their heirs, passing over the descendants of his elder sister Margaret Queen of Scots, failing these to "the next rightful heirs." Mary and Elizabeth, however, were not to succeed unless they acted by consent of the king's son's Privy Council in their marriages.

The following were appointed his executors and privy councillors to his son Edward: The Archbishop Cranmer, the Lord Chancellor Wriothesley, Lord St. John, the Earl of Hertford, Lord Russell, Viscount Lisle, Tunstall, Bishop of Durham, Sir Antony Brown, Sir Edward Montagu, Chief Justice of the Common Pleas, Justice Bromley, Sir Edward North, Sir William Paget, Sir Anthony Denny, Sir William Herbert, Sir Edward Wootton, Master Doctor Wootton. (Rymer xv. 110.)

There was some attempt in this list of councillors to combine the more forward reforming and the reactionary party, Tunstall and Wriothesley belonging decidedly to the latter, though such a strong partizan as Gardiner was omitted.

AUTHORS

Strype's *Annals of the Reformation* preserve a large number of original documents, proclamations, &c., bearing on the history from Henry VIII. to Elizabeth.

Ranke's *History of England*, Book II., gives the best résumé of a period obscured by controversial writing.

Dixon's *History of the Church of England*, Hook's *Lives of the Archbishops, Cranmer*, Father Gasquet's *Henry VIII. and the Monasteries*, are all three excellent, but all three written with a certain bias. The most brilliant literary work on the period, Froude's *History*, if used at all, is to be used with the consideration that accuracy of detail and rectitude of judgment are not present in proportion to its graphic and original vigour. The reign of Charles V., so important for English affairs, is best treated in Ranke's *History of the Reformation in Germany*, or in a small handbook form in Seebohm's *Era of the Protestant Revolution*, but this covers too much ground to be quite satisfactory.

EDWARD VI. 1547-1553

DOMINIONS

England, Ireland, Calais, and the Boulonnais. In 1547 Roxburgh, Haddington, and some other places in Scotland were occupied, but were recovered by the Scots, or evacuated in the next three years. In 1550 Boulogne was surrendered to the French.

WARS

In 1547 the Protector invaded Scotland to try and enforce a marriage treaty between the king and the young queen Mary of Scotland. The Scots were defeated at Pinkie or Musselburgh, September 10th, but the only effect was to strengthen the French party in Scotland. A desultory war followed with Scotland, in which France joined in 1548, until 1550.

In 1549 there were serious rebellions against the religious policy of the government and because of social grievances. Cornwall, Devonshire, and Somersetshire rose for the mass and the six articles, and were only put down by foreign mercenaries after severe fighting, especially at Crediton, near Exeter. The people of Norfolk rose under Ket, a tanner, on social grounds, and were defeated near Norwich. There were riots, religious and social, in the same year in Yorkshire, Kent, Middlesex, Surrey, Sussex, Hampshire, Berkshire, Wiltshire, Oxfordshire, Suffolk.

Owing to the policy of the government in religion, and towards the Lady Mary, relations were strained with her relative the Emperor.

OFFICIALS

Archbishop.—Thomas Cranmer, 1547–1553.

Chancellors.—Lord Wriothesley, Earl of Southampton, 1547; Lord St. John, afterwards Earl of Wiltshire and Marquis of Winchester, Keeper, 1547; Lord Rich, 1547; Bishop of Ely, Thomas Goodrich, Keeper 1551, Chancellor 1552.

Lord Treasurers.—Earl of Hertford, 1547; Earl of Wiltshire, afterwards Marquis of Winchester, 1551.

Edward Seymour, Earl of Hertford (Duke of Somerset, February 16th), Protector of the Realm, February 1, 1547.

John Dudley, Duke of Northumberland, Lord President of the Council, February 2, 1550.

ACTS AND DOCUMENTS

1547. The first book of Homilies published by authority to be read in Churches.

These Homilies, though advocating the doctrines of the Reformation, are not Calvinistic, according with the first Prayer book which followed two years later.

Edward VI. 1 c. 1. An Act commanding the administration of the Holy Communion in both kinds to the laity.

Ed. VI. 1, c. 2. Bishops to be appointed by Letters Patent.

Ed. VI. 1, c. 3. Act against vagabonds. A person loitering without work for three days could be adjudged as a slave for two years to the person who informed against him. If he tried to escape he could be adjudged a slave for life, in either case by two Justices of the Peace. If he tried to escape a second time he could be punished as a felon. A clerk convict to be a slave for a year, or in the second case for five years. Impotent folk were to be provided with lodging, and licensed to beg in their parishes.

The Act was partly directed against the expelled monks. It was modified by Ed. VI. 3 and 4, c. 16, and repealed under Elizabeth.

Ed. VI. 1, c. 12. Treasons limited to the offences made treason by the Acts of Ed. III. and Hen. IV.

Ed. VI. 1, c. 14. An Act for the vesting of the property of all Chantries, Hospitals, Colleges, Free Chapels, Fraternities, Brotherhoods, and Guilds in the King, with exceptions in favour of the Colleges in Oxford and Cambridge, Windsor, Winchester, Eton, Chapel-in-the-Sea in Ely, Cathedrals, and Chapels of Ease not endowed with land.

The subsequent foundations of schools and hospitals were partly to restore the mischief which this act and the previous suppressions of Henry's reign had done to the educational and charitable machinery of the country.

1548. A commission issued for visiting the Universities and Eton and other colleges for regulating the funds, expelling members, and amalgamating foundations. Money employed in supporting the Fellows was to be diverted to lectures in Philosophy or other studies. Rymer, xv. 178.

Ed. VI. 2 & 3, c. 1. An Act of Uniformity setting forth the first Prayer-book of Edward VI.

This book was drawn up by Cranmer chiefly, and founded upon the Breviary, the Sarum Missal, certain foreign Reformed Services, the Bible, and services already prepared in English in the late reign. To follow the progress of the Reformation it should be compared with the second Prayer-book, *vide infra*, set forth after foreign reformers had come to England and gained the ear of the Government. The first Prayer-book was accepted by the Convocation of the clergy before the passing of the Act.

Both books have been re-published by Messrs. Rivington.

Ed. VI. 5 & 6, c. 1. An Act of Uniformity setting forth the second Prayer-book of Edward VI., April, 1552.

The book had been printed Sept., 1551, and considered by Convocation in the autumn probably.

1553. Forty-two Articles of Religion set forth by the king's authority, including an Article (35th) confirming the late Prayer-book and Ordination office, and accepted by Convocation, according to the testimony of Convocation itself in 1562 and 1566.

The Articles are printed in the Parker Society's publications, 1844.

The Acts given above are all printed in the Statutes.

WILL OF EDWARD VI.

Under the influence of the Duke of Northumberland, Edward VI., without parliamentary concurrence, made a will devising the crown differently from the provisions of his father's will. He passed over both his sisters, and his cousin the Lady Frances, the Duchess of Suffolk, and settled the crown upon her daughter, the Lady Jane, for the obvious reason that she was married to Guildford Dudley, the son of Northumberland, saving only the rights of any male heir born to the Lady Frances in the King's own lifetime.

Letters Patent, under the Great Seal, were issued to this effect.

Edward's will is printed in the Camden Society's publication, *Queen Jane and Queen Mary*.

AUTHORS

As in the latter part of the reign of Henry VIII. The volume of Froude's history dealing with the reign of Edward is less influenced by love of paradox than the preceding volumes.

MARY. 1553–1558

Married Philip of Spain, Burgundy, and the Netherlands, son of the Emperor. Philip and Mary, July 25, 1554–1558.

DOMINIONS

England, Ireland, Calais. The last was taken by the French in 1558. In 1556 by the abdication of Charles, Spain, the two Sicilies, Milan, Burgundy, and the Netherlands came under the rule of Philip, the Queen's husband, king in England, *iure maritae*.

WARS

In 1554 Sir Thomas Wyatt raised an insurrection in Kent against the Queen's intended marriage with Philip, which if successful must have ended in her deposition. He was joined by some Londoners, but his forces were dispersed after failing to fight their way into London, Feb. 7, 1554.

In 1557 England joined with Philip in the war against France, Scotland, and the Pope, Paul IV. On August 10, the Spaniards and the Netherlanders with the assistance of a small English contingent defeated the French at St. Quentin. On Jan. 7, 1558, Calais surrendered to the Duke of Guise. On July 13 the French were defeated at Gravelines by the Spaniards and Netherlanders, with the assistance of an English fleet.

OFFICIALS

Archbishops.—Thomas Cranmer, 1553–1555; Reginald Pole, 1556–1558.

Chancellors.—Stephen Gardiner, Bishop of Winchester, 1553–1555; Nicholas Heath, Archbishop of York, 1556–1558.

Lord High Treasurer.—Marquis of Winchester, 1553–1558.

ACTS AND DOCUMENTS

From the Accession of Mary to the Settlement of Religion under Elizabeth.

The attempt to tamper with Henry's arrangement for the succession failed, and Mary's reign is dated from the day of Edward's death, July 6th, 1553.

She styles herself, " Mary, by the Grace of God, Queen of England, France, and Ireland, Defender of the Faith, and of the Church of England, and also of Ireland, in earth the Supreme Head." Rolls of Parliament.

The last clause of the title was dropped after the first year of her reign, but it was not a mere form, for on Sept. 28,

1553, the Queen, by her own authority, restored to the see of Exeter John Voysey, who had resigned in 1551, *cum omnibus Juribus tam spiritualibus quam temporalibus ad eundem Episcopatum pertinentibus.* (Rymer, xv., 340.)

Mary 1, sess. 2, c. 2. An Act repealing the late ecclesiastical changes, the appointment of bishops by letters patent, the act abolishing images, that allowing the marriage of priests, Edward's Acts of Uniformity, &c. Setting up such services as were commonly used in the last year of King Henry.

This Act was passed simply by Parliament without any ecclesiastical co-operation whatever, except the votes of a very limited number of bishops in the House of Lords. Not even Papal sanction was asked or given for it. (Printed in the Statutes.)

1554, March 13–15. The Bishops of Bristol, Chester, St. David's, Gloucester, Hereford, Lincoln, and the Archbishop of York deprived. (Rymer, xv. 370.)

Mary 1, sess. 3, c. 2. The marriage treaty between the queen and Philip of Spain confirmed, vesting all royal power in the queen as fully after her marriage as before. All royal instruments are to be drawn in the names of Philip and Mary, but are to be invalid without the Queen's sign manual. The treaty itself provided that any male heir born of the marriage was to succeed in the Netherlands and Burgundy as well as in England, and any female heir likewise, if she should marry with the consent of her half-brother, Don Carlos, and his council. (Statutes and Rymer, xv. 393.)

Philip and Mary 1 and 2, c. 6. An Act for punishment of heresy, reviving the Lollard Statutes, Richard II. 5, c. 5; Henry IV. 2, c. 15; and Henry V. 2, c. 7. (Printed in the Statutes.)

Philip and Mary 1 and 2, c. 8. An Act for repealing all acts against the See of Rome since the 20th of Henry VIII., saving all prerogatives, jurisdictions, and authorities, &c. of the Crown existing prior to that year, and in the same Act confirming the possession of ecclesiastical lands to their present lay possessors. (Printed in the Statutes.)

Philip and Mary 2 and 3, c. 4. An Act restoring firstfruits to the Church. (Printed in the Statutes.)

Philip and Mary 2 and 3, c. 5. An Act for relieving the impotent and poor in their parishes by voluntary charitable offerings every week. (Printed in the Statutes.)

THE MARIAN PERSECUTION

The persecution was set on foot at the beginning of 1555, and continued to the end of the reign. With the exception of a few Church dignitaries the great majority of the sufferers belonged to the poorer classes; some were foreigners settled in England, many persons living in or near the ports trading with the Netherlands. Foxe, the martyrologist, has collected the names of 277, whose local distribution is most marked.

In the diocese of	London	there were	112
,, ,,	Canterbury	,,	56
,, ,,	Norwich	,,	34
,, ,,	Chichester	,,	23
,, ,,	Coventry and Lichfield	,,	7
,, ,,	Bristol	,,	6
,, ,,	Rochester	,,	6
,, ,,	Salisbury	,,	6
,, ,,	Gloucester	,,	5
,, ,,	Oxford	,,	4
,, ,,	Chester	,,	3
,, ,,	Ely	,,	3
,, ,,	Peterborough	,,	3
,, ,,	Winchester	,,	3
,, ,,	St. David's	,,	2
,, ,,	Lincoln	,,	2
,, ,,	Exeter	,,	1
,, ,,	Llandaff	,,	1

In the Eastern and South-Eastern counties, in Canterbury, Rochester, Chichester, London, Ely, Norwich, and Winchester, there were 237, or about six-sevenths of the whole. Of the three in Winchester two belonged to Southwark, and the other was a native of the coast of Sussex. Of the four who suffered in Oxfordshire three were the Bishops, who did not represent a local opinion. The one in St. David's was the Bishop, Ferrar.

No martyrs are recorded in the dioceses of York, Carlisle, Durham, Sodor and Man, Worcester, Hereford, Bath and Wells, Bangor, St. Asaph.

The three first-named dioceses, with Chester and Lincoln, had been almost universally in rebellion against the reforming government of Henry VIII. Cornwall, Devonshire, and Somersetshire, with one martyr between them, were the counties which had been in arms against the religious reforms of Edward VI. Middlesex with 59 martyrs, and Kent with 58, were the only counties where any effective rebellion was raised against Mary's Spanish marriage.

Though Foxe's lists are probably not quite complete nor accurate the inference is plain, that doctrinal Protestantism, of a complexion sufficiently pronounced to cause its adherents to actively dissent from the laws in religion laid down by government, was practically confined to certain clergy, and to the counties trading with the Netherlands.

ACTS AND DOCUMENTS OF 1559-1563

By Eliz. 1, c. 1, "The ancient Jurisdiction over the Estate Ecclesiastical and Spiritual" was restored to the Crown, and "all foreign powers repugnant to the same" abolished. The Act Philip and Mary 1 and 2, c. 8, restoring the Papal Supremacy was repealed by this act, but the statutes of Henry VIII. and Ed. VI. repealed by Philip and Mary 1 and 2, c. 8, were not all re-enacted by this statute. An oath acknowledging the Royal Supremacy, however, was required by this act from all office holders, civil and ecclesiastical. By clause 18 of the act it was enacted that "the Queen may assign Commissioners to exercise Ecclesiastical Jurisdiction." By clause 36 such Commisioners, or other persons, were not to adjudge any matter to be heresy, "but only such as heretofore have been determined, ordered, or adjudged to be heresy by the authority of the Canonical Scriptures, or by the first four General Councils, or by any of them, or by any other General Council wherein the same was declared heresy by the express and plain words of the said Canonical Scriptures, or such as hereafter shall be ordered, judged, or determined to be heresy by the High Court of Parliament of this Realm, with the assent of the clergy in their Convocation." (Printed in the Statutes.)

By an Admonition in 1559 the Queen explained that no authority was challenged by this act save what was of ancient time due to the Imperial Crown of this Realm; that is, under God, to have the sovereignty and rule over all manner of persons born within these her realms . . . of what estate ecclesiastical or temporal soever they be, as no other foreign power shall or ought to have any superiority over them." (Printed in Cardwell, *Documentary Annals*, i. 199.) This Admonition was confirmed by Eliz. 5, c. 1.

In 1559 a Commission had been issued for imposing the Oath of Supremacy upon the clergy. (Rymer, xv. 518.)

From 189 to 243 (variously estimated) persons refused it, and were deprived or resigned. Subsequently a large number of parochial clergy who had been intruded upon livings in succession to the married clergy deprived under Queen Mary, were removed to make room for the former incumbents.

Elizabeth 1, c. 2. An Act of Uniformity restoring the second Prayer Book of Edward VI., with certain modifications, expunging a petition against "the Bishop of Rome and all his detestable enormities," combining the presentation sentences in the Communion Service of the Books of 1549 and 1552, and restoring "the ornaments of the church and of the ministers thereof" as they were in 1549. (Printed in the Statutes.)

The purely civil Act of Mary 1, sess. 2, c. 2, *vide supra*, was repealed by a similar civil Act.

In 1562-63 the Articles of King Edward were re-cast by Convocation into Thirty-nine. (See Wilkins, *Concil.* iv. 76.)

The following Table will show the extent of the changes in the higher ministry of the Church as the various religious changes and counter changes proceeded.

Under Henry VIII.

Hugh Latimer, bishop of Worcester, resigned in 1539.

Thomas Stanley, bishop of Sodor and Man, was deprived in 1545. [This was not the same Thomas Stanley who was bishop 1556-1570].

John Bell, bishop of Worcester, resigned in 1543.

Under Edward VI.

George Day, bishop of Chichester, was deprived in 1551.
John Voysey, bishop of Exeter, resigned in 1551.
Edmund Bonner, bishop of London, was deprived in 1549.
William Rugg, bishop of Norwich, resigned in 1549.
Stephen Gardiner, bishop of Winchester, was deprived in 1549.
Nicholas Heath, bishop of Worcester, was deprived in 1551.
Cuthbert Tunstall, bishop of Durham, was deprived in 1551.

Under Mary

Thomas Cranmer, archbishop of Canterbury, was deprived in 1555.
Robert Holgate, archbishop of York, was deprived in 1554.
William Barlow, bishop of Bath and Wells, resigned in 1553.
Paul Bushe, bishop of Bristol, resigned in 1554.
John Scory, bishop of Chichester, deprived in 1554.
Robert Ferrar, bishop of St. Davids, deprived in 1554.
Miles Coverdale, bishop of Exeter, deprived in 1553.

John Hooper, bishop of Gloucester and Worcester, deprived in 1553.
John Harley, bishop of Hereford, deprived in 1554.
John Taylor, bishop of Lincoln, deprived in 1554.
Nicholas Ridley, bishop of London, deprived in 1553.
John Poynet, bishop of Winchester, deprived in 1553.
John Birde, bishop of Chester, deprived in 1554.

Several Sees were vacant at the time of Mary's accession; more at the time of the accession of Elizabeth, when the reaction of the above revolution came.

Under Elizabeth

Nicholas Heath, archbishop of York, was deprived in 1560.
Thomas Goldwell, bishop of St. Asaph's, resigned 1559.
Gilbert Bourne, bishop of Bath and Wells, was deprived in 1559.
Ralph Bayne, bishop of Coventry and Lichfield, was deprived in 1559.
Henry Morgan, bishop of St. David's, was deprived in 1559.
Thomas Thirlby, bishop of Ely, was deprived in 1559.
James Turberville, bishop of Exeter, was deprived in 1559.
Thomas Watson, bishop of Lincoln, was deprived in 1559.
Edmund Bonner, bishop of London, was deprived in 1559.
David Pole, bishop of Peterborough, was deprived in 1559.
John White, bishop of Winchester, was deprived in 1559.
Richard Pate, bishop of Worcester, was deprived in 1559.
Owen Oglethorpe, bishop of Carlisle, was deprived in 1559.
Cuthbert Scot, bishop of Chester, was deprived in 1560.
Cuthbert Tunstall, bishop of Durham, was deprived in 1559.

The only bishop who held the same see undisturbed from Henry VIII. to Elizabeth was Antony Kitchin, consecrated to Llandaff in 1545, died 1565. He and Thomas Stanley, who became bishop of Sodor and Man in 1556, the deprived bishops Barlow, Scory, and Coverdale, and Hodgkins, bishop Suffragan of Bedford, took the oaths to Elizabeth.

In 1559 Matthew Parker was consecrated to the see of Canterbury by Barlow, cons. 1536; Hodgkins, cons. 1538; Scory, cons. 1551; Coverdale, cons. 1551.

The additional sees of Gloucester, Bristol, Oxford, Peterborough, Westminster, and Chester were erected by Henry VIII. Gloucester and Bristol were subsequently united 1836, and there was only one Bishop of Westminster.

In 1534, Hen. VIII. 25, c. 14, an act was passed allowing the erection of Suffragan bishoprics in certain specified towns. This act has been put in force in the present century to give titles to several Suffragan bishops. (Printed in the Statutes.)

AUTHORS

The volume of Froude's *History* dealing with Mary's reign is the best of the whole book. Hook's *Lives of Cranmer, Pole, and Parker* may be read in connexion with the ecclesiastical changes, but these matters are the subject of controversy. Ranke's masterly summary in Book ii. of his *History of England* will serve to keep the most important issues and conditions clear.

ELIZABETH. 1558-1603

DOMINIONS

England and Ireland. The latter was practically conquered in this reign, and at the beginning of the next, by the rebellion and conquest of the Earl of Desmond in Munster, killed in 1583, and of the Earl of Tyrone in Ulster, submitted in 1603. From September, 1562, to July, 1563, English troops held Havre in Normandy. In 1585 the Queen, who had refused the sovereignty, accepted the protection of the Netherlands, and the towns of Flushing, Brill, and Rammekins, were put into her hands for the rest of her reign. She bore the title of Queen of Virginia, by which name was meant the coast of North America from North Carolina to New England inclusive, but no permanent colonies were established there in her reign.

WARS

Elizabeth on her accession found herself engaged in the war with France begun in the previous reign, in alliance with Spain. Mary of France and Scotland, Queen of France part of 1559-60, had laid claim to the English throne, on the plea of the illegitimacy of Elizabeth, and the anti-French interests of Spain compelled Philip to continue the alliance with England. An English fleet and army aided the Scotch lords to expel the French garrison from Leith, 1560.

In 1562 English troops were sent into Normany to help the Huguenots against the party of the Guises; and in 1563 they defended Havre in a two months' siege.

In 1569 the Northern Counties rose for Queen Mary under the Earls of Northumberland and Westmoreland, and the revolt was only suppressed after considerable desultory fighting, which extended into Scotland, where the Queen's party supported the English rebels.

In 1585 war with Spain was openly begun, and Drake took St. Domingo and Carthagena in the West Indies.

In 1586 a skirmish at Zutphen was made remarkable by the death of Sir Philip Sidney.

In 1588 the Armada was defeated.

In 1589 Drake and Norris led an abortive expedition against Lisbon. In 1596 Lord Howard of Effingham and the Earl of Essex took Cadiz. In 1598 Sir Henry Bagenal was defeated at Blackwater by the Irish under the Earl of Tyrone, which led to the appointment of Essex to the command in Ireland.

In 1600 the Stadtholder of the United Provinces, Maurice of Nassau, with the aid of Sir Francis and Sir Horace Vere, defeated the Spaniards at Nieuport, and established at least military equality with them for the future.

Elizabeth

OFFICIALS

Lord Chancellors

1558. The Queen, Keeper.
1558. Sir Nicholas Bacon, Keeper, with the authority of Lord Chancellor, by statute, Elizabeth 5, c. 18.
1579. The Queen, Keeper.
Lord Burleigh and the Earl of Leicester, Keepers.
Sir Thomas Bromley, Chancellor.
1587. Lord Hunsdon, Lord Cobham, Sir Francis Walsingham, Keepers.
Lord Burleigh, the Earl of Leicester, Sir Francis Walsingham, Keepers.
Sir Christopher Hatton, Chancellor.
1591. Lord Burleigh, Lord Hunsdon, Lord Cobham, Lord Buckhurst, Commissioners of the Great Seal.
1592. Sir John Pickering, Keeper.
1596. Sir Thomas Egerton, Keeper.

Lord Treasurers and Chancellors of the Exchequer

1558. The Marquis of Winchester, Treasurer.
Richard Sackville, Chancellor of the Exchequer.
1566. Sir William Mildmay, Chancellor of the Exchequer.
1572. Lord Burleigh, Treasurer, till his death in 1598.
1589. Sir John Fortescue, Chancellor of the Exchequer.
1598. Lord Buckhurst, afterwards Earl of Dorset, Treasurer.

Secretaries of State

1558. Sir William Cecil, afterwards Lord Burleigh, till 1572.
1572. Sir Thomas Smith.
1574. Sir Francis Walsingham.
1578. Thomas Wilson, in addition.
1586. William Davison, in addition.
1590. Robert Cecil, afterwards Earl of Salisbury, acting
1596. Secretary of State.
1596. Robert Cecil, Chief Secretary of State, to the end of the reign.

Elizabeth

The Archbishops cease to be of the great political importance of earlier times. With the exception of William Laud, 1633-1644, Cardinal Pole was the last Archbishop who took a great part in the government of the kingdom. The chief influence in the government is not necessarily to be found in any one office at this period. No Lord Chancellor under Elizabeth was a statesman of the first rank, and influence was without doubt exerted on the government by favourites and advisers of the Queen who held no high office. She was herself, however, the chief framer of her own policy. Her most trusted advisers, Burleigh and Walsingham, did not fully enter into the reasons for the moderate course which she wished to keep in religion, nor into the temporizing policy which she succeeded in following for so long in foreign politics. Here her justification is the brilliant success of the end of her reign.

ACTS AND DOCUMENTS
(After the settlement of religion).

1559. Peace of Cateau Cambresis with France. The French made numerous cessions to the Spaniards of places in Italy, and made and received restitution of places taken in the war in France and in the Low Countries. The French agreed to restore Calais to England in eight years if no war intervened. The aid of Elizabeth to the Huguenots in 1562 justified the French in refusing to make the restitution. A supplementary treaty was concluded with the King and Queen of Scots, the Dauphin and Mary Stewart. (Rymer, xv. 505.)

1560. The treaty of Edinburgh was concluded between Elizabeth and the Scotch "Lords of the Congregation," the Reforming and anti-French lords, acting in the name of the Queen Mary, for confirming the Peace of Cateau Cambresis, for the evacuation of Scotland by the French, and for the dropping of the title of Queen of England, assumed by Queen Mary. Philip of Spain was expressly included in the treaty. (Rymer, xv. 593.)

1564. A treaty concluded at Troyes between France and England, after Elizabeth's interference on behalf of the French Huguenots, binding the two powers not to support or harbour rebels against the other. (Rymer, xv. 640.)

This treaty may be considered the beginning of the approach between the English and French monarchies, in face of the common danger of Spanish power co-operating with the Guises in France, and with Mary Stewart, a Guise through her mother, in Scotland. The policy of Catherine de Medicis, Charles IX., and Henry III., was swayed at different times by various motives, but the more decidedly Spain and the Guises became Catholic in policy, the more the French monarchy was inclined to toleration of the Huguenots and to an understanding with England.

1564. Publication of the decrees of the Council of Trent, confirming the schism between Romanists and Protestants. The policy of the Jesuits, founded in 1547, triumphs, and Catholic Recusancy becomes very general in England, the conservative religious party largely withdrawing from the church services. The Decrees of Trent are printed in *Concilii Tridentini Canones et Decreta.* Gauthier, Paris, 1832. See also Father Paul Sarpi's *History of the Council of Trent.*

1570. Elizabeth excommunicated and deposed by Pope Pius V. The Bull is printed in Burnet, *History of the Reformation.* It reiterates the complaint of Northumberland and Westmoreland, in 1569, that the Queen was swayed by "ignoble councillors." Compare the language of the old nobility in the Pilgrimage of Grace. Though it exposed the Queen to great immediate danger, it identified her rule with national independence, to the great ultimate advantage of both her power and of the Reforming party.

1571. Eliz. 13, c. 1. An Act making it high treason to call the Queen Heretic, Schismatic, Infidel, Usurper, &c., and to affirm the right in succession to the crown in some other than the Queen.

Eliz. 13, c. 2. An Act against the introduction of Papal Bulls, and against reconciling anyone with Rome.

1581. Eliz. 23, c. 1. An Act making it treason to reconcile anyone to Rome. Saying or hearing Mass, and absence from Church punished by fines.

1583. The Court of High Commission for exercising the Queen's Ecclesiastical authority finally constituted. See Eliz. 1, c. 1, clause 18, and Strype, *Annals*, iii. 180.

1584. Eliz. 27, 2. An Act against Jesuits and Seminary Priests. Jesuits and Seminary Priests banished on pain of treason, to aid or receive them made felony, all persons being educated in foreign seminaries to return and take the oath of supremacy in six months, on pain of treason.

1585. The Queen accepts the Protectorate of the Netherlands. The Petition of the States-General of the Netherlands is printed in Rymer, xv. 793. It is followed by the Queen's Commission appointing Sir Philip Sidney and Sir Thomas Cecil, Governors of the cautionary towns to be placed in her hands, Flushing, Rammekins, and Brill.

1593 Eliz. 35, c. 1. An Act against Puritans attending Conventicles or disputing the Queen's ecclesiastical authority, who are to be imprisoned till they conform, for three months, then refusing to conform to abjure the realm on pain of death.

Eliz. 35, c. 2. A further Act against Popish recusants, confining them to the neighbourhood of their houses, and banishing them if they cannot pay the fines for non-attendance at church.

1600. A Charter granted to certain merchants for exclusive trade with India and China. The foundation of the East India Company.

The Charters of the East India Company, grants, treaties, &c., were printed in London, 1774.

1601. Eliz. 43, c. 2. An Act for the relief of the poor, enabling the Justices to appoint Parish Overseers with power to levy a compulsory poor rate, to provide houses for impotent poor. The foundation of the Poor Law system as it existed down to 1834. The above Acts are printed in the Statutes.

In 1598 Henry IV. of France made the treaty of Vervins with Spain, whereby he was acknowledged as King of France. The treaty was based on that of Cateau Cambresis. In the same year by the Edict of Nantes an equal political position and local freedom of worship, with strong securities for their protection, was accorded to the Huguenots. They were to be tolerated everywhere, but were only to perform public worship in certain towns, and on the estates of certain seigneurs.

The Treaty of Vervins and the Edict of Nantes are printed *in extenso* in *Dumont*, vol. v. pt. 1, pp. 561 and 545 respectively.

AUTHORS

Hallam's *Constitutional History* is learned and impartial on the reign of Elizabeth, but by far the most powerful review of her reign is that contained in Book iii. of Ranke's *History of England*.

The history of Mary Stewart is surrounded by controversy, and the *Histoire de Marie Stuart* by Mignet, and *Mary Queen of Scots and her Accusers*, by Hosack, with the view in Froude's *History*, the whole corrected by the learning and sense of Ranke, will leave the reader to form a fair judgment for himself.

The history of the Netherlands, so closely connected with that of England, is to be found in Motley's *Dutch Republic and United Netherlands*. But, as is usual in the case of the extremely controversial views which have been taken of characters and actions in this age, those who have access to foreign books may find a very different estimate of Philip II. and his policy in the works of M. Kervyn de Lettenhove. (Belgian.)

The last six volumes of Froude's *History*, covering from 1558 to 1588, must be read with the usual caution, but are superior to the volumes upon Henry VIII.

There are two good small books upon the reign, with slightly different aims. The *Age of Elizabeth*, by Bishop Creighton, groups European history round that of England in this period. It is published in Longmans *Epochs Series*.

Queen Elizabeth, by Professor Beesley, in the *English Statesmen Series*, deals more exclusively with the character and policy of the Queen.

The chapters upon the reign in Green's *Short History* are exceptionally good, especially upon the social and literary side. They are expressed more fully in the larger history of the same author.

JAMES I. 1603-1625
Married Anne of Denmark.

DOMINIONS

England, Scotland, Ireland. As a consequence of the peace with Spain successful colonization began in America. In 1605 Barbadoes was occupied, in 1607 Virginia was re-occupied, in 1609 possession was taken of Bermuda by Sir George Somers, in 1612 a small colony was planted in Newfoundland, which had long been a nominal possession of England. In 1620 the colony of Plymouth, in what was then called North Virginia, was settled by the Pilgrim Fathers. Nearer home the colony in Ulster was planted by English and Scotch in 1611.

WARS

The first twenty-one years of James' reign are distinguished as being free from foreign or domestic wars, with the exception of troubles in Ireland in 1608. No similar period of peace is recorded before, and no such time has elapsed since without a war of some description. The time of the ascendancy of Sir Robert Walpole is the nearest approach to such a peace since, and then there was actual though not declared war with Spain in 1727. Between Elizabeth's peace with France in 1564 and formal war with Spain in 1585, there was rebellion in England in 1569–70, war on the Scotch border, and practically a naval war in the West Indies with Spain. In the so-called forty years' peace of the present century, from 1815 to 1854, occurred two great Sikh wars, an Afghan war, two Burmese wars, a Mahratta war, a Caffre war, the battle of Navarino, the bombardment of Acre, and many smaller conflicts.

The energies of the King were constantly bent on preserving the peace of Europe, which the ambition of Henry IV. of France, the chaos of Germany, the decline of the Protestants in Germany, the intrigues of the Jesuits and the progress of Catholic schemes in their hands, made increasingly difficult. The intentions of James were wiser than his measures. The Thirty Years' War broke out in 1618, on Frederick the Elector Palatine accepting the Bohemian throne, and England was involved in 1624, but no operations of importance ensued. Abroad James' son-in-law, the Elector Palatine, was driven out of Bohemia by the battle of Prague, 1620, the Palatinate was overrun by the Spaniards, and war recommenced in the Netherlands between the Spaniards and the Dutch.

OFFICIALS
Lord Chancellors

- 1603. Sir Thomas Egerton, afterwards Lord Ellesmere and Viscount Brockley, Keeper, Lord Chancellor, July 24.
- 1617. Sir Francis Bacon, afterwards Lord Verulam and Viscount St. Albans, Keeper.
- 1618. Sir Francis Bacon, Lord Verulam, Chancellor.
- 1621. Sir Julius Caesar and Sir John Ley, afterwards Earl of Marlborough, Commissioners to hear causes in Chancery.
    Viscount Mandeville, afterwards Earl of Manchester, the Duke of Richmond and the Earl of Arundel Commissioners of the Great Seal, May 1 to July 10. John Williams, Dean of Westminster, afterwards Bishop of Lincoln and Archbishop of York, Keeper, July 10.

Lord Treasurers

1603. Earl of Dorset, Treasurer.
Lord Hume and Sir Fulke Greville, Chancellors of the Exchequer.
1608. The Earl of Salisbury, Treasurer.
1612. The Earl of Northampton, first Commissioner.
1614. Lord Ellesmere, Lord Chancellor, Commissioner.
July 11, The Earl of Suffolk, Treasurer.
1618. George Abbott, Archbishop of Canterbury, Commissioner.
1620. Sir Richard Weston, afterwards Lord Weston and Earl of Portland, Chancellor of the Exchequer.
Sir Henry Montagu, afterwards Earl of Manchester, Treasurer.
1621. Lord Cranfield, afterwards Earl of Middlesex, Treasurer.
1624. Sir Richard Weston, Treasurer.
Dec. 11. Sir James Ley, afterwards Earl of Marlborough, Treasurer.

Secretaries of State

1603. Sir Robert Cecil, afterwards Earl of Salisbury.
1609. **Sir Alexander Hay.**
1612. **Thomas Hamilton.**
1616. Sir Ralph Winwood, till 1618.
Sir Thomas Lake, till 1619.
1618. Sir John Herbert.
Sir Robert Naunton, *vice* Herbert, till 1622.
1619. Sir George Calvert, afterwards Lord Baltimore.
1622. Sir Edward Conway, afterwards Lord Conway.

Robert **Kerr**, Viscount Rochester 1611, Earl of Somerset 1613, Privy Councillor 1612, Acting Secretary of State 1612–15, Acting Lord Keeper of **the** Privy Seal 1614. Prisoner in the Tower **1615–1622.**

George Villiers, Viscount Villiers 1616, Earl of Buckingham 1617, Marquis 1619, Duke 1623, Privy Councillor 1617, Lord High Admiral 1619.

ACTS AND DOCUMENTS

1604. Jac. I. 1, 33. Tunnage and Poundage granted to the King for life.

A Conference on religion held at Hampton Court to examine into the grievances of the Puritan party. It resulted in some slight changes in the Prayer Book, and in an order for an amended (the present authorized) version of the Scriptures. (Rymer, xvi. 565, 574.)

In the same year Convocation drew up Canons to which the clergy were required to subscribe.

The Canons have been published by the Christian Knowledge Society, 1841.

Peace of London concluded with the King of Spain, and the Archdukes, Albert and Isabella, rulers of the Spanish Netherlands. The cautionary towns in the Netherlands in English hands were to be at present considered neutral. The Inquisition was to be restrained in dealing with English sailors and merchants in Spanish ports. The American trade was finally passed over in silence, with the result that the English traders continued to go to America at their own risk, and the Buccaneers, or independent pirate traders of the West Indies were the speedy result.

Another result of the peace was the desperation of the Recusants in England, who felt themselves abandoned by the Spaniards, and some of whom were shortly in consequence to enter upon the Gunpowder Plot. (Rymer, xvi. 585.)

1606. An important decision was given in the Court of Exchequer, in the case of Bate, a Levant merchant, who refused to pay an imposition upon currants levied by royal authority. The Judges decided that it was within the King's prerogative to make such impositions, and it had been undoubtedly done in the previous reign. Bate's case in *State Trials*, ii. 371. An instance under James is seen in the imposition of six and eightpence in the pound upon Tobacco. (Printed in Rymer, xvi. 601.)

1608. James made a treaty with the United Provinces, with a view to recovering the money spent for them by Elizabeth and terminating their war with Spain. (Rymer, xvi. 667, 673.)

1609. Consequently the Truce of Antwerp was concluded between the United Provinces and Spain for twelve years, on the mediation of France and England. The independence of the Provinces and their East Indian trade were practically admitted by Spain for that time. (*Dumont*, v. part ii. 99.)

1619. The Synod of Dort in Holland was held to settle the questions between Calvinists and Arminians. English divines were present, and the decisions were generally, though not authoritatively, accepted in England, and not only by the Puritan party, as defining the faith of Protestantism. The complete condemnation of the Arminians at Dort undoubtedly strengthened the Puritan party here, all their opponents being stigmatised as Arminians, though Laud always repudiated the description for himself. Motley, *John of Barnevelde*, contains a full account of the circumstances of the Synod and a brief *résumé* of its conclusions.

1624. Jac. I. 21, 3. An Act for the abolition of Monopolies, of which much complaint had been made since the late reign. Patents for new inventions and licenses for keeping taverns excepted.

The act was passed by the parliament, in the course of their attack upon the policy and advisers of the marriage between Prince Charles and the Infanta. The Earl of Middlesex was impeached soon afterwards. The latter part of this reign saw the revival of parliamentary impeachment, which had been in abeyance since Henry VI.'s reign, in the case of Bacon in 1621, and the Earl of Middlesex 1624.

THE GUNPOWDER PLOT

The plot vulgarly associated with the name of Guy Fawkes, though Robert Catesby was its principal organizer, was the result of the failure of James to carry out the complete suspension of the Penal Laws, as the Catholics expected him to do. The peace with Spain had also rendered them desperate, by depriving them of foreign help. The Plot was not prepared by the leading Catholics, nor by the authority of the Church. The conspirators were either ruined men, or men with little to lose, with the exception of Digby and Tresham, and the latter probably betrayed them. The famous letter to Lord Monteagle was not the first intimation to the Government of some design. It was probably a device by moderate Catholics, who wished neither for the consummation of the crime nor for the arrest of the criminals, to give the latter notice that they were discovered, and so induce them to leave the country.

Students may consult Jardine, *The Story of the Gunpowder Treason* (London, 1857), and Gardiner's *History*, vol. i.

AUTHORS

Ranke and Hallam are valuable as before, but the student here gets the aid of Dr. S. R. Gardiner's *History of England* from 1603–1642, which supersedes all other English writers.

Green's *Short History* begins to become less valuable after Elizabeth.

A brief account will be afforded by Gardiner's *Puritan Revolution*, or by the same author's *Student's History*.

CHARLES I.   1625–1649
Married Henrietta Maria of France.
DOMINIONS

England, Scotland, Ireland. The American colonies, as in his father's reign, with the Bahamas, Montserrat, Antigua, a small settlement in Guiana, part of Gambia in Africa, and Madras. New England was further settled by Puritan refugees in 1628 and subsequent years. In 1629 the English

Charles I.

captured Quebec and all the French settlements on the coast of North America, but they were restored to France in 1632.

WARS

Charles succeeded to his father's war with Spain, and incidentally with the Catholic League and the Emperor in Germany, though no actual declaration of war was ever made with the Emperor. The great Thirty Years' War, of which this was a part, vitally affected the whole policy of the reign, and was one cause of the English Civil Wars.

In 1625 an abortive expedition under Viscount Wimbledon and the Earl of Essex was sent against Cadiz. In the same year English ships co-operated with the French Government against the Duc de Soubise and the Huguenots of La Rochelle, whose rebellion prevented France from acting against Spain and the Empire.

In 1626 Christian of Denmark, relying in vain on English supplies, which the quarrels between Charles and his parliament made it impossible to send, was entirely defeated by the Imperialists at Lütter.

In 1627 Charles quarrelled with France, and sent the first abortive expedition to aid La Rochelle.

In 1628 the second expedition to help La Rochelle failed, and after the murder of Buckingham the third expedition failed, and La Rochelle surrendered.

The Imperial generals overran all North Germany and the mainland of Denmark, but Stralsund made a successful defence against them.

In 1630, after the dissolution of his third parliament, the king perforce made peace with France and Spain, but English and Scotch regiments still continued to take part in the German war, and the discontent of the Puritan party in England was allayed or exasperated in proportion as the general cause of Protestantism abroad seemed to triumph or be defeated in the hands of the Swedes and Germans. The most important of these events were as follows. In 1630 Gustavus Adolphus of Sweden took up the cause of the German Protestants. In 1631 he defeated Count Tilly at Leipsic; in 1632 he again defeated and killed him at the passage of the Lech, and invaded Bavaria. In the autumn of the same year he barely defeated Wallenstein at Lutzen, and was himself killed in the battle. In 1634 the Imperial troops defeated the Protestants at Nordlingen. In 1635 the Protestant Saxons went over to the Emperor, and the French began their decisive interference in Germany in alliance with Sweden against the Emperor and the Spaniards. Charles, perceiving truly that the war had ceased to be a war of religion, began to intrigue against the French and Dutch, in favour of the retention of the southern Netherlands by Spain, and for the balance of power. The French in return encouraged the resistance of Scotland to his ecclesiastical authority, to keep him occupied at home. In 1638 the French took the German so-called Protestant army of Duke Bernhard of Saxe Weimar into their own service. In 1639 the Dutch, in violation of English neutrality, defeated a Spanish fleet in the Downs. In 1640 Spain was crippled by the revolt of Catalonia and of Portugal, the latter attaining independence.

The importance of the war to England and Scotland, lay not only in the passions which it engendered and the occasions for quarrel over the raising of money and over foreign policy which it offered. The military training of most of the chief leaders in the civil wars, and of many of the soldiers, was gained in the Low Countries and Germany, and the religious opinions of the parliamentary army were affected by the contact of such as had served abroad with these opinions in Holland, the original seat of some of the sects which became prominent in England. Compare the distribution of the Marian Martyrs in England (*supra*) and the supporters of the King and Parliament respectively (*infra*), as an indication of the effects of foreign religious opinion here.

Among the principal leaders in the Civil Wars who had seen service abroad were—

On the King's side, the Princes Rupert and Maurice, the Earl of Lindesey, Patrick Ruthven Earl of Brentford and Forth, Sir Jacob Astley, General Goring, Sir Charles Lucas, Sir George Lisle.

On the Parliamentary side, the Earl of Essex, Sir Thomas Fairfax, Sir William Waller, General Skippon, General Monk, General Massey.

Among the Scots, Alexander Leslie Earl of Leven, David Leslie, the Duke of Hamilton.

Of the two great military geniuses who appeared, one—the Marquis of Montrose—had seen very little service abroad, and the other—Oliver Cromwell—had seen none at all.

THE CIVIL WARS

The Civil Wars beginning in Charles' reign fall into three main divisions, continuing after the King's death.

First, the wars between England and Scotland in 1638-39 and 1640.

Secondly, the Civil Wars from 1642 to 1646, during the whole of which Irish rebellion, begun in 1641, was going on.

Thirdly, the renewed war in 1648 in England, continued in the smaller British islands, Ireland and Scotland, to 1651.

In the first of these the Scots almost unanimously opposed the king's ecclesiastical policy, partly upon religious grounds, partly upon national, objecting to a system originated in and supported from England. The French encouraged the Scots and assisted them in bringing back Scotch officers and soldiers from the German war. A cessation of arms was agreed upon at York.

The war broke out again in 1640, and the Scots forced the passage of the Tyne at Newburn. A cessation was agreed upon at Ripon.

THE IRISH REBELLION

The native Irish Catholics broke out in rebellion on October 23rd, 1641. The alleged complicity of the King, and the obvious need of an army to be sent to Ireland helped to precipitate civil war in England.

THE CIVIL WARS
Division of Parties.

In Religion, for the King were the people who were not Puritans, both High Churchmen and Broad Churchmen, if we may borrow names which were not used then; also the Roman Catholics.

For the Parliament were the Puritans, including those who were in favour of a further Calvinistic reform in the Church, Presbyterians, Sectaries who were not in accord with the old-fashioned Puritan party, and the more intellectual of whom touched the Royalist Broad Churchmen more nearly.

In Race, for the King were the more Celtic parts of the kingdom, Wales and Cornwall, ultimately many of the Scotch Highlanders and the native Irish.

For the Parliament were the purely Teutonic parts of the kingdom as a rule.

In Geographical Distribution, for the King were generally speaking the North and West.

For the Parliament the East and South.

In Class. It was not a war of classes; but for the King were many country gentlemen, about two-thirds of the nobility, and many country people.

For the Parliament were many townsmen and mercantile people, for Puritanism was strong in the larger towns, some influential country gentlemen and nobility, as John Hampden, the Earls of Warwick, Northumberland, Holland, Manchester, Essex, Pembroke, Salisbury, Bedford, Leicester, Stamford, etc., and many of the farmers of the East and South.

Roughly speaking the King had with him two-thirds of the

House of Lords and one-third of the House of Commons; the Parliament *vice versa*.

The King had with him all the members returned in Rutland, Flintshire, Carnarvonshire, Merionethshire, Montgomeryshire, Radnorshire, Brecknockshire, Caermarthenshire; a majority of those returned in Northumberland, Westmoreland, Nottinghamshire, Cheshire, Shropshire, Staffordshire, Herefordshire, Somersetshire, and Cornwall. Durham returned no members, but was chiefly Royalist. The representation of Cumberland, Yorkshire, Monmouthshire, Anglesea, and Glamorganshire was equally divided.

The Parliament had with them all the representatives of London, Middlesex, Essex, Hertfordshire, Bedfordshire, and Denbighshire; and the majority of the representatives from all the rest. This, and the distribution of the Peers, applies to the beginning of the war.

The general geographical distribution is plain.

The general objects of the two sides were to possess themselves of as much country as possible, so as to give opportunity to their friends in each district to aid them, to levy contributions and raise supplies, and to cut off a source of supply from the enemy. The King had the further great object of recovering London, which would no doubt have been fatal to the Parliament. They aimed at the King's headquarters at Oxford, the taking of which, though a heavy blow, need not have been so immediately fatal to his cause as the taking of London to theirs.

The campaign of 1642 was marked by the indecisive battle at Edgehill, October 23rd, the march of the King towards London and his capture of Brentford, November 12th, and his retreat to Oxford. Minor operations took place in Yorkshire and many other counties.

1643. The Earl of Essex advanced from London towards Oxford and took Reading, April 27th, but was unable to besiege Oxford, and was harassed by the King's cavalry. Hampden killed in a skirmish at Chalgrove, June 18th.

A Royalist army organized in Cornwall defeated the Earl of Stamford at Stratton, May 16th, Sir William Waller at Lansdown, July 5th, and at Devizes, July 13th. Bristol surrendered to Prince Rupert, July 27th.

In the North the Marquis of Newcastle defeated Fairfax at Adwalton Moor, June 30th, and invaded Lincolnshire. The three Royalist armies formed the three sieges of Plymouth, Gloucester, and Hull, instead of converging upon London, and failed in all three. Essex, having obliged Charles to raise the siege of Gloucester, was intercepted by the King at Newbury on his return, September 20th, and after a desperate battle got his army through, owing to the failure of the Royalist ammunition.

"Ormond's cessation" in Ireland, to allow troops from Ireland to join the King, September 13th, and the treaty between the Parliament and the Scots, September 25th, gave a new character to the war. (See *Acts and Documents*.)

1644. The Scots invaded the North in January, and drew off the Marquis of Newcastle from Yorkshire to oppose them. English troops from Ireland landed at the mouth of the Dee to aid the King, and were defeated by Fairfax at Nantwich, January 25th.

The Earl of Forth and Lord Hopton were defeated at Cheriton in Hampshire by Sir William Waller, March 29th. Essex and Waller marched upon Oxford, but divided their forces. Waller was defeated by the King at Cropredy Bridge, June 30th. Essex, going into the West, was followed by the King, and lost his army, the infantry surrendering in Cornwall, September 30th, the horse cutting their way through, the commanders escaping by sea.

Rupert marching in aid of Newcastle, relieved Newark, and Lathom House in Lancashire, took Liverpool and Bolton, raised the siege of York and joined Newcastle in that city, but insisting on going out to fight was defeated by the combined forces of the Scots, Fairfax, and the Associated Eastern

Counties at Marston Moor, July 2nd. The royal cause was thereby ruined in the North.

The army of the Associated Counties came south to help Waller, and an indecisive battle was fought with the king at Newbury, October 27th. The consequent dissensions among the Parliamentary Commanders led to a New Modelling of their army under Fairfax and Cromwell. A force of professional soldiers strongly impressed with a sectarian character being the result; the old aristocratic commanders, with the Presbyterian interest, being put on one side.

1645. The King marching from Oxford relieved Chester and took Leicester, May 31st, but having divided his forces was caught with inferior numbers by Fairfax at Naseby, June 14th, and utterly defeated, his infantry being cut to pieces. Fairfax marched into Somersetshire, and the Scots after taking Carlisle invaded the Royalist counties on the Welsh border. Bristol surrendered by Prince Rupert Sept. 10th. The King's horse defeated on Rowton Heath, near Chester, Sept. 23rd.

MONTROSE IN SCOTLAND

On the agreement of the Scots to help the Parliament becoming known, 1643, Hamilton, who had undertaken to prevent it by peaceful means, was imprisoned by the King. Montrose, who had before advocated an armed attempt to prevent it, repaired to Scotland, and joining a body of Irish who had crossed over to the Highlands, raised the King's standard in 1644, appealing to the hatred felt by neighbouring Highlanders for the Campbells, whose head Argyle was a leader of the Covenanters. The loyalty of the clans was usually in proportion to their proximity to and fear of the Campbells. On the other side of Scotland the Gordons, though they from jealousy did not cordially co-operate with Montrose, made their neighbours Covenanters, being themselves Royalists. Montrose defeated the Covenanters at Tippermuir, near Perth, Sept. 1st, and at Aberdeen Sept. 13th, but was compelled to fall back into the Highlands. In January, 1645, he invaded Argyle's country, and defeated the Campbells at Inverlochy, Feb. 2. He took Dundee, and harried the East Coast, and on May 9th won a victory at Auldearne, on July 2 at Alford, and on August 15th at Kilsyth. By the last battle he became for the moment master of Scotland; but the Highlanders left him to bestow their plunder, the Scotch horse returned out of England, and on Sept. 13th surprised and defeated him at Philiphaugh. He maintained himself for about a year in the Highlands, till ordered to lay down his arms by the King.

1646. Fairfax forced Lord Hopton to a convention at Truro, March 14th. Sir Jacob Astley, with the last Royalist force in the field, was defeated at Stow-in-the-Wold, March 22nd. On June 10th the King, in the hands of the Scottish army, gave orders for the surrender of the Royalist garrisons.

THE SECOND CIVIL WAR

1648. The failure of the King, Parliament, and Army to come to terms among themselves, and the consequent treaty between the King and the Scots, produced a renewed war, in which English Royalists, Scotch Presbyterians, and many of the more moderate of the old English Parliamentary party were arrayed against the English Army and the more extreme of the Parliamentary party. As the composition of the parties was new, so the parts of the country affected were new, London and the South-East being full of this new Royalist party. It is noteworthy that it was this combination which failed in 1648, which finally triumphed, in 1660, in the Restoration. Now the superior leadership, discipline, and unity of the army was fatal to them.

March 23rd. Colonel Poyer, formerly a Parliamentary officer, declared for the King at Pembroke.

April 9th. Armed riot in London for the King.

April 28th and 29th. Berwick and Carlisle seized by Royalists.

Charles I. 141

May 8th. The Royalists defeated at St. Fagan's, in Glamorganshire.

May 21st. East Kent rose for the King.

May 27th. The fleet in the Downs hoisted the Royal Standard.

June 1st. Fairfax stormed Maidstone, and Kent was rapidly reduced.

June 3rd. Pontefract Castle seized for the King.

June 13th. The remains of the Kentish force, which had crossed the Thames and joined the Essex Royalists, checked Fairfax at Colchester, but were shut up in the town.

July 4th to 6th. Abortive rising in Surrey.

July 11th. Surrender of Pembroke.

August 17th to 20th. The Scots defeated in Lancashire, at Preston, on Wigan Moor and at Winwick.

August 27. Surrender of Colchester.

Minor Royalist movements had been attempted and failed in North Wales, Herefordshire, Cornwall, Northamptonshire, Lincolnshire, Suffolk, and Sussex.

OFFICIALS

Lord Chancellors

1625. The Bishop of Lincoln, Keeper, resigned Oct. 30.
   Sir Thomas Coventry, afterwards Lord Coventry, Keeper.
1640. Sir John Finch, afterwards Lord Finch, Keeper.
1641. Sir Edward Lyttelton, afterwards Lord Lyttelton, Keeper.
1642. The King, Keeper.

Lord Treasurers

1625. Lord Ley, afterwards Earl of Marlborough.
1628. Sir Richard Weston, afterwards Lord Weston and Earl of Portland.
   Sir Francis Cottington, afterwards Lord Cottington, Chancellor of the Exchequer.

1635. The Archbishop of Canterbury, the Earl of Manchester, Lord Cottington, Sir John Coke, Sir Francis Windebanke, Commissioners.
1636. William Juxon, Bishop of London.
Lord Newburgh, Chancellor of the Exchequer.
1641. Sir Edward Lyttelton, the Earl of Manchester, Sir John Bankes, Lord Newburgh, Sir Henry Vane (the elder), Commissioners.
1642. Sir John Colepepper, Chancellor of the Exchequer.
1643. Sir Edward Hyde, afterwards Earl of Clarendon, Chancellor of the Exchequer.
Lord Cottington.

Secretaries of State

1625. Sir Albert Morton.
Lord Conway.
Sir John Coke, *vice* Morton, Nov. 9th.
1630. Sir Dudley Carleton, afterwards Lord Carleton and Viscount Dorchester, *vice* Conway.
1632. Lord Cottington, *vice* Dorchester.
Sir Henry Vane, *vice* Coke.
Sir Francis Windebanke, *vice* Cottington.
1641. Sir Edward Nicholas, *vice* Windebanke.
1642. Viscount Falkland, *vice* Vane.
1643. Lord Digby, *vice* Falkland.

Duke of Buckingham, Lord High Admiral, 1625–1628.

Sir Thomas Wentworth, afterwards Lord Wentworth, 1628, and Earl of Stafford, 1640, Councillor of the North, 1625, Lord President of the Council of the North, Dec., 1628–1641, Privy Councillor, Nov. 9, 1629, Lord Deputy of Ireland, 1632, Lord Lieutenant of Ireland, 1640.

The Earl of Essex, Privy Councillor, Feb. 19, 1641, General of the Army of the Parliament, 1642–1645.

The Earl of Northumberland, Admiral 1636, Chief Commissioner of the Office of Lord High Admiral for the Parliament, 1645.

The Earl of Warwick, Admiral for the Parliament, 1642.

The Earl of Forth and Brentford, Commander-in-Chief of the King's army, 1642–1644.

Prince Rupert, Commander-in-Chief of the King's army, 1644–1645.

Duke of Ormonde, Commander-in-Chief in Ireland, 1641, Lord Lieutenant of Ireland, 1643–1647, 1648–1650.

Marquis of Montrose, Lieutenant-General of the Kingdom of Scotland, 1644–1646.

William Lenthal, Speaker of the House of Commons, 1641–1653.

Sir Thomas Fairfax, General for the Parliament, 1645–1650.

Earl of Manchester, General of Horse for the Parliament, 1643–1645.

ACTS AND DOCUMENTS

Dr. Gardiner's *Constitutional Documents of the Puritan Revolution*, 1628–1660, fills the place for this reign and the Commonwealth, which is filled by Stubbs' *Select Charters* for the period from William I. to Edward I. It is indispensable to all who have not access to large libraries, and useful to them as containing much in a readily-accessible form which is otherwise only to be found scattered through Rushworth's *Collections*, the Statutes, Parliamentary Histories, and State Papers.

1628. The Petition of Right. Car. I. 3, c. 1. Against the exaction of any gift, loan, benevolence, tax, or such like charge without consent of Parliament; against imprisonment without cause shewn; billeting of soldiers in private houses; and exercise of martial law.

The Petition of Right was intended to deal with the special instances of grievances which had arisen since Charles' accession. It avoided the question of the Impositions (see James' reign) and Tunnage and Poundage, which had been granted to the King for a year only in 1625, instead of for life, as had been the custom since the accession of Edward IV.

Printed at the end of Stubbs, *Select Charters*, and in Gardiner, *Const. Documents*, page 1.

1628. The King's Declaration on the Articles, intended to silence controversy between the Puritan, or Calvinistic, and the Arminian party in the Church. The government, acting in the spirit of the declaration, suppressed controversial books, with some impartiality, but the Puritan party justly complained that while both sides were muzzled, one only, the Arminian, was promoted.

Printed at the beginning of the Prayer Book and in Gardiner, *Const. Documents*, 9.

1629. Resolutions on Religion by the House of Commons. Printed in Gardiner, *Const. Documents*, 11.

Protestation of the House against Arminianism, and against the levying of Tunnage and Poundage without Parliamentary consent. Printed in Gardiner, *Constitutional Documents*, 16.

These Resolutions of the House shewing an intention of regulating the religious policy of the government, and traversing the contention of the King that, pending the passing of a Tunnage and Poundage Act, he was justified in raising Tunnage and Poundage for the defence of the realm, led to the dissolution and suspension of Parliament for eleven years.

1629. Peace between England and France, on the mediation of the Republic of Venice. Rymer, xix., 86–88.

1630. Peace between England and Spain. Rymer, xix., 219.

By the peace with France, the French claim to interfere in the household arrangements of the Queen, Henrietta Maria, was dropped; and Charles I. gave up all claim to interfere on behalf of the Huguenots.

By the Spanish peace the relations of 1604 were to be restored, and a vague promise was given in the negotiations that the interests of Charles' sister in the Palatinate were not to be lost sight of.

1633. The Declaration of Sports was issued, in favour of

dancing, archery, and athletic sports after the time of divine service on Sundays and Holidays. Puritan Justices of the Peace had interfered with them, and the Puritan party was deeply offended at the declaration.

Printed in Gardiner, *Const. Documents*, 31.

1634. The first Ship-Money writs issued to maritime towns and counties for providing a fleet. The maritime counties had been called upon to provide ships for the defence of the country on many occasions—1626 was the last instance. The payments were trifling in amount and fairly assessed, but the Government's intentions were distrusted, and no actual war was going on, though English commerce needed protection from pirates both Algerine and European.

In 1635 the Ship-Money writs were extended to the inland counties, which was an innovation. The fleet provided by the successive levies fell into the hands of the Parliament when the Civil War began, and formed the body of the fleet with which Blake and others defeated the Dutch and Spaniards under the Commonwealth and Protectorate. A specimen Ship-Money writ is printed in Gardiner, *Const. Documents*, 37.

1638. The Scottish National Covenant was made, in renewal of that of 1580, in defence of the Kirk of Scotland. It avoided any direct mention of Episcopacy.

Printed in Gardiner, *Const. Documents*, 54.

1640. New Canons framed by the clergy in Convocation, sitting after the dissolution of the Short Parliament. They inculcated Non-Resistance, and attacked the Sectaries. The Convocation also voted money to the King. The oath imposed by the Canons upon beneficed clergy against alterations in doctrine and Government is printed in Rushworth's *Collections*, iii. 1186. For the Canons themselves see *State Papers, Domestic*, Charles I. 1640.

The Long Parliament met on November 3rd, 1640, and by the following acts not only did away with the means of unparliamentary government, but established itself as a part of the government equally irremovable with the King, unless by its own consent.

Car. I. 16, c. 1. An Act by which parliaments were to meet every three years at least. This Act, often called a Triennial Act, is not to be confounded with the Act William and Mary 6 and 7, c. 2, by which parliament was not to sit more than three years.

Car. I. 16, c. 7. An Act by which the present parliament was not to be dissolved without its own consent. This Act was suggested by a well-founded fear of a violent dissolution, but was disastrous to a regular settlement of difficulties, in that it erected two indissoluble and supreme powers in the state.

Car. I. 16, c. 8. The Tunnage and Poundage Act, declaring the Impositions (see James' reign), without parliamentary grant, to be illegal, and granting Tunnage and Poundage for a short time.

Car. I. 16, c. 38. Act of Attainder passed against the Earl of Strafford in the Commons, April 21, 1641, in the Lords, April 29. Received the royal assent May 10. The previous impeachment appeared likely to result in some punishment short of death. The most fairly balanced view of the proceedings against Strafford is to be found in Hallam, *Const. Hist.* ch. ix. The whole of the proceedings are in Rushworth, vol. viii., which is solely devoted to the Trial and matters connected with it.

Car. I. 16, c. 10. An Act abolishing the Star Chamber, the Council of the North, the Court of the Marches of Wales, the Court of the Duchy of Lancaster, and the Court of the Exchequer of the County Palatine of Chester.

Car. I. 16, c. 11. An Act abolishing the Court of High Commission.

This was the court through which the Ecclesiastical supremacy of the Crown had been chiefly exercised. The House of Commons had already taken to itself Ecclesiastical authority by issuing a Commission for removing ornaments, &c., from Churches. Jan. 23, 1641.

Car. I. 16, c. 14. An Act making Ship-Money illegal.

Car. I. 16, c. 20. An Act abolishing fines for refusing to take the order of Knighthood. The government had compelled persons qualified to take Knighthood to do so, in order to secure the feudal dues and services ensuing.

Aug. 13, 1641. Thirteen Bishops impeached by the Commons for their share in the Canons of 1640.

Dec. 1. 1641. The Grand Remonstrance presented. This was substantially a vote of want of confidence in the Government, in spite of alterations in the Ministry. The logical result should have been the removal of the King or the dissolution of Parliament and fresh elections. Both proceedings however were unattainable by lawful means, since the Act Car. I. 16, c. 7. (Gardiner, *Const. Doc.* 127.)

Jan. 3, 1642. Articles of high treason and other offences exhibited on the part of the King against one member of the House of Lords and five members of the Commons. This was an attack upon the leaders of the one half of the irremovable government by the other half.

Car. I. 16, c. 27. An Act disabling all clergy from exercising any temporal authority. This Act, expelling the Bishops from Parliament and from the Council, made a complete revolution in the system of government, as it had formerly existed.

March 5, 1642. The Parliament, contrary to precedent, nominated Lords-Lieutenant of the several counties with power to levy the militia.

June 1, 1642. The Nineteen Propositions sent by the Parliament to the King, demanding practically that the Ministry should be appointed by Parliament, and all civil and ecclesiastical authority vested in their hands. The obvious refusal of the King, and many others, to agree to this, marks the necessary outbreak of civil war. (Gardiner, *Const. Doc.* 170.)

After the breaking out of the Civil War the following

negotiations and treaties mark the attempts at accommodation or the bringing of new forces into play.

Feb. 1, 1643. Treaty of Oxford attempted; the result of a brief experience of war. The Parliament demanded the abolition of Episcopacy, the exclusion of certain persons from office, the appointment of other certain persons to judicial office. (Gardiner, *Const. Doc.* 182.)

Sept. 15, 1643. Ormonde's Cessation in Ireland. A truce with the rebels on the basis of *uti possidetis*, to enable the English troops employed against them to come over to help the king. (See Carte, *Ormonde*.)

Sept. 25, 1643. The Solemn League and Covenant taken by the Parliament as the basis of an alliance with the Scots. This went further than the Scotch Covenant, in directly stipulating for the abolition of Episcopacy and for the establishment of uniformity of religion in England, Scotland, and Ireland. On this latter account it was distasteful to the rising party of Sectaries in the English army. (Gardiner, *Const. Doc.* 187.)

Jan., 1645. The Treaty of Uxbridge attempted. The Parliament desired the abolition of Episcopacy, the taking of the Covenant by the King, permanent parliamentary control of ministerial appointments, parliamentary power of declaring peace and war, a permanent Committee of the two kingdoms to control military affairs; the attainder of 58 persons by name, and of all Papists in arms, and all persons concerned in the Irish rebellion; the permanent exclusion from office and deprivation of the estates of 48 persons by name, and of several large classes of persons.

The King's counter propositions suggested a return to the Constitution as it stood in August, 1641, the preservation of the Prayer-book, a bill for the relief of tender consciences, and a trial by law of all persons against whom offences were alleged. (Gardiner, *Const. Doc.* 193 and 204.)

April 3, 1645. The Self-Denying Ordinance passed to exclude all members of both Houses from civil and military office. This Act, which was in fact a victory for the Sects and more thoroughgoing revolutionary party, separated again the legislative and executive powers which the Houses had tried to combine. (Gardiner, *Const. Doc.* 205.)

The overthrow of the King's armies in the field was followed by protracted negotiations between him, the Parliament, the Scots, and the Army Leaders for the settlement of the country.

Aug. 1, 1647. Proposals were drawn up by the Army Officers for a redistribution of seats, biennial parliaments, freedom of religion, except with regard to Romanists, and a nominated Ministry for seven years. Though the Proposals were refused by the Parliament as a basis of negotiation they are noteworthy as illustrating the progress of liberal opinion in the Army. (Gardiner, *Const. Doc.* 232.)

Dec. 26, 1647. The King made an Engagement with the Scots, stipulating, in return for his restoration to the ancient monarchical power, as limited in 1641, for a three years' trial of Presbyterianism, and a subsequent settlement of religion by Parliament and certain Divines, and the suppression of the Sects. This was the agreement which produced the alliance of Royalists and Presbyterians in the war of 1648. (Gardiner, *Const. Doc.* 259.)

Dec. 5, 1648. The Lords and Commons voted that the King's concessions made to their negotiators at Newport were a sufficient basis for peace. By this agreement an Amnesty was stipulated for, the control of the military force was given to the Parliament for twenty years, Presbyterianism was to be established for three years, the bishops excluded from the House of Lords, but the episcopal order and property were not to be finally abolished and alienated.

The proposals fell through owing to the Purge of the Parliament by the Army, and the subsequent execution of the King. They are noteworthy as the last constitutional attempt at settlement before military force overthrew Parliament and King together. The original aims of the old Puritan party, the Calvinistic reform of the Church and the control of the government of the King by a Puritan parliament, were never so near being accomplished in a regular legal manner, and failing now, failed entirely.

A complete account of the Newport Negotiation by Sir Edward Walker, clerk to the King, was published in *Historical Dissertations relative to King Charles I.* 1705.

The Acts of Parliament above which received the royal consent are printed in the Statutes.

Oct. 24. 1648. The peace of Westphalia closed the Thirty Years War, with which the beginnings of the English Civil War had been so closely connected. If it did not affect England immediately, it had European effects in which England could not long be unconcerned. It closed the era of religious wars, it fixed the limits of Catholic and Protestant rule in Germany, going back to the *status quo* of Jan. 1, 1624. It formally separated the Netherlands, Switzerland, and French Lorraine from the Empire, slightly increased the territories of Brandenburg (Prussia of the future), and largely aggrandized France and Sweden, on the Rhine and Baltic respectively. France became, in fact, the leading European power.

See Koch et Schoell, *Histoire Abrégée des Traités*, vol. i. ch. ii. §§ 3, 4.*

AUTHORS

Gardiner's *History of England* from 1603-1642, and his *History of the Great Civil War*, supersede all other English books.

Ranke's *History*, however, is still invaluable for its complete and impartial grasp of all the sides of the contest, from a point of view superior to any which can be reached by an Englishman.

Hallam's *Constitutional History* is very fair and very

---

* Koch et Schoell, *Histoire Abrégée des Traités depuis* 1648, &c., fifteen vols., is a diplomatic history of Europe from 1648 to 1815, giving a *résumé* of important treaties and the complete text of some.

learned upon Constitutional points. The period is one in which contemporary writers are in reach of the ordinary reader. Clarendon's *History of the Rebellion* (Royalist), Whitelocke's *Memorials of English Affairs* (Moderate Parliamentary), Ludlow's *Memoirs* (Independent), Cromwell's *Letters and Speeches*, Carlyle ed., are all easily available, and are equally useful during the Commonwealth and Protectorate time following, except Clarendon, who is less valuable after the war was over, when he was absent from England. The Clarendon State Papers are a collection of documents made by Clarendon for the purpose of his history.

Rushworth's *Collection*, the most ample body of State Documents and contemporary notes of the period, was made by John Rushworth, a barrister, in the employment of the Long Parliament, and later a member of Parliament.

The *Thurloe Papers* are a collection of Letters, Despatches, &c., made by John Thurloe, Secretary in turn to the Council of State and the two Protectors.

THE COMMONWEALTH. 1649–1653

DOMINIONS

At the time of the execution of the King the whole of England was in the hands of the Parliament and Army, with the exception of Pontefract Castle and the Scilly Islands, which were reduced March 21st, 1649, and May, 1651, respectively. The island of Guernsey was captured in October, Man in November, Jersey in December, 1651. Barbadoes and Virginia were also reduced in 1651.

These islands and colonies were altogether, or had long practically been, dependencies of England, but the Commonwealth proceeded to foreign conquest when the army was sent to conquer Ireland in 1649, against such a combination of Irish and Anglo-Irish as has never been seen before or since. The conquest was assured in 1649, though hostilities continued for many years. The independent kingdom of Scotland was mostly conquered in 1650 and 1651, though opposition continued in the Highlands.

WARS

The naval war, to reduce the Royalist islands and colonies, easily merged into a war with the Dutch, who traded with the colonies while in Royalist hands, and were jealous of English maritime power. The war broke out in 1652; there were several severe and indecisive naval actions, till, in 1653, the English got the upper hand. From February 18th to February 21st there was a running fight between Blake and Van Tromp from off Portland Bill to off Cape Blanc Nez; on June 2nd and 3rd the Dutch were again defeated off the North Foreland by Blake, Deane (killed in the action), Monk, and Penn; on July 31st the Dutch fleet was nearly destroyed and Van Tromp killed, by Monk and Penn off the Texel, 1653.

In 1649 Cromwell invaded Ireland, and by the storm of Drogheda and massacre of the garrison and population, September 11th, and by the storm of Wexford, October 9th, broke the neck of resistance.

In 1650 he invaded Scotland, and after a fruitless attempt upon Edinburgh was out-manœuvred by David Leslie and forced back upon the sea at Dunbar, where the over eagerness of the Scots gave him a great victory on September 3rd. In 1651 Charles II., with the Scotch army, marched into England, but were overtaken and entirely defeated by Cromwell and Lambert at Worcester September 3rd; Monk meanwhile reduced most of Scotland.

OFFICIALS

Feb. 8th, 1649. Commissioners of the Great Seal, Bulstrode Whitelocke, John Lisle, Sergeant Keeble.

Feb. 14th, 1649. A Council of State was erected by

Parliament consisting of John Bradshaw, made President, March 10th, and 40 other persons.

June 26th, 1650. Oliver Cromwell Lord General, *vice* Fairfax retired.

In 1653, after the expulsion of the Parliament and the dissolution of the Council of State by Cromwell, a new Council of State was erected, consisting of Oliver Cromwell, eight officers and four civilians, with John Thurloe as secretary, who summoned the Parliament of Nominees, commonly called Barebones' Parliament.

ACTS AND DOCUMENTS

1649, Feb. 1. The Members excluded by Pride's Purge formally by vote expelled from the House.

March 17. The office of King abolished.

March 19. The House of Lords abolished.

The two latter Acts are printed in Gardiner, *Const. Doc.*, &c., pp. 296-7.

1651, Oct. 9. The Navigation Act passed, forbidding the importation of goods into England from any European country, except in English ships or in the ships of the country producing the goods, and forbidding trade with the colonies except in English ships. It was aimed at the Dutch carrying trade, and the Dutch trade with the English colonies. It was re-enacted after the Restoration as Car. II. 12, c. 18.

THE PROTECTORATE. 1653-1659

The title of Lord Protector was not new in England. Humphrey Duke of Gloucester had been Protector in the minority of Henry VI., Richard Duke of York had been Protector during the incapacity of the same king, Richard Duke of Gloucester had been Protector during the minority of Edward V., and the Duke of Somerset had been Protector during the minority of Edward VI.

The title had thus been borne as the mark of a temporary authority to tide over a crisis; but in the case of the Duke of York its wearer had looked forward to the crown, in the case of Richard duke of Gloucester he had used it as the stepping-stone to the crown.

In this case the Protectorate was practically a return to monarchy, first elective, and then hereditary, but in either case depending upon the support of the army.

DOMINIONS

Great Britain, Ireland and the British Isles. The colonies previously settled or acquired. Jamaica, taken in 1655; Dunkirk, taken in 1658.

WARS

Desultory warfare in the Highlands with the Royalists under the Earl of Glencairn and General Middleton 1653–55.

Penruddock's Royalist rising in the West of England, 1655.

Peace was made with Holland in 1654.

War was begun against Spain, 1655. In this year Hispaniola was unsuccessfully attacked and Jamaica taken. In 1657, April 20th, Blake won a naval victory over the Spaniards at Santa Cruz in the Canaries. On June 4th, 1658, the English aided the French in a victory over the Spaniards near Dunkirk, and the town was taken on June 17, and handed over to England. England was included in the peace of the Pyrenees between France and Spain in 1659.

OFFICIALS

Dec. 16, 1653. Oliver Cromwell becomes "His Highness the Lord Protector of the Commonwealth of England, Scotland, and Ireland."

May 25, 1657. Oliver Cromwell, Lord Protector, &c., with power to appoint his successor.

Sept. 3, 1658. Richard Cromwell declared Lord Protector by the Council.

PARLIAMENTS OF THE PROTECTORATE

Dec. 13, 1653. The Parliament of Nominees resigned its power into the hands of the Lord General.

Sept. 4, 1654. The Protector's first Parliament opened.

Jan. 31, 1655. Parliament dissolved, owing to its quarrel with the Protector as to the source of his authority.

Sept. 17, 1656. The Second Parliament meets. Many of the elected members arbitrarily excluded.

Feb. 4, 1658. The Parliament dissolved, owing to dissensions between the Commons and the revived Second Chamber, or House of Lords.

Jan. 29, 1659. The Parliament of Richard Cromwell meets.

April 22, 1659. Parliament dissolved owing to the opposition of the army.

ACTS AND DOCUMENTS

1653, Dec. 16. The Instrument of Government. This was an attempt to found a permanent written Constitution. The Government was to be in the hands of a Protector, appointed for life, a Council of State, nominated in the Instrument for life, and a Parliament representing the three countries of England, Scotland, and Ireland, elected upon the basis of a redistribution of seats, and a property franchise in the counties, the old franchises in the boroughs being unaltered. Vacancies in the Council were to be filled up by a choice made by the Protector and the Council out of a list presented by the Parliament. The executive power was to be in the hands of the Protector and Council, legislative power in those of the Parliament. Taxation was to be under Parliamentary control, with the important exceptions that a fixed revenue was to be settled upon the Protector for civil government, and a yearly revenue was to be settled for maintaining an army of 30,000 men and a fleet. This was part of the Constitution, so that a standing army was established, beyond the future control of Parliament. Some Christian Church was to be established and supported by public money, according to a plan to be agreed upon in the future. Religious toleration was made part of the Constitution, but was not to extend to Popery nor Prelacy; that is, it was not to be accorded to the great majority of the Irish, nor to what was shortly to appear to be the dominant party in England.

There was no provision for altering these fundamental laws, nor any proof that they represented the wishes of England, much less those of Scotland and Ireland.

The whole constitution is interesting as embodying the views of what had become the revolutionary party, and as bearing on the face of it the confession of their failure to conduct what they called a popular government, without an overwhelming military force to suppress popular opinion. It is printed in Gardiner, *Const. Documents*, 314.

1654, April 12. An Ordinance by the Protector for the Union of England and Scotland. Published in accordance with the Instrument of Government. (Printed in Gardiner, *Const. Documents*, 325.)

1654, June 27. Ordinances by the Protector for the election of members of the United Parliament in Scotland and Ireland. (Printed in Gardiner, *Const. Documents*, &c., pp. 329, 332.)

1654. The Treaty of Westminster put an end to the Dutch War. (Printed in *Dumont*, vol. vi. pt. ii. 74.)

1655. An Ordinance of the Protector imposed an income tax of 10 *per cent.* upon the Royalists, irrespective of former compositions, called the Decimation of the Royalists. England was also by Ordinance divided into eleven districts, under Major-Generals Lambert, Desborough, Whalley, Goffe, Fleetwood, Skippon, Kelsey, Butler, Worseley, Berry, and Barkstead, for the collection of this tax and the maintenance of order, and the suppression of popular amusements. (See *Order Books of the Council*, v. 49, and *Thurloe Papers*, iii. 701.)

In 1657 Parliament refused to vote money for the maintenance of this extraordinary military administration.

1657, May 25. The Humble Petition and Advice, and on

June 26 the Additional Petition and Advice, were presented by Parliament to the Protector. By these the Instrument of Government was modified, in spite of its self-asserted fundamental and permanent character. The Protector was to nominate his own successor; the name of the Council of State was changed to the old style of the Privy Council. It was to be filled up by the Protector, with the consent of the Council itself, and with the subsequent confirmation of the appointments by Parliament. Members of the Council were only to be removable by Parliament. A second Chamber, or House of Lords, was to be nominated by the Protector.

By this means the Monarchy was completely re-established, with the additional strength of a House of Lords nominated *en bloc* by the Monarch, and an established irreducible standing army. A ministry appointed by the Monarch, but subject to Parliamentary approval and control, was likely to be an efficient check upon monarchical power in proportion to the personal vigour or the contrary of the Monarch.

It marked the abandonment of all pretence of Republicanism, for the title of King was offered to the Protector, though refused, and it made the restoration of the old royal family nearly certain. If there was to be a monarchy, most people would prefer the old laws and limited prerogatives of the ancient monarchy to this new military dominion. The Petition and Advice is printed in Gardiner, *Const. Documents*, 334.

1659. The Peace of the Pyrenees put an end to the war between France and Spain, in which England had taken part. (See *Koch et Schoell*, vol. i. ch. 2.)

FURTHER STEPS IN THE RESTORATION

1658, Sept. 3.   Death of Oliver Cromwell.
                  Richard declared Lord Protector.
1659, Jan. 29.   Parliament meets.
     April 22.   Parliament dissolved.
     May 7.   The Members of the Long Parliament expelled in 1653 re-assemble.

May 13.	A Council of State of 15 soldiers and 16 civilians appointed by parliament.
May 25.	Richard retires from the Protectorate.
Oct. 13.	Fleetwood and Lambert expel the Parliament.
Dec. 26.	The Army restores the Parliament.
1660, Feb. 3.	Monk arrives in London with the Army from Scotland.
Feb. 13.	The Engagement to be true to the Commonwealth voted by Parliament.
Feb. 21.	The Members of Parliament expelled in 1648 re-admitted.
Feb. 22.	All votes of the Parliament since the forcible exclusion of these members rescinded, including the votes which abolished Monarchy and the House of Lords.
March 13.	The Engagement repudiated.
March 16.	The Long Parliament dissolves itself.
April 4.	The Declaration of Breda published by the King, making general promises of indemnity, except to such as shall be excepted by Parliament, a parliamentary settlement of religion, the retention of the ancient laws, security for the occupiers of lands acquired during the *interregnum*, and offering service to the army. (Printed in Gardiner, *Const. Documents*, &c. p. 351.)
April 25.	The Convention Parliament assembles, including the House of Lords.
May 1.	The King invited to return by Parliament.
May 25.	The King lands at Dover.
May 29.	A bill confirming Privilege of Parliament, Magna Charta, and the Petition of Right, passes the second reading, and is committed by the House of Commons. The King returns to London.

FAMILY CONNEXION OF SOME OF THE PARLIAMENTARY NOBILITY

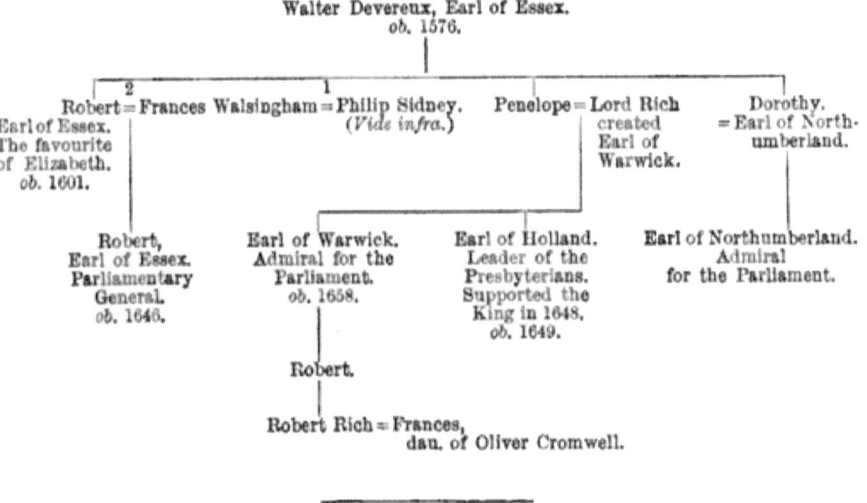

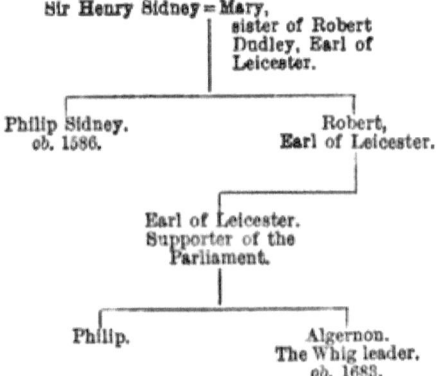

THE HOUSE OF CROMWELL, WITH THEIR CONNEXIONS

Members of the family actively engaged against the King are printed in heavier type. For a complete account see Noble, *Memoirs of the Protectoral House of Cromwell.*

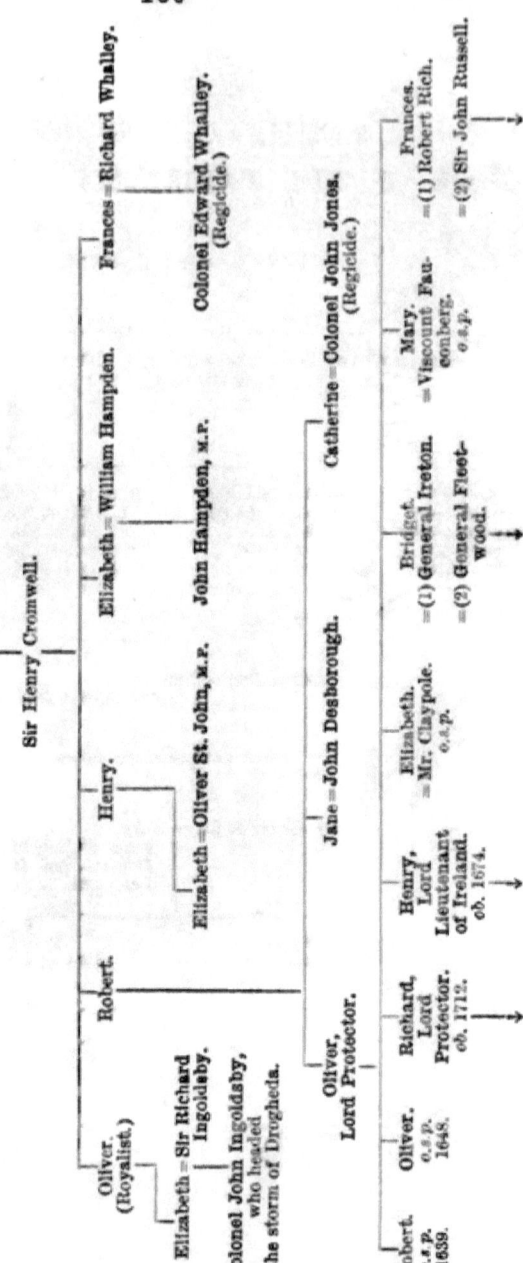

AUTHORS ON THE COMMONWEALTH AND PROTECTORATE

Ranke's *History of England*, Bks. xi. xii. xiii., is invaluable for a temperate survey of the whole period, with full knowledge of foreign as well as of English affairs.

Guizot's *The Republic and Cromwell*, is also free from the almost inevitable prepossessions of English writers.

Carlyle's *Cromwell's Letters and Speeches* is indispensable for a knowledge of Cromwell.

Hallam's *Constitutional History*, though needing correction and modification here and there, is here as always a work of great learning and wonderful balance of judgment, unbiassed by any enthusiasm.

As a small text-book Gardiner's *Puritan Revolution* is still the best.

The contemporary writers, Whitelocke, *Memorials of English Affairs;* Ludlow, *Memoirs;* Evelyn, *Diary;* Mrs. Hutchinson, *Memoirs of Colonel Hutchinson;* all are now available for the ordinary reader. Clarendon's *History of the Rebellion*, always prejudiced, becomes of less value during this period, when the author was absent from England.

CHARLES II. 1660-1685
Married Katharine of Braganza.

DOMINIONS

England, Scotland, and Ireland. The coast of North America from the borders of Florida (undetermined) to the borders of Nova Scotia (undetermined), with the exception of the Dutch settlements in and about New York. Part of Honduras, part of Guiana, Jamaica, Barbadoes, Bahamas, Montserrat, Anguilla, Antigua, Nevis, all in the West Indies. Bermuda, Madras, part of Gambia in Africa, Dunkirk, sold to the French in 1662. In 1661 Bombay and Tangiers (evacuated 1683) were acquired as the marriage portion of the Queen.

Cape Coast Castle, Accra, and Dix Cove were taken from the Dutch in 1664. In 1665 St. Helena, and in 1666 Tortola and the Virgin Islands, were conquered from the Dutch. In 1664 New Amsterdam, since called New York, was taken from the Dutch, and confirmed to England by treaty in 1674.

WARS

Commercial rivalry with the Dutch led to hostilities in 1664 and formal war in 1665. On June 3rd, 1665, the Duke of York, Prince Rupert, and the Earl of Sandwich defeated the Dutch fleet off Solebay. In 1666 the French joined the Dutch, and we were defeated, June 1st to 4th, 1666, in the Downs. Prince Rupert and Monk (Duke of Albemarle) defeated the Dutch on July 25th, off the North Foreland. June 11th to 29th, 1667, the equipment of the English fleet being neglected, the Dutch attacked Sheerness, Chatham, and other places in the mouth of the Thames, doing much damage. Peace was concluded the same year. In 1672 Charles joined France in an attack on Holland. An indecisive naval action was fought on May 28th, 1672, between the Duke of York and the Dutch in Southwold Bay, the Earl of Sandwich being killed. In 1673 partial actions with various success were fought off the Dutch coast. Peace was made in 1674.

In 1679 the troubles with the Covenanters in Scotland assumed the form of civil war, after the murder of Archbishop Sharpe. A skirmish at Loudon Hill, June 3rd, resulted in the defeat of a squadron of the royal cavalry, but the insurgents were defeated in a pitched battle at Bothwell Brig, near Glasgow, on June 22nd, by the Duke of Monmouth.

OFFICIALS AND MINISTERS

The Restoration had been a restoration not only of the King, but of the Parliament and laws, the relative positions of King and Parliament being substantially those which had been reached in the summer of 1641, before the outbreak of civil

Charles II.   163

war, with the exception that Parliament had no longer the power of self-dissolution. The King, however, had to govern with regard to the wishes of Parliament, and his ministers from this time onward became more and more dependent upon Parliamentary support.

In 1661, when the elections to the new Parliament had returned a decided majority of High Churchmen and Cavaliers, the following may be considered as the administration, enjoying the confidence of the two Houses.

Edward Hyde, Earl of Clarendon, Lord Chancellor, 1660–1667. On the disgrace of Clarendon Sir Orlando Bridgeman was Lord Keeper, 1667-1672. George Monk, Duke of Albemarle, sworn a Privy Councillor May 26th, 1660, was Captain General of the King's Forces by land and sea, 1660–1670; First Lord of the Treasury 1669–1672. James Duke of York was Lord High Admiral 1660–1673. Prince Rupert was sworn a Privy Councillor April 28th, 1662, was Admiral of the Fleet on the resignation of the Duke of York 1673, and First Lord of the Admiralty 1673–1679. In 1679 he was sworn a member of the New Privy Council of 30. The Earl of Southampton was Lord High Treasurer 1660–1667. Lord Ashley, afterwards Earl of Shaftesbury, was Chancellor of the Exchequer 1661-1667, a Commissioner of the Treasury 1667–1672. Sir Edward Nicholas was Secretary of State 1660–1662; Sir William Morrice 1660–1668; Sir John Trevor 1668–1672.

By 1670, after the fall of Clarendon in 1667, the ministry had been gradually reconstructed on an anti-high church basis.

The Earl of Shaftesbury, a Commissioner of the Treasury 1667–1672, was Lord Chancellor 1672–1673. Lord Clifford, a Commissioner of the Treasury and Comptroller of the Household 1667–1672, was Lord High Treasurer 1672–1673. Henry Bennet, Earl of Arlington, was Secretary of State 1662-74. George Villiers, Duke of Buckingham, had been re-sworn a member of the Privy Council 1667. He had been already sworn in 1662, and had been struck out in 1666. John Maitland, Earl (afterwards Duke) of Lauderdale, was a Privy Councillor and Secretary of State for Scotland 1660, President of the Secret Council of Scotland for life 1671.

The above five formed the Cabal ministry. Their common interest was opposition to the Church. Clifford was an ardent Romanist, Arlington a Romanist of less zeal, Buckingham, a man of no principles, posed as a favourer of the Sects, Ashley (Earl of Shaftesbury) was a freethinker, Lauderdale a moderate Presbyterian by birth and antecedents, though he of course favoured the moderate Episcopacy established in Scotland. They were some of them driven from office, and the ministry practically displaced, by the Test Act of 1673, when a High Church Cavalier Ministry again succeeded under Sir Thomas Osborne, afterwards Earl of Danby, Marquis of Carmarthen, Duke of Leeds, Lord High Treasurer 1673–1679. Sir Heneage Finch, afterwards Earl of Nottingham, Lord Keeper 1673–1675, Lord Chancellor 1675–82.

After the impeachment of the Earl of Danby 1678–1679 the Privy Council was dissolved, and a new Council of 30 nominated, of which the Earl of Shaftesbury was President April 21st to October 15th, 1679. The Earl of Essex was First Lord of the Treasury March 26th to November 21st, 1679. Robert Earl of Sunderland became a Secretary of State 1678–1681, and again 1683–85.

The Thirty included the leading noblemen and gentlemen of all parties, but were never effective as a ministry.

As the struggle over the Popish Plot and the Exclusion Bill gradually turned in the King's favour, he relied upon what was now beginning to be called a Tory ministry.

Lord Keeper, Sir Francis North, Lord Guildford, 1682–1685. First Lord of the Treasury, the Earl of Rochester, 1679–1684; Sidney Earl of Godolphin, 1684–1685 (Secretary of State 1684). Lord Privy Seal, Marquis of Halifax, 1682–1685.

Charles II.

Lord President of the Council, Earl of Anglesea, 1679–1684. Earl of Rochester 1684, 1685.

ACTS AND DOCUMENTS

1660. Car. II. 12, c. 11. An Act of general pardon and oblivion, with certain exceptions, especially of the Regicides.

Car. II. 12, c. 30. An Act of attainder against the Regicides, who as members of the court or otherwise took part in the execution of Charles I.

Of these 12 were executed, Colonels Harrison, Axtell, Jones, and Hacker, Cook, Scot, Carew, Clement, Scroop, Hugh Peters, chaplain to the Court, and Barkstead and Okey later. Colonel Hutchinson was excepted from the Act of Attainder, but was afterwards arrested on suspicion of being concerned in a plot of the Sectaries, and died in prison.

Vane and Lambert, though not Regicides, were condemned, Vane executed, Lambert allowed to reside in Guernsey. Of the other leading men of the Army party George Fleetwood, Goffe, and Whalley resided unmolested in New England, Charles Fleetwood in England. Lisle and Ludlow went abroad, where the former was murdered. Richard and Henry Cromwell retired abroad, but returned and died in England, Richard at a great age in 1712. See Noble, *History of the Regicides* and the *State Trials*.

Car. II. 12, c. 24. Feudal tenures and dues abolished, and a revenue settled on the king in their place.

Oct. 25, 1660. A declaration published by the king favouring a compromise among religious parties. There had been at first attached to it a recommendation of toleration, but the old school of Puritan clergy, headed by Baxter, refused to consider a toleration extended to Socinians, Anabaptists, and Romanists. The Declaration was proposed as a Bill to the House of Commons and was rejected, Nov. 28th, 1660. See Baxter's own account in his *Life*, p. 276 and *Old Parl. Hist.* xxiii. 28.

1661. Car. II. 13, Stat. 2, c. 1. Office holders in corporations compelled to take the Holy Communion according to the rite of the Church of England, and to abjure the Covenant.

1662. Car. II. 14, c. 4. The Act of Uniformity, approving the Prayer Book as recently revised by Convocation, requiring assent to it, and episcopal ordination by all persons holding ecclesiastical preferment.

In consequence of this Act, and the Act Car. II. 12, c. 17, restoring ejected clergy to their livings, from 1400 to 1500 ministers resigned their livings.

Car. II. 14, c. 33. Printing regulated, all books to be licensed by authority.

1664. Car. II. 16, 1. An act passed that Parliament should be called at least once in three years.

Car. II. 16, c. 4. The Conventicle Act, severely punishing persons present at an unlawful assembly. It was a re-enactment with variations and less severe penalties of the act, Eliz. 35, c. 1.

1665. The right of the clergy to tax themselves in Convocation tacitly abandoned. See Hallam, *Const. Hist.* iv. 60.

Car. II. 17, c. 2. The Five Mile Act, forbidding persons who had held ecclesiastical preferment, and who refused the oath of non-resistance, to come within five miles of any corporate town except when travelling, and prohibiting them from keeping schools.

This Act was passed in a panic, at the prospect of a descent of Republican exiles from Holland during the Dutch war, and in common with the Conventicle Act was the result not only of the rebound of popular opinion in favour of the Church, but of the attempted insurrection in London of 1661, and at Newcastle in 1663, and the knowledge that a large number of disbanded soldiers were about the country.

1667. The Treaty of Breda ended the war with Holland. See *Koch et Schoell*, vol. i. ch. 3.

1668. The Triple Alliance negotiated by Sir William Temple between England, Holland, and Sweden.

This Alliance was not so entirely anti-French in its design as is sometimes represented. It was entered into with a view of arresting French progress in the Spanish Netherlands, dangerously near the Dutch frontier, but also with a view of compelling Spain to give up something to France, lest by continuing to resist she might bring on a general European war.

The Peace of Aix-la-Chapelle was the consequence of the alliance, by which part of Flanders was ceded by the Spaniards to France. See *Koch et Schoell*, vol. i. ch. 6, and *Dumont*, vii. pt. 1, p. 107, for the formal treaty between England, Holland, and Sweden.

1670. Secret Treaty of Dover, negotiated through Charles's sister Henrietta, Duchess of Orleans, by which Charles in return for support in money, and men when needed, from Louis XIV., undertook to support the latter against Holland, to procure the repeal of the penal laws against the Catholics, and to declare himself a Catholic. Certain colonial and foreign possessions in America, Minorca, Ostend, and other places were to be secured to England if the Spaniards, as was probable, joined the Dutch; and the rights of the Prince of Orange, Charles' nephew, were to be considered in Holland, where the anti-Orange party was now in power. The whole of the Cabal Ministry were privy to the scheme of war against Holland; only Clifford and Arlington, the two Catholics, were admitted to the full contents of the treaty.

The English reader will find the best review of the negotiations in Ranke, *Hist. of England*, B. xv. ch. 6.

1672. Declaration of Indulgence issued by the King in favour of the Noncomformists. See *Parl. Hist.* iv. 515.

1673. The Test Act, Car. II. 25, c. 2, passed to nullify the Declaration, and make the Tests imposed upon all taking office more severe.

1674. Peace with Holland. The Dutch paying an indemnity and yielding certain colonies to England. The King's Catholic schemes having been checked by the Test Act, and his nephew having been placed at the head of the Dutch state, he threw over the French king. See *Koch et Schoell*, vol. i. ch. 7; *Dumont*, vii. pt. 1, p. 283.

1676. Secret treaty with Louis XIV., by which Louis pays the King to subordinate his foreign policy to that of France. Another treaty was made in 1678, but Charles kept the money and not the conditions. For the impeachment of Danby, springing out of the Treaties, see *Parl. Hist.* iv. 1060, and Hallam, *Const. Hist.* ch. 12.

1678. The Continental war ended by the Peace of Nimuegen, by which the powers wronged by France compound with her, but France fails to gain all that she had hoped to attain by the help of England. See *Koch et Schoell*, vol. i. ch. 7.

1679. Car. II. 31, c. 2. Habeas Corpus Act. "For better securing the liberty of the subject, and preventing imprisonment beyond the seas." The writ of *Habeas Corpus* was no new thing in England, and the principle is recorded in the Magna Charta, clause 29, but by this Act the law was put upon a plain and unequivocal basis.

At the time of its passing its authors were inciting prosecutions, during the Popish Plot agitation, in defiance of justice and reason. The Act was suspended in times of confusion, on nine occasions from 1688-1746, from 1794-1800, and in 1817. Besides appearing among the Statutes, the Act is printed at the end of Stubbs, *Select Charters*.

The Acts given above are printed in the Statutes.

AUTHORS

Ranke's *History of England* and Hallam's *Constitutional History* hold the first place for foreign affairs and constitutional history respectively.

Macaulay's *History* comes into the field, but the student must remember that it is avowedly a party history, and further unconsciously disfigured with some inaccuracies. No study of the time is complete without it, however.

James II. 169

The *Diaries* of John Evelyn and Samuel Pepys are accessible to the general reader, and illustrate the history and social life of the age on every side.

The *Parliamentary History*, referred to above, 1660, was published first in 1752. William Cobbett projected a *Parliamentary History*, which incorporated many earlier publications, and came down to 1803. Since that date it has been continued under the name of *Hansard*.

JAMES II. 1685–1688
Married (1) Anne Hyde. (2) Maria d'Este of Modena.

DOMINIONS
As under Charles II.

WARS

In 1685 the Earl of Argyle made a descent from Holland upon Scotland, and the Duke of Monmouth upon England. Argyle was taken without fighting. Monmouth gathered a considerable force, but was defeated at Sedgemoor, in Somersetshire, on July 6th, in what is the last action deserving the name of a battle fought in England.

OFFICIALS

Lord Guildford, Lord Keeper till Sept. 5, 1685.
George, Lord Jeffreys, Lord Chancellor, 1685.
Earl of Rochester, Lord Treasurer, 1685–1687.
Lord Belasyse, First Lord of the Treasury, 1687.
Marquis of Halifax, President of the Council, 1685.
The Earl of Sunderland, President of the Council, Dec. 4th, 1685.
Richard Talbot, Earl of Tyrconnell, Lord Lieutenant of Ireland, 1686.
The Earl of Tyrconnell, the Earl of Powis, the Earl of Castlemaine, all Romanists, and Father Petre a Jesuit, were

illegally sworn members of the Privy Council in 1686, and with the Earl of Sunderland, who betrayed him, shared the inner counsels of the King.

ACTS AND DOCUMENTS

1686, June 21. The Judges, in the case of Sir Edward Hales, affirm the power of the King to dispense with the provisions of the Test Act in particular cases. (*State Trials*, xi. 1165.)

1686. The League of Augsburg formed on the Continent to check the ambition of Louis XIV. This League included the Emperor and Princes of the Empire, the Kings of Spain and Sweden, the Duke of Savoy, and ultimately Holland and the Pope, Innocent XI. It was begun by the Prince of Waldeck, and completed by the Prince of Orange and the Elector of Brandenburg. It played an important part in the English Revolution, for the events of the previous war, 1672–1678, had shewn the necessity of including England in the alliance, and the allies of Augsburg furnished the army by which the invasion of England by the Prince of Orange was successfully accomplished. (See *Koch et Schoell*, vol. i. ch. 8, and *Dumont*, vii. pt. 2, 131.)

1686, July 14th. A Court of Ecclesiastical Commission erected by the King, contrary to the Act of 1641, consisting of the Lord Chancellor, the Archbishop of Canterbury, the Bishops of Durham and Rochester, the Earls of Sunderland and Rochester, and the Lord Chief Justice, Sir Edward Herbert.

1687, April 4th. A Declaration of Indulgence suspending the Test Act, and other acts against Romanists and Nonconformists, issued by the King. (See *London Gazette*, April 7, 1687.)

1688, April 25th. The Declaration republished, and commanded to be read in Churches, May 4th. This re-issue of the Declaration led to the Petition and the trial of the Seven Bishops.

AUTHORS

As on the reign of Charles II.

GENEALOGY OF THE HOUSE OF ORANGE

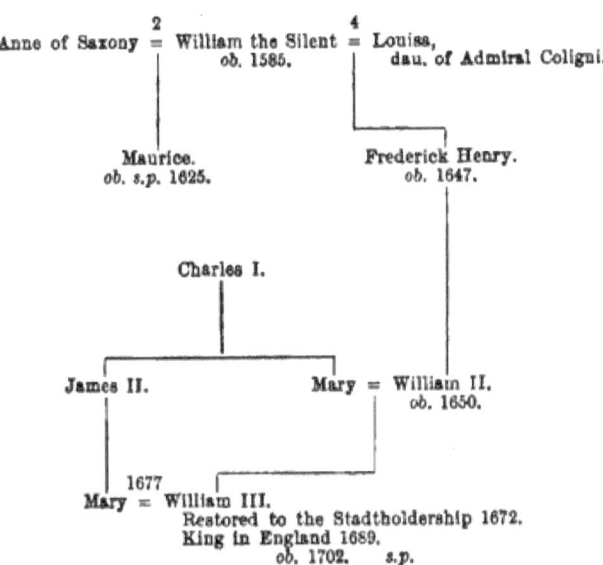

On the death of William III. the Stadtholdership was again abolished. It was revived (1748) in the person of William IV., a descendant of a daughter of Frederick Henry and of a brother of William the Silent. He married Anne, daughter of King George II. of England, and his grandson became first King of the Netherlands in 1815.

WILLIAM III. AND MARY II. 1689–1694
WILLIAM III. 1694–1702

DOMINIONS

The same as under Charles II., but the greater part of Ireland continued to acknowledge James II., and was not finally conquered till 1691.

A small district in Bengal was acquired in 1697. St. Kitt's in the West Indies, which had been disputed between English, French, and Spaniards since Charles the First's reign, was acquired by the Peace of Ryswick in 1697.

WARS

The Revolution had to be imposed upon Ireland by force of arms. Londonderry was successfully defended by the Protestants till the siege was raised on July 30th, 1689, and the same day the Protestants of Enniskillen defeated the Irish at Newtown Butler. On July 1st, 1690, William defeated James at the Boyne, but was forced to raise the siege of Limerick on Aug. 30th. The Earl of Marlborough took Cork and Kinsale in the autumn. In 1691 General Ginkell took Athlone, defeated the French and Irish at Aghrim, July 12th, took Galway, and ended the war by the surrender of Limerick, Oct. 5th, on terms which were partly evaded by the Irish and English parliaments later.

In Scotland Viscount Dundee raised the Highlands for King James, but was killed in a victory at Killiecrankie, July 27th, 1689, after which the conflict dwindled down into partisan warfare, till a pacification was made in 1691.

On the Continent war with France began in 1689, being part of the understood terms on which the Revolution was carried out. William was to restore Parliamentary government in England, and England was to act with the allies against France.

William and Mary

1690, June 30th. The English and Dutch fleets were defeated off Beachy Head by the French. The same day the Allies under the Prince of Waldeck were defeated by Luxembourg at Fleurus.

1692, May 19-24th. The French fleet defeated and many men of war and transports destroyed at La Hogue.

1692, Aug. 3. William defeated at Steenkirke by Luxembourg.

1693, July 28. William defeated at Landen or Neerwinden by Luxembourg.

1695, Sept. 1. William took Namur.

OFFICIALS

The two parties, now called Whigs and Tories, had united in supporting William and Mary, and the King at first drew his advisers from both parties. He was, however, in fact his own Prime Minister, presiding in the Council when in England, and his own Minister of War and Foreign Affairs.

In 1689 Viscount Mordaunt was first Lord of the Treasury till 1690; the Marquis of Carmarthen, afterwards Duke of Leeds, formerly Earl of Danby, Lord President of the Council till 1699; the Marquis of Halifax, Lord Privy Seal till 1690; the Earl of Torrington, first Commissioner of the Admiralty, till 1690; the Earl of Nottingham, Secretary of State, till 1693.

The Great Seal was in Commission.

1690. The Earl of Godolphin was First Lord of the Treasury till 1696, and again 1700-1701.

Charles Montague, afterwards Earl of Halifax, was a Lord of the Treasury, 1692-1697; Chancellor of the Exchequer, 1694 to 1697; First Lord of the Treasury, 1697 to 1699.

Lord Somers was Lord Keeper, 1693-1697; and Lord Chancellor from 1697 to 1700.

Robert, Earl of Sunderland, Privy Councillor, 1697.

The Earl of Shrewsbury, afterwards Duke, Privy Councillor, 1689–92; a Secretary of State, 1689–1690; and again 1694–1699.

John Lord Churchill, afterwards Earl and Duke of Marlborough, Privy Councillor, 1689–1692; Commander in Chief in England, 1690–1692. Restored to the Privy Council, 1698. Commander in Chief in the Netherlands, 1701.

William Bentinck, Earl of Portland, Privy Councillor, 1689.

ACTS AND DOCUMENTS

Gul. & Mar. 1, c. 5. The first Mutiny Act, to regulate the discipline of the army. Passed in consequence of the refusal of Dumbarton's (Scotch) regiment to obey the (certainly illegal) order of the English government to embark for Flanders. Passed as an annual act it necessitated the annual meeting of parliament.

Gul. & Mar. 1, c. 18. The Toleration Act. This Act while not altering the Test and Corporation Acts, nor repealing the penal laws against the Romanists, allowed the meeting of dissenters from the Church for public worship with open doors on certain conditions. Deniers of the Trinity were, however, still excluded from the benefit of the act. Taken in conjunction with the expiration of the law against unlicensed printing, which lapsed in 1695, it marks the abandonment by the government of the hardest part of its work, the maintenance of its own view of truth, which had perplexed all governments since Henry VIII., if not since the passing of the Lollard statutes. The small number of Romanists and Socinians made their exception of no practical importance. The benefits of the policy were not extended to Ireland, where the Romanists were a majority.

Gul. & Mar. 1, sess. 2, c. 2. The Bill of Rights. This is practically the same as the Declaration of Rights which had been presented to the sovereigns as a condition of their receiving the crown, and which put the monarchy of the Revolution upon a different basis from that of the monarchy by birthright of the Stewarts. It settled, in the sense desired by the Whig party, the questions concerning the Suspending and Dispensing power, the maintenance of a standing army in time of peace, the freedom and constant assembling of Parliaments, and the liberty of the subject, laying down the law distinctly on many points in opposition to the views upheld by the Judges and Crown lawyers under the Stewarts. It also regulated the succession to the crown according to a definite plan. In effect it marked the transference of influence from the Crown to the aristocracy who controlled Parliament.

It is printed at the end of Stubbs, *Select Charters*.

Gul. & Mar. 2, sess. 2, c. 11. Commissioners appointed to audit the public accounts. These were appointed subsequently year by year till 1785, when a Permanent Board of Public Accounts was erected.

1691. The Treaty of Limerick, promising certain liberties to the Irish Catholics. The treaty was subsequently much modified by the action of the Irish Parliament.

See Lecky, *History of England*, vol. ii., chaps. 6, 7, for a comment on the results of the Irish War.

The Treaty is given in Leland, *History of Ireland*, 619.

Gul. & Mar. 5 & 6, c. 20. An Act incorporating certain Merchants with special privileges, on condition of their supporting the Government with money for the war. They were incorporated by Royal Charter as the Bank of England on July 27th, 1694.

Gul. & Mar. 6 & 7, c. 2. The Triennial Act, limiting the duration of parliaments to three years.

Gul. III. 7 & 8, c. 3. An Act regulating trials for treason. Persons accused of treason to be furnished with a copy of the indictment and to be allowed counsel, and otherwise protected. Trials for treason had up to this time been little better than an authorised form of murder. The old habit of taking unfair advantage of the prisoner in such cases continued to make itself felt long afterwards.

In 1696 as Sir John Fenwick could not have been convicted of treason under the new Act, he was condemned by Act of Attainder. (Gul. III. 8 & 9, c. 4.)

1697. The Peace of Ryswick, between France and the Allies. William recognised as King in England, and the Protestant succession after him accepted by France. France yielded all her conquests since the Treaty of Nimuegen, but retained Strassburg and other places which she had acquired by a form of law, supported by violence, in time of peace. It was the first peace for fifty years by which France had not been aggrandized, and was so far a triumph for the Allies. (See *Koch et Schoell*, vol. i. chap. 9.)

1698 and 1700. The Partition Treaties, for a partition of the Spanish Monarchy, arranged between William and Louis XIV. These treaties, disregarding the rights of the Spanish crown and people, were negotiated with the privity of only a very few of the King's advisers, though they were certain to involve England in war. The Earl of Portland and Lord Somers were impeached in 1701 for their share in them, a mere vote of the House of Commons not being yet sufficient to remove a Minister. The French king disregarded the Treaties so soon as it suited his schemes to do so. (See *Koch et Schoell*, vol. ii. chap. 10.)

1701. The Act of Settlement. Resettling the Protestant Succession, recapitulating several points of the Bill of Rights, and incapacitating persons holding offices of profit under the Crown from sitting in the House of Commons. Privy Councillors were also to be individually responsible for the acts taken on their advice.

This act illustrates the so far imperfect conception of Ministerial government and united Cabinets as now understood. Ministers were by it considered independent advisers of the Crown, not sitting in the House of Commons.

It is printed at the end of Stubbs, *Select Charters*.

All the Acts given above are printed in the *Statutes*.

THE CHURCH OF ENGLAND AND THE NON-JURORS

The clergy had as a body so strongly upheld the duty of non-resistance that it was difficult for them consistently to take part in the Revolution.

Some of the ablest and most conscientious of the High Churchmen refused to take the oaths to William and Mary, and were deprived of their sees and livings. They founded and continued in existence the separate body of Non-jurors. They were headed by the Archbishop of Canterbury, Sancroft, Ken the Bishop of Bath and Wells, author of the *Morning and Evening Hymns*, the Bishops of Ely, Peterborough, Chichester, Gloucester, Norwich, Worcester. The first five of these had been among the Seven Bishops prosecuted by James II.

The secession of so influential a body, and the evident tergiversation of many who took the oaths, contributed to the decided decay of the influence of the Church, which began to make itself felt by the reign of George I. The reign of Anne, a High Churchwoman herself, had brought the Church and government into close alliance again, but the Jacobitism of the ablest prelate, Atterbury of Rochester, and the promotion by William III. and George I. of Low (*i.e.* Broad) Churchmen to bishoprics, against the wishes of the mass of the clergy and country gentlemen, increased the inefficiency of the Church. Jeremy Collier and Carte the historical writer, and William Law by far the most eminent divine of the earlier eighteenth century, were Non-jurors. See Lathbury, *History of the Non-jurors*.

THE STANDING ARMY

There was no permanent army in England till the Instrument of Government—see 1653—incorporated the army into the machinery of government by a fundamental constitutional law. The armies during the Civil Wars had been avowedly raised for temporary emergencies, though no doubt an army would have remained after the struggle, whoever had won. In 1660 this army was paid off and disbanded by Car. II. 12, cc. 9, 10, 15, 20, 27, but twenty-six garrisons were maintained, and a small force permanently in regiments, supported out of the fixed revenues of the Crown. Monk's regiment was immediately re-embodied after disbandment as the Coldstream Guards. One regiment of Foot-guards, now the Grenadier Guards, and two regiments of Horse Guards, now the First Life Guards and the Blues, were raised from members of the old Cavalier forces and Royalist refugees. Dumbarton's Foot, a Scotch regiment originally serving in France, and then under Gustavus Adolphus, subsequently in France again, came home, and became known as the First Royal Regiment of Foot in Scotland, late the first of the Line, now the Royal Scots. A regiment of Scottish Life Guards, now the Second Life Guards, and subsequently other regiments, were raised in Scotland.

A regiment of Dragoons, now the First Royal Dragoons, and of Foot, late the Second Queen's Regiment, now the Royal West Surrey, were raised for service at Tangiers; and a regiment of Foot, subsequently the Bombay Fusileers, then the 103rd Regiment, now the 2nd Batt. R. Dublin Fusileers, for service at Bombay.

During the Dutch wars, and in the reign of James II., the standing army was increased, but diminished again in 1678 and at the Revolution. The Buffs, however, lately the 3rd Regiment of Foot, now the East Kent Regiment, were permanently added to the Army, and six English regiments which had been maintained in the Dutch service were brought home.

Under William III. the annual **Mutiny Acts** gave a cohesion to the Army which had not formerly existed, and with the Bill of Rights and the Act of Settlement brought the existence and pay of the army under Parliamentary control. There was great jealousy, however, on the subject of a standing army, and its numbers were constantly reduced at every peace to absurdly small proportions, to be raised hurriedly, inefficiently, and expensively, as each war broke out. Down to the Wars of the French Revolution the military disasters in the beginning of most of our wars may be traced to this practice.

For a complete account see Article *Army, Encyclopædia Britannica*, new edition, 1875, &c.

AUTHORS

On the Revolution and reign of William III.

The Constitutional side of the History may still be best followed in Hallam, *Const. History*. The general and European side in Ranke, *History of England*.

Lord Macaulay enters upon his principal subject with the reign of James II., and, though to be used with the cautions suggested above on Charles II., can never be surpassed for graphic description of events viewed from the standpoint of the Whigs.

The opening chapters of Lecky, *History of England in the Eighteenth Century*, should be read for a philosophic review of the causes and effects of the Revolution.

Coxe, *Life of Marlborough*, is painstaking and generally correct.

For small text-books Gardiner's *Student's History of England* and the edition of 1878 of the *Student's Hume* are the most satisfactory.

QUEEN ANNE. 1702-1714
Married Prince George of Denmark.

DOMINIONS

At her accession as under William III.

By the treaty of Utrecht in 1713, Gibraltar, taken in 1704, Minorca, taken in 1708, and Hudson's Bay Territory, Nova Scotia, Newfoundland, and St. Kitt's in the West Indies, all previously disputed territories, were added to the Crown of Great Britain.

WARS

The great war of the Spanish Succession occupies the greater part of Anne's reign. The Alliance comprised England, Holland, the Emperor, the Electors of Brandenburg and Hanover, the Elector Palatine, the Duke of Baden, some lesser German Princes, the King of Denmark, and after a short time Portugal and the Duke of Savoy. The Allies also had the sympathies of the Catalans in Spain, and of some of the Aragonese who were jealous of Castile.

On the side of France were the Castilians and most of the Spaniards, the Electors of Bavaria and Cologne.

The avowed object of the Allies at the beginning of the war was to carry out the principles of the Partition Treaties, giving the throne of Spain to the Austrian candidate, the Archduke Charles, and extensive compensations to the French and their candidate, Philip Duke of Anjou. The French tried to grasp the whole Spanish Monarchy for the Duke of Anjou. As the war progressed favourably for the Allies they tried to grasp the whole for the Archduke, falling into the same mistake as the French in aiming at too much. The war ended in a recognition of the principle of a Partition, though not as originally agreed.

The real objects of the war, however, so far as England was concerned, were to punish Louis for recognizing the son of James II., contrary to the Peace of Ryswick, generally to check French power, and to prevent the grant by the Spaniards of exclusive trade privileges to the French in America. These objects were fully attained.

1702-3. The war was confined to sieges in the Netherlands and on the Lower Rhine, but the French in 1703 were victorious on the Upper Rhine and in Bavaria.

1704. The Duke of Marlborough marched from the Netherlands into Bavaria, defeated the Bavarians at Schellenberg on July 2, and in concert with Prince Eugene, the Emperor's general, completely routed the French and Bavarians at Blenheim, Aug. 2. Sir George Rooke took Gibraltar, July 23, and defeated the French fleet off Malaga, Aug. 13.

1705. Barcelona taken, Oct. 4, and the east of Spain overrun by the Allies.

1706. Marlborough defeated the French at Ramilies, May 12. The Allies occupied Madrid, but retired again. Prince Eugene defeated the French at Turin, Sept. 7.

1707. The Allies completely defeated at Almanza, in Spain, by the Duke of Berwick, April 14. Naples conquered by the Emperor's troops, who however unsuccessfully invaded south-east France. The French successful on the Upper Rhine.

1708. The French seized part of Flanders, but were defeated by Marlborough at Oudenarde July 11. Lille taken by Marlborough Dec. 29. Sardinia and Minorca taken by an English fleet.

1709. Marlborough and Eugene defeated the French at Malplaquet, Sept. 11, with heavy loss on their own side.

1710. A war of sieges on the north-east frontier of France. In Spain the Allies won Almenara and Saragossa, but were destroyed by the Duc de Vendôme at Brihuega, Dec. 10, and Villa Viciosa, Dec. 20.

1711. A war of posts and sieges on the French frontier. Marlborough deprived of his command.

1712. Eugene, deserted by the English, was defeated by Villars at Denain, in France, and the latter re-captured the late conquests of the Allies within the French frontier.

MINISTERS

In the reign of Anne the system of homogeneous party Ministries may be said to have established itself, owing to the difficulty of working the government, when Ministers belonged to different parties, under a sovereign whose sex and want of great capacity prevented her from presiding as effectually as William had done.

In 1702 the Ministry was considered to be one of moderate Tories.

Lord Keeper, Sir Nathan Wright, 1702–1705.

Lord Treasurer, Earl of Godolphin, 1702–1710.

Lord President of the Council, Earl of Pembroke and Montgomery, 1702–1708.

Secretaries of State, Earl of Nottingham, 1702–1704; Sir Charles Hedges, 1702–1706; Robert Harley, afterwards Earl of Oxford, 1704–1708.

Secretary at War, Henry St. John, afterwards Viscount Bolingbroke, 1704–1708.

Generalissimo of the Allied Forces, Master General of the Ordnance. Privy Councillor, John Duke of Marlborough, 1702–1711.

The Ministry, engaged in a war which was more popular with the Whigs than with the Tories, inclined towards the former party, and began to drop its more pronounced Tory Members about 1704 and onwards, taking in Whig leaders in their place.

Lord Keeper, Earl Cowper, 1705–1707, became Lord Chancellor, 1707–1710.

Lord President, Lord Somers, 1708–1710.

Secretaries of State, Earl of Sunderland, 1706–1710; Henry Boyle, afterwards Lord Carleton, 1708–1710.

Secretary at War, Robert Walpole, 1708–1710.

In 1710–1711 a strongly Tory Ministry succeeded.

Lord Keeper, Sir Simon Harcourt, 1710–1713.

Lord Chancellor as Lord Harcourt, 1713–1714.

Lord Treasurer, Earl Poulett, 1710–1711.

Chancellor of the Exchequer, Robert Harley, 1710–1711.

Lord Treasurer, Harley Earl of Oxford, 1711–1714.

Chancellor of the Exchequer, Robert Benson, afterwards Lord Bingley, 1711–1714.

Lord President, Earl of Rochester, 1710–1711; Duke of Normanby and Buckinghamshire, 1711–1714.

Lord Privy Seal, John Robinson, Bishop of Bristol, afterwards of London, 1711–1714. Plenipotentiary at Utrecht, 1712–1713. The last prelate to fill high civil office in England.

Secretaries of State, Earl of Dartmouth, 1710–1713, and Henry St. John, Viscount Bolingbroke, 1710–1714; William Bromley, vice Earl of Dartmouth, 1713–1714.

Secretary at War, Sir William Wyndham, 1712–1714.

Commander of the Forces, Duke of Ormonde, 1712–1714.

The Tory Ministry becoming Jacobite under Bolingbroke's guidance, the Earl of Oxford was deprived of the Treasury, but the Duke of Shrewsbury was appointed Lord High Treasurer, July 29, 1714, three days before the Queen's death, and the Dukes of Argyle and Somerset, acting on their right as Privy Councillors, attended the meeting of the Council to arrange for the accession of George I.

ACTS AND DOCUMENTS

1703. Methuen Treaty with Portugal, a commercial treaty to induce Portugal to support the Allies. Noticeable as the cause of what became the national habit of port wine drinking to the neglect of French wines. (See *Koch et Schoell*, ii. 36.)

1703. First Fruits restored by the Crown to the Church by Letters Patent, see Henry VIII. 26, c. 3. The foundation of Queen Anne's Bounty, confirmed by Act of Parliament, Anne 2 and 3, c. 20.

Anne 6, c. 11. The Union with Scotland. A complete Parliamentary and Commercial Union between the two kingdoms, leaving the domestic law of each unaltered. The maintenance of the Episcopal Church in England, including Wales, and of the Presbyterian Church in Scotland, made integral articles of the Union.

Such an Act had become inevitable since the Revolution of 1688–89 had transferred real supremacy in government to the two parliaments in their respective countries. One crown had been a kind of guarantee of common action in the two countries, while the crown was the real depository of power. Whenever formerly, as in 1638 and 1648-49, and when now, this had ceased to be the case, the two countries tended rapidly towards separation. The Scotch Act of Security, 1704, had pointed to a possibly different monarch in Scotland and England after the death of Queen Anne.

The same arguments were not yet applicable to the case of Ireland; for from its unpopular composition, and from Poyning's Act (see Henry VII. 1494), the Irish Parliament was completely dependent upon the English Government.

One of the greatest effects of the Act of Union was the increase of English commercial and Colonial enterprise by the admission of the poor and energetic Scotchmen to share in it. This was especially felt in the forthcoming development of our Indian Empire.

Anne 9, c. 5. A high property qualification established for Members of the House of Commons. Repealed Victoria 21 and 22, c. 26.

Anne 10, c. 2. An Act against Occasional Conformity, to punish Dissenters who should qualify for office by taking the Communion in Church, and should afterwards frequent conventicles.

It was repealed under George the First, but is important as the great index of Whig and Tory leanings in this reign. It was several times passed by the House of Commons, and thrown out by the House of Lords, but was carried before the creation of 12 new Tory Peers, Dec. 31, 1711, to swamp the Whig Majority in the Upper House.

1713. The Treaty of Utrecht, ending the War of the Spanish Succession. The Duke of Anjou was left in possession of the throne of Spain, which he actually held, and where the sympathies of the population, except in Catalonia, were unmistakeably for him. The Austrian candidate had become Emperor, which in itself would have been an argument for reverting to the Partition scheme and for not giving him the whole Monarchy. He was amply compensated in the Netherlands and Italy. A barrier of garrisons was secured for the Dutch in the Netherlands.

England acquired considerable Colonial possessions, see on *Dominions*, and the right of carrying on the slave trade and some general trade in the Spanish colonies, from which France was excluded. This trade was easily in effect expanded into a considerable illicit trade, especially between the English and Spanish colonies in America, which led to much future trouble.

The new king of Spain was barred from the French succession, the Protestant succession guaranteed in England, and the interests of the Regent in France, who took up the government in 1715, enlisted on the side of the maintenance of the Treaty and of the Protestant succession, for he and Philip of Spain were likely to be rival heirs in France in the event of Louis XV. dying as a child, which seemed likely.

Above all, the events of the war had prevented France from being a real menace to Europe for another eighty years.

The manner of obtaining the Treaty, behind the backs of the Allies, can only be palliated by the fact of the Emperor having tried to do the same first.

The Treaty is printed in *Dumont*, viii. 339, and see *Koch et Schoell*, ii. 79, etc.

The Acts given above are printed in the Statutes.

AUTHORS

The history of Queen Anne's reign has been very fully written in the present century. *The History of the Reign of Queen Anne*, and *The War of the Succession in Spain*, by Earl Stanhope, are singularly fair. The latter, and the Essay upon it by Lord Macaulay, are however vitiated by their acceptance of Carleton's *Memoirs* as genuine. A better view of the Earl of Peterborough is given in Colonel Parnell's *Life of Peterborough*. *The Life of the Duke of Marlborough*, by Archdeacon Coxe,

THE HOUSE OF BRUNSWICK

SHOWING THEIR SERVICES AS SOLDIERS TO THE EMPIRE

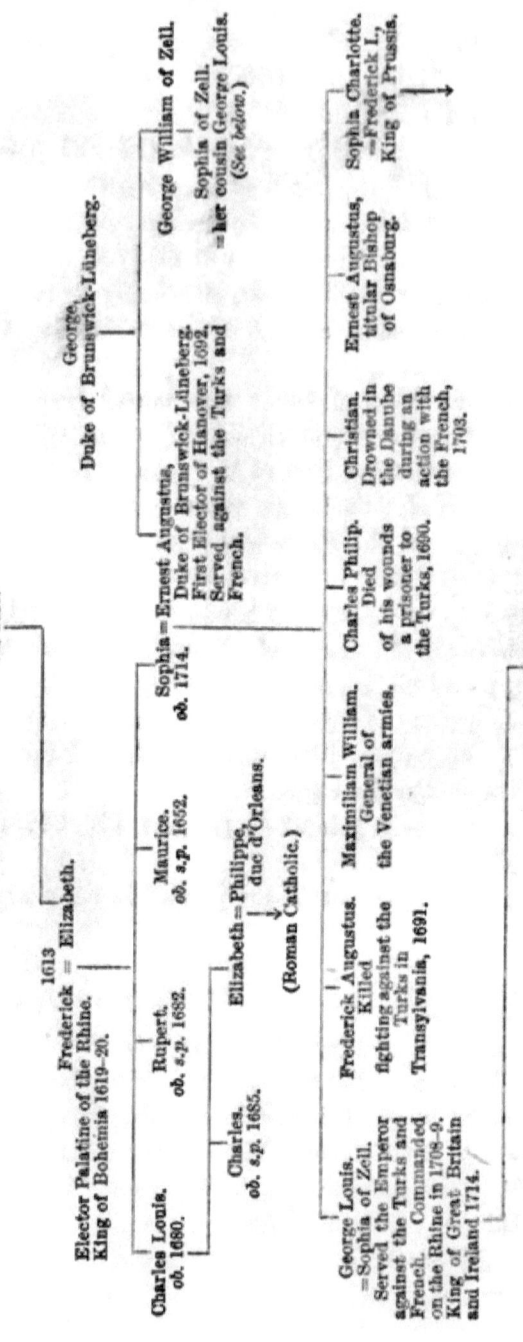

Burton's *History of the Reign of Queen Anne*, and Wyon's *History of the Reign of Queen Anne* are all to be depended on.

Swift's *History of the last four Years of Queen Anne's Reign*, and his pamphlet, *On the Conduct of the Allies*, are vigorous party contributions to the history of the latter part of the reign and of the war.

Among small histories, Morris's *Age of Anne*, Longmans' *Epochs Series*, is among the best of the series.

GEORGE I. 1714–1727

Married Sophia Dorothea of Zell.

DOMINIONS

Great Britain and Ireland, with Gibraltar and Minorca, and the colonial possessions as guaranteed by the Treaty of Utrecht. The Electorate of Hanover. The Duchy of Brunswick-Lüneburg had been raised to the *status* of an electorate by the Emperor in 1692, and the electoral family had been, as their genealogy shews, zealous supporters of the House of Austria. In 1715–1719 they acquired the bishoprics of Bremen and Verden, during the break up of the Swedish dominions in Germany, and thereby made Charles XII. of Sweden a supporter of the cause of the Stewarts, who might have become dangerous to the dynasty of Hanover in England had he lived. The connexion of Hanover with England was simply that the King was also Elector. The foreign policy of the two was supposed to be distinctly managed, but in fact England was influenced by a regard for Hanoverian interests.

WARS

The efforts of the English government were devoted to maintaining the settlement of Utrecht, in conjunction with the French Regency and the United Provinces, and for a time with the Emperor, against the efforts of Spain to recover portions of the old Spanish monarchy. Sweden and even Russia were in alliance with Spain for a time. In 1718, with no declaration of war, an English fleet defeated the Spaniards off Cape Passaro in Sicily, and war ensued in name till 1720. In 1727 Spain and the Emperor combined, and the Spaniards tried to recover Gibraltar with no declaration of war.

In 1715 a Jacobite insurrection broke out in Scotland and England, owing chiefly to the feeling against the Union in Scotland, and to the proscription of the Tory leaders in England, which seemed to give the Tories no hope of power under the new dynasty. The English Jacobites, reinforced by a detachment of the Scots under Brigadier McIntosh, were forced to surrender at Preston, November 13th, and on the same day an indecisive battle was fought between the Duke of Argyle and the Earl of Mar at Sherrifmuir in Scotland, but the incapacity of Mar led to the rapid collapse of the insurrection.

In 1719 there was a Jacobite rising in the Highlands, supported by Spanish troops, and a skirmish was fought in Glenshiel.

In 1715 the Jacobite feeling in Scotland was very strong. Of 46 Scotch Peers 21 were actually "out" or suspected of sympathy with the cause; of 18 principal Highland chiefs 15 were "out" with an armed following of between 14000 and 15000 men. An able military commander in Mar's place would have mastered Scotland and overpowered Argyle, in time to co-operate with the English Jacobites. In England, nobility and gentry of position and wealth were actually engaged, and the whole Tory party was sympathetic. Success, for a time at least, was within reach of the Jacobites, had their king and leaders been capable. The composition of their forces then is worth comparison with those they had in 1745, when they did so much more with so much less, though they had no prospect then of real success. France, however, was favourable in 1745, and opposed to them in 1715. A standing army

George I.

on both occasions gave an immense advantage to the government.

MINISTERS

The age of Cabinet Government had now definitely set in. The King, ignorant of English, ceased to preside at the meetings of the Privy Council, except for formal business. A meeting of the principal Minsters, making an informal Committee of the Council, really directed public affairs.

1714. Earl of Halifax, first Lord of the Treasury, d. May 19, 1715, succeeded by Earl of Carlisle till October 10, 1715. Lord Chancellor; Lord Harcourt, deprived Sept. 21 1714, succeeded by Lord Cowper, afterwards Earl Cowper, till 1718; Earl of Nottingham, Lord President; Marquis of Wharton, Lord Privy Seal; General, afterwards Earl Stanhope, and Viscount Townsend, Secretaries of State; Sir Richard Onslow, Chancellor of the Exchequer; Sir Robert Walpole, Paymaster-General.

1715. Sir Robert Walpole, First Lord of the Treasury and Chancellor of the Exchequer, October 10, 1715 to April 15, 1717.

1717. Lord Stanhope, First Lord of the Treasury and Chancellor of the Exchequer, till March 1718.

1718. Earl of Sunderland, first Lord of the Treasury; Charles Aislabie, Chancellor of the Exchequer; Lord Parker, afterwards Earl of Macclesfield, Lord Chancellor till 1725; Lord Stanhope, a Secretary of State.

1720. Sir Robert Walpole, Paymaster-General.

1721. Sir Robert Walpole, first Lord of the Treasury and Chancellor of the Exchequer till 1742; Lord Townshend and Lord Carteret, afterwards Earl Granville, Secretaries of State.

1724. Duke of Newcastle, Secretary of State, *vice* Lord Carteret, till February 10, 1746, again Feb. 14, 1746–1754; The Hon. Henry Pelham, Secretary at War.

1725. Lord King, Lord Chancellor.

ACTS AND DOCUMENTS

1716. Septennial Act to prolong the existence of Parliament to seven years. (See Triennial Act, Wil. & Mar. 6 & 7, c. 2.) Passed owing to the popular excitement and the strong Tory feeling manifested in England after the suppression of the rising in 1715, the Government fearing lest the pending elections should return a House of Commons dangerous to the dynasty. This prolonging of its own existence by the Parliament was violently objected to, but see the remarks of Hallam, *Const. History.* Act 1 Geo. I. s. 2, c. 38.

1719. An Act declaring the power of the Parliament of Great Britain to legislate for Ireland, completing the dependence of the Irish upon the English government. Act 6 Geo. I. c. 5.

1720. A bill was introduced to limit the power of the Crown to add to the Peerage, and so to make the House of Lords a strictly limited class assembly. It was, however, thrown out. See *Parl. Hist.* vii. 589.

The Acts given above are printed in the Statutes.

1717. The Triple Alliance between England, France, and Holland, becoming, by the addition of the Emperor, in

1718, the Quadruple Alliance, to maintain the settlement of Utrecht, but giving Sardinia to the house of Savoy in place of Sicily. See *Koch et Schoell,* ii. 179 and 184 respectively.

1725. The Treaty of Vienna was formed between the Emperor and Spain, with secret articles for a marriage between the families, the recovery of Gibraltar and Minorca for Spain, and the support of the Stewarts. The Czarina Catherine subsequently adhered to this alliance. Printed in *Dumont,* viii. pt. 2, 114.

The same year, in consequence, the Treaty of Hanover was made between England, France, and Prussia to counteract the Treaty of Vienna. It is one of the points of "Hanoverian policy" which was zealously attacked in Parliament, but the attacks were made in ignorance of the secret clauses of the Treaty of Vienna, which the King knew, and communicated to Townshend and Walpole. Holland and Sweden subsequently adhered to the Treaty of Hanover, and the Emperor abandoned the Spanish alliance, 1727. See *Koch et Schoell*, vol. ii. p. 205.

The Suppression of Convocation (see on the Church and the Non-jurors, William III.). The antagonism between the Whig bishops and the Tory lower clergy had led to the suspension of Convocation from 1689–1700, and to continual conflicts since. In 1717 the determination of the Lower House to censure Dr. Hoadley, Bishop of Bangor, for Broad Church sermons, led to the suspension of Convocation. It met formally till 1741, but then ceased to be summoned at all till 1861. The "Bangorian controversy" is principally important now as having called forth the answers of Dr. Law to Bishop Hoadley, which embody the views of the Tractarian party of the present century, and may be said to have preserved the continuity of Anglican doctrines in the Church.

AUTHORS

Earl Stanhope's *History of England*, from 1714–1783, is calm and judicious, accurate in facts, but wanting in a wide and profound view of the bearing and cause of events. This characteristic is supplied exactly by Mr. Lecky's *History of England in the Eighteenth Century*, which is most valuable as illustrating all the forces at work in forming the history of the nation, but is apt to insist too strongly sometimes on the effects of minor causes. The conclusion of Hallam's *Constitutional History* deals with the Constitution under the House of Hanover.

Mr. Leslie Stephens' *History of English Thought in the Eighteenth Century*, is invaluable for one side of the history.

Professor Seeley's *Expansion of England* gives a comprehensive view of the real bearing of the apparently complicated foreign politics of the age from the Revolution onwards.

Thackeray's well-known *Lectures upon the Four Georges* are most useful studies of social life, but valueless as contributions to political history.

For short histories Gardiner's *Student's History of England*, or, with more detail, Morris's *Early Hanoverians* (Longmans' *Epochs Series*) are trustworthy.

GEORGE II. 1727–1760

Married Caroline of Anspach.

DOMINIONS

Great Britain and Ireland. Foreign and Colonial possessions as settled by the Treaty of Utrecht. In 1739 Georgia was settled in North America, encroaching upon territory which the Spaniards claimed as part of Florida. In 1745 Cape Breton was taken, but restored in 1748 to the French. In 1746 the French took Madras, but restored it in 1748. Minorca was lost in 1756, but restored at the peace in exchange for Belleisle. The conquests of the Seven Years' War were not confirmed till the peace in the following reign.

WARS

The war with Spain which had been in progress at the time of the death of George I. was concluded with no further active operations, the siege of Gibraltar by the Spaniards being scarcely serious. A general peace was concluded at Seville in 1729. Sir R. Walpole succeeded in keeping England at peace during the War of the Polish Succession, 1733–1735, when under the guise of supporting a native candidate for the throne of Poland, France and Spain were carrying out one of the objects of the Secret Family Compact, the aggrandisement of the House of Bourbon in Europe. Walpole knew that a

George II.

foreign war would mean a Jacobite movement, and that every year of peace would help to consolidate the dynasty.

In 1739 the second great object of the Family Compact appeared, the curtailment of English commerce and colonial and maritime power. A maritime war began with Spain, countenanced though not at first actively aided by France. In 1742 the war merged into the great European war of the Austrian Succession, in which England and France were arrayed on opposite sides, though war was not actually declared between them till 1744.

In 1739 Admiral Vernon took Porto Bello, but failed before Carthagena in 1741. Admiral Anson's voyage round the world, 1740-1744, resulted in some injury to Spanish towns and shipping in the Pacific.

In 1743, July 27th, the English and Hanoverian army extricated themselves from a nearly hopeless position at Dettingen, on the Maine, by hard fighting and the mistake of a French general. It was the last occasion on which an English king was engaged with his army. The last before this was when William III. took Namur. Omitting civil wars, the last before that reign was when Henry VIII. took Boulogne. Before that Edward IV. had led an army abroad without fighting. From Henry V. upwards to William I. every English king, except Stephen, had commanded an army in foreign warfare.

In 1745, April 30th, the Duke of Cumberland was defeated at Fontenoy, near Tournay, by the French under Marshal Saxe.

1745 Louisbourg and Cape Breton in America taken by the English.

In 1746, on Oct. 12th, the French defeated the English and their allies at Roucoux; in 1747, on June 20th, at Laufeld.

In 1747 Anson defeated the French fleet off Finisterre, and Hawke defeated them off Belleisle. The war was concluded by the Peace of Aix la Chapelle in 1748.

THE 'FORTY FIVE

In 1745 the Jacobite Insurrection predicted by Walpole took place, Prince Charles Edward landing in the West Highlands on July 25th with seven men, and being joined by some of the clans. On Sept. 21st he defeated Sir John Cope at Preston Pans; on November 18th he entered Carlisle; on Dec. 4th he reached Derby, having out-manœuvred two English armies; on the 6th he left Derby in retreat; on the 21st returned to Scotland; on Jan. 17th, 1746, he defeated General Hawley at Falkirk; on April 16th he was defeated by the Duke of Cumberland at Culloden, or Drumossie Muir; on Sept. 20th he set sail again for France.

CLANS "OUT" IN THE 'FORTY FIVE

The Camerons; Stewarts of Appin; Macdonalds of Clanranald, Glengarry, Keppoch, and Glencoe; the MacGregors; the Maclachlans; Farquharsons; Macphersons; Macintoshes; Frasers; Ogilvies; some of the Athol men, Gordons, Macleans, Macleods and Mackenzies. Of these the Frasers had not been "out" in the 'Fifteen; but in that year all the Athol men, Gordons, Mackenzies, Macleans, and Macleods; the Macdonalds of Sleat, the MacEwens, Chisholms, Breadalbane men, the Earl of Mar's men in Braemar, and several minor clans, had been in arms on the Jacobite side, besides a considerable number of influential noblemen and gentlemen in the Lowlands.

It may be certainly said that the Jacobites had never any chance of ultimate success in 1745. Extraordinary skill and fortune got them safely to Derby, and back again. A continuance of the same conditions might have put them in temporary possession of London, had they advanced, but more probably they would have been destroyed by the regular troops in the open country of England. Lord George Murray brought more military skill to their side than they had ever had since the death of Dundee, but even in Scotland the very general and respectable support which they had in 1715 was wanting now, and in England the Tory party was not inclined to venture anything for them. The French, intent on the conquest of the Austrian Netherlands, gave them very slight assistance.

Chronic hostilities continued between the English and French East India companies, and the rival colonists in America, resulting in the Seven Years War, which, like the previous war, merged in a European contest. The events are carried on to the end of the war, after the death of George II.

In 1755, July 9th, General Braddock's army was surprised and destroyed by the French and Indians when marching on Fort Duquesne on the Ohio.

In 1756 war was declared. On May 20th Admiral Byng engaged the French unsuccessfully off Minorca. On June 27th Minorca surrendered to the French.

In 1757 the Duke of Cumberland was defeated by the French at Hastenbeck in Hanover, July 26th, and forced to capitulate at Closter Seven, Sept. 10th.

In Sept., 1757, we unsuccessfully attacked Rochefort.

In 1758 Louisbourg was taken in July. Aug. 15, an expedition destroyed Cherbourg, but was defeated at St. Malo, Sept. 27th. On June 23rd Prince Ferdinand of Brunswick at the head of a combined English and German army defeated the French at Crefeld in Westphalia.

Dec. 20th. Goree taken by the English.

1759. Ferdinand was defeated at Bergen, April 13th, but won a decisive victory over the French at Minden, Aug. 1st.

Sept. 13th. The battle of the Heights of Abraham was followed by the surrender of Quebec, Sept. 18th.

May 1st. Guadaloupe was taken.

Aug. 18th. Boscawen defeated the French off Lagos.

Nov. 20th. Hawke defeated the French in Quiberon Bay.

1760, Sept. 8th. Montreal surrendered, and the conquest of Canada was completed.

1761, June 4th. Dominica taken.

June 7th. Belleisle surrendered.
1762, Feb. 16th. Martinique taken.
Aug. 13th. Havana taken.
Oct. 5th. Manilla and the Philippines taken.

THE EAST INDIAN WAR

In the course of the 17th century the great empire of the Moghuls in India was rapidly breaking up. Native adventurers like the Mahratta leaders, or foreign rulers like the Nizam of the Deccan, the Nawab of the Carnatic, or the Nawab of Bengal, were scrambling for local power, and the European traders in the country sought their own advantage and intrigued for their own protection in the confusion.

The rivalry of the English and French East India Companies involved them in disputes, apart from the wars between the two countries. By interference in the politics of the Carnatic and the Deccan, M. Dupleix at the head of the French administration founded French power in Southern India, and sent M. de Bussy with troops who occupied the Circars. The genius of Clive however defeated the other French officers, Dupleix was recalled in disgrace, Lally, who went out in military command in 1757, recalled Bussy from the Circars, but was ultimately defeated himself in the Carnatic, while the Circars fell to Colonel Forde during Bussy's absence. Clive had meanwhile established English influence in Bengal by the victories at Chandernagore, Plassey, and Chinsura.

BATTLES IN INDIA

1746, Sept. 25th. Madras taken by the French.

1751, Aug. 31st. Clive captured Arcot. Nov. 14th, Clive's victory at Arcot, followed by numerous defeats of the French and their allies in the Carnatic by Clive and Lawrence.

1757, May 24th. Clive took the French post of Chandernagore.

June 23rd. Clive's victory at Plassey in Bengal.

George II.

1758. Lally took Fort St. David, June 1st. Oct. 20th to April 7th, 1759, Colonel Forde drove the French out of the Circars.

1759, Feb. 17th. The French raised the siege of Madras. Clive and Forde defeated the Dutch at Chinsura in Bengal, Nov. 3rd.

1760, Jan. 22nd. Lally defeated by Colonel Coote at Wandewash.

1761, Jan. 16. Pondicherry surrendered to the English, and the French political power in India came to an end.

MINISTERS

In 1727 Sir Robert Walpole was First Lord of the Treasury and Chancellor of the Exchequer.

Lord King was Lord Chancellor.

The Duke of Devonshire was Lord President.

Viscount Townshend and the Duke of Newcastle Secretaries of State.

In 1730 Lord Trevor, and on Dec. 31st the Earl of Wilmington, were Lords President, and Lord (afterwards Earl) Harrington succeeded Lord Townshend as Secretary of State. The Rt. Hon. Henry Pelham became Paymaster-General.

In 1733 Lord Talbot was Lord Chancellor.

1737 Lord Hardwicke was Lord Chancellor.

In 1742 the long power of Sir Robert Walpole came to an end. The Earl of Wilmington was First Lord of the Treasury. Samuel Sandys Chancellor of the Exchequer. The Earl of Harrington Lord President. The Duke of Newcastle and Lord Carteret (afterwards Earl Granville), Secretaries of State.

In 1743 the Right Hon. Henry Pelham was First Lord of the Treasury and Chancellor of the Exchequer.

In 1744 the Earl of Harrington succeeded Lord Carteret as Secretary of State.

In 1745 the Duke of Dorset was Lord President.

In 1746 Pulteney, Earl of Bath, formed a ministry which

lasted only four days, Feb. 10th to 14th, when Pelham and his colleagues returned to power.

In 1746 the Earl of Chesterfield succeeded Lord Harrington as Secretary of State.

In 1748 the Duke of Bedford succeeded Lord Chesterfield as Secretary of State.

In 1751 the Earl of Holderness succeeded the Duke of Bedford, and continued till the end of the reign.

Earl Granville became Lord President, and continued till the end of the reign.

In 1754 Mr. Pelham died. The Duke of Newcastle, his brother, became First Lord of the Treasury. Lord Lyttelton Chancellor of the Exchequer till 1756, when the Rt. Hon. H. B. Legge became Chancellor of the Exchequer, and continued till the end of the reign. Sir Thomas Robinson succeeded the Duke of Newcastle as Secretary of State.

In 1755 the Rt. Hon. Henry Fox (afterwards Lord Holland) succeeded Sir Thomas Robinson as Secretary of State.

In 1756 the Duke of Devonshire was First Lord of the Treasury, William Pitt and the Earl of Holderness Secretaries of State.

In 1757 William Pitt resigned in April, and became Secretary again in June, and was the practical head of the Administration during the war.

The Duke of Newcastle was First Lord of the Treasury. The Duke of Devonshire, Lord Chamberlain. Earl Temple, Privy Seal. Lord Anson, First Lord of the Admiralty. Lord Henley, Lord Keeper. Henry Fox, Paymaster.

ACTS AND DOCUMENTS

1729. The Treaty of Seville. The lingering war between England and Spain was concluded, and a defensive alliance formed between England, France, Spain and Holland, Spain repudiating the alliance of the Emperor, re-establishing the Assiento in our favour and being guaranteed certain rights in

Italy. In fact, however, the alliance marks the conclusion of the estrangement between France and Spain, which had prevailed since 1715, and was the occasion for the first beginning of the Family Compact between the two branches of the House of Bourbon, for their aggrandisement in Europe and for the diminution of English maritime and colonial power. The Treaty was followed in 1731 by that of Vienna between England, Spain, and the Emperor, by which the last agreed to the arrangements of Seville. See *Koch et Schoell*, ii. 214, etc.

In 1733 the actual Family Compact, "eternal and irrevocable," was signed. (A French Version, MS., is in the British Museum, Add. MSS. 27731.) It was immediately followed by the war of the Polish Succession. It was renewed in 1743, just before England and France were formally engaged in the war of the Austrian Succession, but was practically in abeyance from 1746 to 1759 during the reign of Ferdinand VI. Students should consult an Article by Professor Seeley in Vol. I. of the *English Historical Review*, headed "The House of Bourbon."

In 1730 Walpole passed a bill allowing the direct exportation of rice in British vessels from Carolina and Georgia to Southern Europe. This beginning of a more liberal colonial policy led to the increase of prosperity in the plantations, and if extended as Walpole desired might have prevented the subsequent troubles in America. 3 Geo. II. c. 28.

1746. An Act was passed disarming the Highlands and forbidding the wearing of the national dress. 19 Geo. II. c. 39.

Disarmament had been partially carried out in 1725 by General Wade, but while it had been general among the clans well affected to Government, Campbells, Gunns, Munroes, etc., it had been largely evaded by the Jacobite clans. Even after 1746 many hidden stores of arms were preserved.

In 1740 various independent companies of Highlanders had been embodied in a regiment known familiarly as the Black Watch, and numbered first as the 43rd and then the 42nd of the Line, now the Royal Highlanders. In 1757 Pitt extended the practice of encouraging Highland noblemen and gentlemen to raise regiments, whose ranks were rapidly filled by the attractions of adventure, the national dress and arms.

1747. Heritable Jurisdictions were abolished in the Highlands, so breaking down the authority of the chiefs. 20 Geo. II. c. 43.

1748. The Peace of Aix-la-Chapelle ended the war between England and the Bourbon powers. A mutual restoration of conquests was arranged. The right of search, which had been the pretext for the original quarrel of England and Spain, was not mentioned. See *Koch et Schoell*, ii. 411, etc.

1751. The Calendar was reformed. The year was to begin on Jan. 1 instead of March 25, and 11 days were nominally suppressed in Sept. 1752, to bring the year into accord with the usual reckoning of Western Europe. 24 Geo. II. c. 23.

Some chronological errors have arisen from the use by early chroniclers of various dates ranging from Michaelmas Day to Lady Day, or even to Easter Day abroad, for the beginning of the year. Jan. 1, 1752, was the first legal commencement of the year on that day in England. In Scotland a proclamation of James VI. had declared Jan. 1, 1600, to be the first day of the year, but the New Style had not been accepted in Scotland because it was the work of a Pope, Gregory XIII., and the same reason made it unpopular in England and Scotland in 1751.

Domestic legislation of importance was very rare in the reigns of George I. and George II. Sir Robert Walpole brought about the annual suspension of the Test and Corporation Acts, to relieve Nonconformists from penalties for taking office, and introduced many small financial reforms in the direction of more free trade. His comprehensive Excise Bill was withdrawn, 1733. See, for the Excise Scheme, *Parl. Hist.* viii. 1268, and ix. 1–8. The Acts given above are printed in the Statutes.

George III.

AUTHORS

Lord Stanhope's and Mr. Lecky's *Histories* (see on George I). Coxe's *Life of Sir Robert Walpole* and *Life of Henry Pelham*; Lord Macaulay's *Essays* on Lord Chatham and on Clive; Carlyle's *Frederick the Great*; Sir John Malcolm's *Life of Clive*; Parkman's *Wolfe and Montcalm*, for the Conquest of Canada. Horace Walpole's *Letters*, and his *Memoirs of the Last Ten Years of George II.*, are contemporary writings of the highest value. Mr. Leslie Stephens' *History of English Thought in the Eighteenth Century*, and Southey's *Life of Wesley*, deal with another important side, which is also fully noticed in Mr. Lecky's *History*.

GEORGE III. 1760-1820
Married Charlotte of Mecklenburg-Strelitz.

DOMINIONS

Great Britain and Ireland, Hanover, and dominions in Europe, Asia, Africa, and America, as given above.

By the Peace of Paris, Feb. 10th, 1763, the whole of Upper and Lower Canada, Labrador, Newfoundland, Nova Scotia, New Brunswick, Prince Edward's Island, Hudson's Bay Territory (guaranteed at Utrecht, but disputed since), Florida, and the country lying behind our North American colonies to the river Mississippi were ceded or guaranteed to England, France retaining the islands of St. Pierre and Miquelon, and rights of fishing off Newfoundland and in the St. Lawrence.

In the West Indies we kept Grenada, St. Vincent, Tobago, and Dominica.

In Africa we retained Senegal.

In Europe Minorca was restored to us.

In India we restored the French factories, but they were not to be fortified.

In 1765 the Isle of Man was put directly under the English Crown by purchase from the Duke of Athol.

In 1765 the Great Moghul ceded to the East India Company the administration, revenues, and virtual sovereignty of Bengal, Bahar, and Orissa, and the northern Circars, though the last was not actually occupied till 1768.

1771. Falkland Islands recognized as English.

In 1773 New Zealand and Australia were formally taken into possession by Captain Cook, but the latter was not occupied till 1787, the former only in the present century.

In 1778 what is now British Columbia and Vancouver's Island were claimed, and the right of possession vindicated against Spain in 1789.

In 1783, by the Peace of Versailles, the Independence of the United States was acknowledged. Florida and Minorca were restored to Spain, Tobago and Senegal to France. Negapatam, in India, was ceded to us by the Dutch. All other conquests were restored.

In 1786 Penang was occupied.

In 1787 Sierra Leone.

In 1792 the Malabar Coast and Coorg were ceded to us by Tippoo Sahib.

In 1794-6 Corsica was under the protection of England, and ruled by an English Viceroy.

In 1801-2, by the Peace of Amiens, we retained Ceylon and Trinidad, taken in 1796 and 1797.

Malta, taken in 1800, was to have been relinquished, but was retained by us ultimately.

In India, in 1799, part of the Mysore territory was annexed, and the remainder formed into a protected state under the native line of rulers, the usurping Mohammedan dynasty being destroyed.

In 1801 the direct administration of the Carnatic was taken over.

In 1803 Cuttack, part of Berar, and the Doab were annexed.

In 1806 the Cape Colony was taken finally. It had been taken before, but restored by the Peace of Amiens.

In 1807 Heligoland was taken from the Danes.

In 1809 the Ionian Islands, except Corfu, were occupied.

In 1810 Mauritius, the Seychelles, and Ammirante were taken.

In 1811 Java was taken, but restored to the Dutch in 1814.

In 1814 the Treaty of Paris confirmed the English conquests as above, and restored to the French their West India Islands which we had occupied in the course of the war. All the Ionian Islands were put under English protection. Ascension and Tristan d'Acunha were occupied by us.

1815. The interior of Ceylon was conquered. In India the Ghoorkas ceded part of the Terai.

In India, in 1818, the territories of the Peishwa were annexed, with other great parts of the Mahratta conquests in Central and Western India. The Princes of the remaining Mahratta states, Gwalior and Indore, Guzerat, Baroda, the Nizam of Hyderabad, and the Rajput states were made finally dependant upon English power.

In 1819 Singapore was occupied.

WARS

The War of American Independence

Probably no war in which we were ever engaged depended for its results less upon purely military operations. The battles, so-called, were mostly insignificant from the numbers engaged and the results which followed, with the exceptions of the operations before the surrender of Saratoga and Yorktown. A really capable English commander might at various periods have made military operations decisive, but as it was the issue of the war depended upon political events in England and America, and upon naval actions.

1775, April 19th. An English detachment defeated in a skirmish at Lexington.

June 17th. The Battle of Breed's Hill, miscalled Bunker's Hill, won by the English with heavy loss.

Dec. 31st. The Americans defeated before Quebec.

1776. Boston evacuated by the English in March. Expedition against New York. The Americans defeated on Long Island, Aug. 27. New York taken Sept. 15th. General Howe advanced through New Jersey. Washington defeated the Hessians at Trenton, Dec. 25th.

1777, Jan. 13. Indecisive action at Princetown, in New Jersey, followed by the retreat of the English towards New York.

In the summer General Burgoyne marched from Canada by way of the Hudson river towards New York, and Howe left New York by sea to attack Philadelphia.

Aug. 16th. A detachment of Burgoyne's army was defeated at Bennington.

Sept. 11th. Howe defeated Washington at the Brandywine Creek, and occupied Philadelphia.

Oct. 4th. Howe defeated Washington at Germantown. Partly from his incapacity, but partly from his want of cavalry, which could not be easily transported, with their horses, to America, nor be mounted there, Howe did not succeed in destroying Washington's army, as he might have done at and after these battles.

Meanwhile, on Sept. 19th, Burgoyne fought an indecisive and, on Oct. 7th, an unsuccessful, action at Stillwater with Generals Gates and Arnold, and on Oct. 16th, outnumbered and in want of supplies, surrendered at Saratoga.

1778. Howe evacuated Philadelphia and returned to New York, getting the worst of an action at Monmouth June 28th.

December 29th the English took Savannah, and recovered Georgia in the course of the winter, and invaded South Carolina.

The French had joined the Americans in this year, and Spain followed in 1779, Holland in 1780. The Armed Neutrality of Russia, Prussia, Sweden, and Denmark was practically hostile to us. Troops were withdrawn from North

George III.

America to defend or attack West India Islands, and French fleets appeared on the coasts of America, and in the Channel.

July 27th Keppel fought an indecisive action off Ushant with the French.

In 1779 the active war was almost confined to the sea and the West Indies.

Oct. 9th the French and Americans failed to take Savannah.

1780. May 12th the English took Charleston, and recovered South Carolina.

Aug. 16th Cornwallis defeated Gates at Camden.

Jan. 16th Rodney defeated the Spaniards off Cape St. Vincent.

April 17th and May 19th Rodney fought the French in the West Indies.

1781. Jan. 17th Greene defeated the English at Cowpens.

March 15th Cornwallis defeated Greene at Guildford and marched into Virginia.

Aug. 5th Hyde Parker fought an indecisive action with the Dutch off the Dogger Bank.

Sept. 5th Graves fought the French off the Chesapeake, and was compelled to leave the French fleet on the coast of Virginia. Cornwallis in consequence shut up in Yorktown Sept. 28th, and forced to surrender Oct. 19th.

The war in America came to an end, the English being unable to attempt anything, and the Americans being unable to try to drive us from New York, Charleston, Savannah, and other posts on the coast.

1782. Feb. 5th Minorca taken by the French and Spaniards.

April 12th Rodney defeated De Grasse off Martinique and saved the West India Islands. Coming a year earlier the victory would probably have saved the Southern States for England.

Sept. 13th the grand combined attack upon Gibraltar, which had been besieged for four years, defeated. The French and Spaniards computed to have lost in one day and night military and naval stores worth £2,000,000.

WARS IN INDIA

Up to the end of the American War.

In 1760 the Moghul, Shah Alum, and the Viceroy of Oude invaded Bengal, but were defeated in several actions by Colonel Caillaud, Captain Knox, and Major Carnac.

In 1763 the Nawab of Bengal, Meer Cassim, intrigued with Shah Alum against us, but was defeated on July 19th at Cutwah, on Aug. 2nd at Gheriah, and on Sept. 4th at Owda Nulla.

In 1764 the Nawab and the Viceroy of Oude were finally defeated on October 22nd at Buxar by Sir Hector Munro. This was the only war in which we were opposed to the Moghul, the nominal ruler of India, till the Sepoys set the old king of Delhi at their head in 1857, and Shah Alum was not in actual possession of his throne and capital at this time.

In 1767-68 the Madras Government was engaged in war with the Nizam of Hyderabad and Hyder Ali the Mohammedan usurper in Mysore. The Nizam was defeated and withdrew, but Hyder dictated his own terms of peace.

In 1772 the Bombay Government began hostilities with the Mahratta chiefs, and with interruptions the war continued till 1782. The taking of Gwalior, Aug. 2nd, 1780, by Captain Popham, was the most striking success achieved.

Meanwhile, however, the renewal of war with France and the capture of Pondicherry and Mahé, 1778 and 1779, brought Hyder again into the field, and on Sept. 10th, 1780, he defeated Colonel Baillie near Conjeveram and forced him to surrender. The Carnatic was saved by Sir Eyre Coote's victory over Hyder on July 1st, 1781, at Porto Novo. Hyder died at the end of the year. The French troops sent to support him under Bussy were defeated at Cuddalore June 25th, 1783, and shortly withdrawn on the news of the Peace of Versailles arriving. Hyder's son Tippoo consented to peace in 1784.

The French fleet using Mauritius (Isle de France) as their

basis had co-operated with the Mysoreans against us, and severe but indecisive engagements had been fought between Admirals Hughes and De Suffrein in 1782, on Feb. 17th, April 12th, July 5th, Sept. 3rd, and June 20th, 1783.

THE FRENCH REVOLUTIONARY WAR

France declared war against England on Feb. 2, 1793. The French navy was to a great extent disorganized by the Revolution, many of the best officers being Royalists. The English army, on the other hand, besides being inefficient from the usual reductions in the time of peace, had been demoralized by the desultory operations and ill-success of the American war. It was only by degrees that the efforts of Abercrombie and Moore above all others restored discipline and *morale*.

In 1793 an English army, under the Duke of York, co-operated with the Emperor's forces against the French in Flanders. They assisted at the capture of Valenciennes, and on Aug. 18th, 1793, fought a successful action at Lincelles, and formed the siege of Dunkirk. The siege was raised owing to the defeat of the covering army. On May 18th, 1794, the English shared in the defeat at Turcoign, and subsequently the Austrian troops retired into Germany, the English to Holland, and thence to Hanover.

On Dec. 18th, 1793, Toulon, which had been defended by a mixed force of allies, including English, supported by an English fleet, was evacuated, the arsenal and French ships in the harbour being destroyed.

On June 1st, 1794, Lord Howe won the victory of the First of June over the French fleet off Ushant.

St. Lucia and Guadaloupe were taken. Tobago had been taken in 1793. Martinique and Corsica were reduced in the course of the year.

1795. From August to December the Cape Colony, Cochin, and Malacca were conquered by us.

1796. Ceylon was taken. St. Lucia, which the French had

recovered in 1795, Grenada, Demerara, and Essequibo, were taken.

1797. Feb. Trinidad surrendered.

Spain had joined France against England, the Family Compact in fact outlasting the Bourbon family in France. The common interest against the overwhelming naval and colonial power of England continued to unite her rivals Republican France, Republican Holland, and Bourbon Spain.

Feb. 14th the Spanish fleet defeated off Cape St. Vincent by Sir John Jervis and Commodore Nelson.

July 22nd and 24th unsuccessful attack by Nelson on Santa Cruz.

Oct. 11th Duncan defeated the Dutch fleet off Camperdown.

In 1798 Irish discontent broke out in armed rebellion, and communications were opened with France. The French, however, failed to send adequate help, and the main body of the insurgents were defeated at New Ross May 25th, and Vinegar Hill June 21st. The small French force which landed was compelled to surrender Sept. 8th, and a French squadron with further aid was defeated off the Irish coast by Admiral Warren, Oct. 12th.

1798. August 1st and 2nd Nelson destroyed the French fleet at Aboukir, the battle of the Nile.

In November Minorca was taken.

1799. In April and May the defence of Acre by Sir Sydney Smith frustrated Napoleon's Eastern schemes.

August 27th an English force landed in Holland, at the Helder, and the Dutch fleet of 8 ships of the line and 17 other vessels was captured at the Texel, a success fully justifying the expedition. A force of Russians co-operated with the English, the Duke of York was in supreme command, but Sir Ralph Abercrombie was the directing genius of the army. On Sept. 19th the French were defeated at Bergen, and on Oct. 2nd at Egmont-op-Zee, but on Oct. 6th the allies failed to force a passage to Haarlem, and large reinforcements arriving for the French, they evacuated the country.

1800. Sept. 5th, Malta surrendered to the English.

1801. In March, St. Thomas, St. Bartholomew, and St. Cruz in the West Indies were taken.

March 21st Sir Ralph Abercrombie defeated the French near Alexandria, but was killed in the action.

Aug. 31st Alexandria surrendered to Abercrombie's army and to the force from India under Sir David Baird.

April 2nd Nelson defeated the Danish ships and batteries at Copenhagen.

The number of minor naval actions during the war, resulting in almost universal success for the English, was about 250.

THE NAPOLEONIC WAR

After the rupture of the Peace of Amiens the war assumed the character of a death struggle between England and Napoleon, in which the actions of Napoleon towards Continental powers were regulated by his plans for the destruction of English commerce. The Emperor took up the old quarrel of the House of Bourbon against our position at sea and in the colonies, his annexation of Spain being merely an attempt to utilise the Peninsula as a means for carrying out the old principles of the "Family Compact," still recognised as expressing the true policy of France and Spain, even in the absence of the Bourbon dynasties. Our war with the United States in 1812, and Napoleon's fatal quarrel with Russia, were consequences of the policy adopted by the two chief combatants. The results of the war, our complete maritime supremacy, the removal of all chance of French interference in India, the undisputed English occupation of Australia, New Zealand, and other places in the South Seas, and the separation of South America from Spain consequent on the destruction of the Spanish marine, marked the final failure of the aims of the "Family Compact," till their revival in a different form by different powers in the colonial arrangements of the last thirty years.

In 1803 the war was renewed. In June Tobago was taken; in September Demerara and Essequibo.

1804. In March Goree was taken; in May Surinam.

1805. July 22nd Sir Robert Calder engaged the French off Ferrol and frustrated the intended combination of their fleets.

Oct. 21st Nelson destroyed the French and Spanish fleets off Cape Trafalgar.

Nov. 4th Sir Richard Strachan defeated the French off Cape Ortegal.

In 1806, Feb. 6th, Sir John Duckworth destroyed the French squadron off St. Domingo.

The naval war henceforward became one of blockade on our part, with occasional attacks upon shipping in the enemies' ports and upon sea coast towns and forts, and actions between single ships.

With the co-operation of the fleet The Cape of Good Hope was taken, Jan. 1806; Alexandria was taken, March 21st, 1807, but evacuated in Sept.; St. Thomas, St. Cruz, and Madeira were taken, Dec., 1807; Cayenne, Jan., 1809; Senegal, July, 1809; the Ionian Islands, except Corfu, Oct., 1809; Guadaloupe, Feb., 1810; Amboyna, Feb., 1810; St. Eustatia and St. Martin, Feb., 1810; Mauritius, Dec., 1810; Java, in Aug., 1811; and some 500 minor naval actions were fought.

On shore in 1806, on July 6th, Sir John Stuart, who had crossed with a small army from Sicily to support the Calabrian insurrection, defeated the French at Maida, after crossing bayonets. A success the moral effect of which on the English army was out of proportion to the material results, which were merely temporary.

1806-07. Expeditions were sent against Monte Video and Buenos Ayres, which after partial success were defeated at Buenos Ayres, July 5th, 1807.

George III. 211

In 1807, August and September, the expedition to Copenhagen under General Cathcart resulted in the surrender of that capital and of the Danish fleet. Sir Arthur Wellesley served as Major-General.

THE PENINSULAR WAR

In 1808 the revolt of the Spaniards against Napoleon's attempt to place a Buonaparte on the Spanish throne, and the French attempt to conquer Portugal, gave us a basis for action on the continent against Napoleon.

Aug. 16th. Sir Arthur Wellesley defeated Laborde at Roliça.

Aug. 21st. Sir Arthur Wellesley defeated Junot at Vimiera, but as he was superseded on the field of battle by Sir Harry Burrard, who was superseded in twelve hours by Sir Hew Dalrymple, the French were allowed to retreat to Lisbon, where they concluded the Convention of Cintra and evacuated Portugal.

Sir John Moore took command of the English army and advanced into Spain, but the Spaniards being defeated at Tudela and elsewhere by Napoleon in person, he was obliged to retreat to the fleet at Corunna.

1809, Jan. 16. Moore defeated Soult and Ney before Corunna, but was killed in the action, and the army embarked during the night and next day.

Sir Arthur Wellesley was reappointed to the command in Portugal in April, on May 12th he forced the passage of the Douro, and drove Soult first out of Oporto and finally out of Portugal. The English marched towards Madrid on the line of the Tagus, co-operating with a Spanish army. On July 27th and 28th Sir Arthur Wellesley defeated Jourdan, Victor, and Sebastiani at Talavera, but the concentration of Soult's, Ney's, and Mortier's corps compelled his retreat into Portugal. The effect of Talavera was to demonstrate the superiority of the English infantry, and the impossibility of counting upon the serious co-operation of Spanish regular troops. Their

Guerilleros, however, continually paralysed French communications, and did therein excellent service.

WALCHEREN EXPEDITION

In July 1809 a powerful expedition left England under Lord Chatham to attack the mouth of the Scheldt, and if possible Antwerp. On Aug. 16th Flushing surrendered, but nothing further could be accomplished, and in December the remains of the army, wasted by sickness, returned.

PENINSULAR WAR (CONTINUED)

1810. The cessation of the war with Austria enabled Napoleon to send Masséna with reinforcements to the Peninsula, with orders to invade Portugal. Cuidad Rodrigo and Almeida were quickly surrendered by the Spaniards and Portuguese, and Lord Wellington retired towards the lines which he had fortified at Torres Vedras covering Lisbon.

On Sept. 27th Masséna attacked Wellington on the ridge of Busaco, and was badly beaten. The French, however, were able to turn the position, and Wellington continued his retreat, concentrating behind the lines of Torres Vedras, on Oct 15th.

Masséna lay for a month in front of Torres Vedras, and for five months in Portugal, which he left in April 1811, having lost 45,000 men by battle, want, and disease.

March 6th, 1811. Graham leaving Cadiz, defeated part of the besieging army of Victor at Barossa.

May 5th, Wellington defeated Masséna at Fuentes d'Onoro, and Almeida was evacuated by the French.

May 16th Beresford defeated Soult at Albuera near Badajos, but the attempt to recover Badajos from the French was unsuccessful. The failures of the Spaniards, and the presence of 300,000 French in Spain, prevented any further success this year.

1812. Jan. 4th. The French forced to raise the siege of Tarifa.

Jan. 19th. Wellington stormed Ciudad Rodrigo.

April 6th. He stormed Badajos.

May 19th. Hill stormed the French works at Almaraz on the Tagus, and broke the bridge, cutting the easiest communication between the French armies in the north and south of Spain.

July 22nd. Wellington defeated Marmont at Salamanca, and entered Madrid in August.

Sept. 21st. Wellington was obliged to raise the siege of Burgos, and retire to Portugal. The effect of the campaign, however, had been to free Southern Spain from the French, and Napoleon's needs in Russia and Germany threw the French upon the defensive in Spain.

1813. An English and Sicilian force landed in the east of Spain to co-operate with the Spaniards, and on

April 13th Murray defeated Suchet at Castalla, but the allies were not able to drive Suchet from Catalonia. Wellington advanced from Portugal, turning the right of the French, and co-operating with the Spanish insurgents in the northern provinces, till on

June 21st he closed upon King Joseph and Jourdan at Vittoria and completely defeated them, driving them from Spain.

Soult, sent to retrieve the disaster, was defeated in the battles of the Pyrenees, from July 25th to August 2nd.

Aug. 31st. San Sebastian was stormed.

Oct. 15th. Pampeluna surrendered.

Oct. 8th. Wellington forced Soult's position on the Bidassoa, and entered France, the first commander of the allied forces to do so.

Nov. 10th. Wellington stormed Soult's positions on the Nivelle.

Dec. 9th to 15th. Wellington defeated Soult in a series of actions on the Nive.

Suchet, who had maintained himself in Catalonia, retired to the Pyrenees, leaving garrisons in several places.

1814. Feb. 27th. Wellington defeated Soult at Orthes.

March 8th. Graham co-operating with the allies in Holland made an unsuccessful attempt to storm Bergen-op-zoom.

April 10th. Wellington defeated Soult at Toulouse.

April 14th. A desperate sally of the French from Bayonne, after Napoleon's abdication had been notified to them, ended the war with useless slaughter.

THE WAR IN FLANDERS

1815. June 15th. The French attacked the Prussian outposts on the Sambre.

June 16th. Napoleon defeated Blucher at Ligny. Wellington checked Ney at Quatre Bras, but was unable to give aid to Blucher owing to the attack.

June 17th. Blucher retired to Wavre, Wellington to Mt. St. Jean. Skirmish at Genappe on the retreat.

June 18th. Wellington, with the co-operation of Blucher in the latter part of the day, defeated Napoleon at Waterloo. Grouchy fought Thielmann at Wavre, but hearing of the defeat at Waterloo retired to France.

THE AMERICAN WAR

In 1812 the disputes with America upon the right of search at sea, enforced owing to the Berlin and Milan decrees and the English Orders in Council, led to war.

A succession of actions between single ships resulted at first in favour of the Americans, whose frigates were more heavily armed than our cruisers on that station. On June 1st, 1813, the taking of the U. S. A. frigate *Chesapeake* by the *Shannon* marked the result of the employment of equal force.

On land invasions of Canada attempted in 1812-13 were defeated after severe skirmishes.

In 1814, Aug. 24th, General Ross defeated a small American force at Bladensberg and took Washington.

George III. 215

1815. Jan. 8th. The English were repulsed in an attack upon New Orleans.

1816. Aug. 27th. Lord Exmouth bombarded Algiers, and caused the release of Christian slaves.

INDIAN WARS

In 1789, Tippoo Sahib, Sultan of Mysore, attacked our ally, the Rajah of Travancore. Lord Cornwallis began war against him in conjunction with the Mahrattas and the Nizam, and Tippoo was driven to peace with the allies in 1792.

In 1798, when Napoleon went to Egypt, the French had made overtures to Tippoo Sahib, and war began in 1799.

On May 3rd, Seringapatam, Tippoo's capital, was stormed by the army under General Harris; Tippoo killed, and the Mysore power finally broken.

In 1803, the Mahratta chiefs of Gwalior and Berar refused to agree to the treaty of Bassein, 1802, by which the Peishwa of the Mahrattas had accepted English Alliance.

Sept. 23. General Wellesley (Wellington) defeated their forces at Assaye.

Sept. 7th. General Lake defeated them near Delhi, took the city, and put the Moghul under English protection.

Oct. 18th. Lake took Agra.

November 1st. Lake defeated the Mahrattas at Laswaree, destroying the infantry trained by French officers.

Nov. 29th. Wellesley defeated them at Argaum in Berar. Peace with the Mahrattas followed; but Holkar, chief of Indore, who had not taken part in the previous war through jealousy of Sindhia of Gwalior, began war in 1804. On Nov. 13, he was defeated at Deeg by Colonel Monson. Lord Lake failed to take Bhurtpore, but Holkar was driven to treat in 1805.

1814–16. Lord Moira (the Lord Rawdon of the American war, afterwards Marquis of Hastings) had to repel the aggressions of the Goorkhas of Nepaul, and succeeded in finally detaching them from the interests of the Mahratta chiefs.

The latter were all intriguing against England. In addition the whole of central India was overrun by Pindharees, many of them Afghans, the remains of soldiery who had come into India with Afghan invaders, or who had served in the old Mahratta armies. These now formed regular armies of freebooters, living on plunder. Their destruction was necessary for the security of the inhabitants of half India, and the Marquis of Hastings began war upon them in 1817. The Peishwa, Holkar, and other chiefs joined the Pindharees, but all the confederates were defeated in a series of sharp actions and vigorous sieges in 1817 and 1818, and Central India was finally brought under English Government or supervision.

ADMINISTRATIONS

1760. The Ministry continued as under George II.

1761. Jan. Lord Henley (afterwards Earl of Northington), Lord Chancellor; March, Earl of Bute, a Secretary of State *vice* Lord Holdernesse; October, Earl of Egremont, a Secretary of State *vice* Mr. Pitt; Viscount Barrington, Chancellor of the Exchequer.

1762. Earl of Bute, First Lord of the Treasury; Sir Francis Dashwood, Chancellor of the Exchequer; Lord Granville, Lord President; Duke of Bedford, Lord Privy Seal; George Grenville, Secretary of State *vice* Earl of Bute.

1763. George Grenville, First Lord of the Treasury and Chancellor of the Exchequer; Earl of Halifax and Earl of Sandwich, Secretaries of State.

1765. Marquis of Rockingham, First Lord of the Treasury; William Dowdeswell, Chancellor of the Exchequer; Earl of Winchelsea and Nottingham, Lord President; Duke of Newcastle, Lord Privy Seal; Duke of Portland, Lord Chamberlain; General Conway and the Duke of Grafton, Secretaries of State; Charles Townsend, Paymaster *vice* Henry Fox Lord Holland, who had held the office since 1757.

1766. Earl of Chatham, Lord Privy Seal; Duke of

Grafton, first **Lord** of the Treasury; Charles Townsend, Chancellor of the Exchequer; Earl of Northington, Lord President; Lord Camden, Lord Chancellor; Duke of Richmond, Secretary of State *vice* Duke of Grafton, June; **Earl** of Shelburne *vice* Duke of Grafton, August; Lord North, a joint Paymaster, he had been a Lord of Treasury from 1759–1765.

1767. Lord North, Chancellor of the Exchequer.

1768. Earl of Bristol, Lord Privy Seal *vice* Chatham; Lord Weymouth, Secretary of State *vice* General Conway; Earl of Hillsborough (afterwards Marquis of Downshire), Secretary of State for the Colonies; Earl of Rochford, Secretary of State *vice* Earl of Shelburne.

1770. Lord North, First Lord of the Treasury and Chancellor of the Exchequer; Earl of Halifax, Lord Privy Seal. The Lord President, Secretaries of State and other chief officers continued as before. The Hon. Charles James Fox was Junior Lord of the Admiralty, 1770–71, and a Commissioner of the Treasury, 1773, at which date he became an opponent of Lord North's Ministry. This Ministry, with some changes, held office through the American War till after the surrender of Yorktown.

1771. Earl of Halifax, Secretary of State *vice* Earl of Sandwich, who became First Lord of the Admiralty; Earl of Suffolk and Berkshire became Lord Privy Seal *vice* Earl of Halifax, Jan.; Duke of Grafton, Lord Privy Seal *vice* Earl of Suffolk; Earl of Suffolk, Secretary of State *vice* Earl of Halifax, June; Lord Apsley (afterwards Earl Bathurst) Lord Chancellor.

1772. Earl of Dartmouth, Secretary of State *vice* Earl of Hillsborough.

1775. Viscount Weymouth, Secretary of State *vice* Earl of Rochford; Lord George Sackville Germaine, Secretary of State *vice* Earl of **Dartmouth**; Earl of Dartmouth, Lord Privy Seal *vice* Duke of Grafton.

1778. Lord Thurlow, Lord Chancellor.

1779. Viscount Stormont, Secretary of State *vice* Earl of Suffolk; Earl Bathurst, Lord President *vice* Earl Gower.

1780. Earl of Hillsborough, Secretary of State *vice* Lord Weymouth.

1782. The failure of the American War led to the resignation of Lord North's Ministry, and the King was obliged to send for the Rockingham Whigs. The Marquis of Rockingham was First Lord of the Treasury; Lord John Cavendish, Chancellor of the Exchequer; Lord Camden, Lord President; Duke of Grafton, Lord Privy Seal; Earl of Shelburne and Charles James Fox, Secretaries of State for Home and Foreign Affairs respectively; Edmund Burke, Paymaster.

In the same year the Marquis of Rockingham died, and "the King appointed" the Earl of Shelburne First Lord of the Treasury, against the wishes of some of the Ministry. Fox, Lord John Cavendish, Burke, and others resigned. William Pitt was Chancellor of the Exchequer; Lord Grantham, Home Secretary; Thomas Townshend (afterwards Viscount Sydney), Foreign Secretary; Isaac Barre, Paymaster.

1783. The "Coalition Ministry" succeeded Shelburne. The Duke of Portland was first Lord of the Treasury; Lord John Cavendish, Chancellor of the Exchequer; Viscount Stormont, President of the Council; Earl of Carlisle, Lord Privy Seal; Lord North, Home Secretary; Charles James Fox, Foreign Secretary; Edmund Burke, Paymaster. Lord Thurlow resigned, and the Great Seal was put in commission.

At the end of the same year the Coalition was dismissed, after Fox's India Bill had been thrown out in the House of Lords by the King's interference.

William Pitt was First Lord of the Treasury and Chancellor of the Exchequer, *aetat 25;* Earl Gower, Lord President; Duke of Rutland, Privy Seal; Marquis of Caermarthen (afterwards Duke of Leeds), Home Secretary; Thomas Townshend, (afterwards Viscount Sydney), Foreign Secretary; Henry Dundas (afterwards Viscount Melville), Treasurer of the Navy;

George III.

William Wyndham Grenville (afterwards Lord Grenville), Joint Paymaster; Lord Thurlow, Lord Chancellor.

1789. W. W. Grenville, Home Secretary *vice* Duke of Leeds.

1791. Lord Grenville, Foreign Secretary *vice* Lord Sydney; Henry Dundas, Home Secretary *vice* Grenville.

1792. Lord Thurlow resigned; the Great Seal in Commission.

1793. Lord Loughborough, Lord Chancellor.

1794. Duke of Portland, Home Secretary, *vice* Dundas.
Dundas, Colonial Secretary and Secretary for War.

1799. George Canning member of the Board of Control.

1801. Mr. Pitt resigned. Henry Addington (afterwards Lord Sidmouth), First Lord of the Treasury and Chancellor of the Exchequer; Duke of Portland, Lord President; Earl of Westmoreland, Privy Seal; Lord Pelham (afterwards Earl of Chichester), Home Secretary; Lord Hawkesbury (afterwards Earl of Liverpool, Foreign Secretary; Lord Hobart, War and Colonial Secretary; Charles Yorke, Secretary at War; Lord Eldon, Lord Chancellor; Lord St. Vincent, First Lord of the Admiralty.

1802. Viscount Castlereagh (afterwards Marquis of Londonderry), President of the Board of Control.

1803. Charles Yorke, Home Secretary, *vice* Pelham.

1804. William Pitt, First Lord of the Treasury and Chancellor of the Exchequer; Lord Sidmouth, Lord President; Earl of Westmoreland, Lord Privy Seal; Lord Hawkesbury, Home Secretary; Lord Harrowby, succeeded in 1805 by Earl of Mulgrave, Foreign Secretary; Earl Camden, succeeded in 1805 by Lord Castlereagh, War and Colonial Secretary; Viscount Melville, succeeded in 1805 by Lord Barham, First Lord of the Admiralty.

William Pitt died January 23rd, 1806.

1806. Lord Grenville, First Lord of the Treasury; Lord Henry Petty, Chancellor of the Exchequer; Earl Fitzwilliam, Lord President; Viscount Sidmouth, Privy Seal; Charles

James Fox, Foreign Secretary; Earl Spencer, Home Secretary; William Windham, War and Colonial Secretary; Earl of Moira (formerly Lord Rawdon, afterwards Marquis of Hastings), Master-General of the Ordnance; Earl of Minto, President of the Board of Control; Sir Charles Grey (afterwards Viscount Howick and Earl Grey), First Lord of the Admiralty; Lord Erskine, Lord Chancellor.

Mr. Fox died Sept. 13th, 1806.

Lord Howick became Foreign Secretary; Thomas Grenville, First Lord of the Admiralty; Viscount Sidmouth, Lord President; Lord Holland, Privy Seal.

1807. Duke of Portland, First Lord of the Treasury; Mr. Spencer Perceval, Chancellor of the Exchequer; Lord Hawkesbury, Home Secretary; Canning, Foreign Secretary; Castlereagh, War and Colonial Secretary; Earl Camden, Lord President; Earl of Westmoreland, Privy Seal; Lord Eldon, Lord Chancellor, an office which he held till 1827.

1809. Spencer Perceval, First Lord of the Treasury and Chancellor of the Exchequer; the Hon. Richard Ryder, Home Secretary; Marquis of Wellesley, Foreign Secretary; Earl of Liverpool, War and Colonial Secretary; Viscount Palmerston, Secretary at War. Lord President and Lord Privy Seal as before.

1812. Mr. Spencer Perceval was murdered in the lobby of the House of Commons, May 11th, 1812.

The Earl of Liverpool became First Lord of the Treasury; Mr. Nicholas Vansittart (afterwards Lord Bexley), Chancellor of the Exchequer; Viscount Sidmouth, Home Secretary; Castlereagh, Foreign Secretary; Earl Bathurst, War and Colonial Secretary; Earl of Harrowby, Lord President; Earl of Westmoreland, Lord Privy Seal; Viscount Melville (son of the former Viscount Melville), First Lord of the Admiralty; Viscount Palmerston continued Secretary at War till 1828.

The Earl of Liverpool continued holding office till his fatal illness, in 1827.

1812. Mr., afterwards Sir Robert Peel, Irish Secretary.
1815. Mr. William Huskisson became a Member of the Board of Trade.
1816. Mr. Canning became President of the Board of Control.
1818. Mr. Frederick J. Robinson (afterwards Viscount Goderich and Earl of Ripon) became President of the Board of Trade.
1819. The Duke of Wellington became Master-General of the Ordnance.

LORDS-LIEUTENANT OF IRELAND IN THE REIGN OF GEORGE III.

1760. Duke of Bedford.
1761. Earl of Halifax.
1763. Earl of Northumberland.
1765. Viscount Weymouth (did not reside).
Earl of Hertford.
1766. Earl of Bristol (did not reside).
1767. Viscount Townsend.
1772. Earl Harcourt.
1777. Earl of Buckinghamshire.
1780. Earl of Carlisle.
1782. Duke of Portland, during whose Lieutenancy the Irish Parliament became independent.
Earl Temple (afterwards Marquis of Buckingham).
1783. Earl of Northington.
1784. Duke of Rutland.
1787. Marquis of Buckingham.
1790. Earl of Westmoreland.
1794. (December 10th) Earl Fitzwilliam.
1795. (March 11th) Earl Camden.
1798. Marquis Cornwallis, during whose Lieutenancy the Union was carried.
1801. Earl of Hardwicke.
1805. Earl Powis (did not reside).

1806. Duke of Bedford.
1807. Duke of Richmond.
1813. Viscount (afterwards Earl) Whitworth.
1817. Earl Talbot.

John Fitzgibbon (Lord Fitzgibbon and Earl of Clare) was Lord Chancellor of Ireland from 1789 to 1802.

GOVERNORS-GENERAL OF INDIA

Colonel Robert Clive (Lord Clive) was Administrator of Bengal June 27th, 1758, to Jan. 24th, 1760, and again from May 3rd, 1765, to Jan. 20th, 1767.

Mr. Warren Hastings was Administrator, April 13th, 1772, and held his first Council as Governor-General, under Lord North's Regulating Act, Oct. 20th, 1774. Resigned Feb. 1, 1785.

1785. Sir John Macpherson.
1786. Earl (afterwards Marquis) Cornwallis.
1793. Sir John Shore (afterwards Lord Teignmouth).
1797. Marquis Cornwallis, appointed, but resigned before sailing.
1798. Sir Alured Clarke (April to May).
1798. Lord Mornington (afterwards Marquis Wellesley).
1805. Marquis Cornwallis (July to October, *died* Oct. 5th).
1805. Sir George Barlow.
1807. Earl of Minto.
1813. Earl of Moira (afterwards Marquis of Hastings) to 1823.

ACTS AND DOCUMENTS

1763. The Peace of Paris concluded the Seven Years' War. The restoration of Havannah and the Philippines to Spain, with the equivalent of Florida only in return, and the restoration to France of Guadaloupe, Martinique, and St. Lucia, of Goree, and of the Newfoundland Fishery, were condemned generally as far too generous. Undoubtedly more might have been taken, and the specious argument of the Duke of Bedford, that had we insisted on severer terms we should have caused all the naval powers ultimately to coalesce against us, as aiming at a monopoly of naval power "as dangerous to the liberties of Europe as that of Louis XIV.," loses its point when it is seen that our actual attitude did lead to such a combination.

Too much has been made of the alleged abandonment of Frederick of Prussia. The coalition against Prussia was broken up. Our really defenceless ally, Portugal, was well cared for. The unpopularity of the Ministry, especially of Bute, led to most of the outcry against the Treaty. (See *Koch et Schoell*, vol. iii. pp. 106, &c.) The Treaties are in the *Annual Register*, vol. v. p. 233.

1764. George Grenville began to reform the revenue laws and administration of the North American colonies. It had always been the practice of European powers to try to regulate colonial trade with strict reference to the supposed advantage of the trade of the Mother Country. The English Navigation Act, 1651, formed the basis of our commercial policy in the colonies; it had been modified to a slight extent by Walpole, but the prosperity of the colonies, of New England in particular, had depended upon a systematic evasion of the revenue laws and upon smuggling. The retention by us of all our West Indian conquests, in 1763, would have had at least this beneficial result, that our Government would have been relieved of the difficulty of trying to regulate American trade with foreign powers.

The re-enactment of a law passed in 1733, and expiring in 1763, to prohibit in fact trade with the French and Spanish islands, increased the dissatisfaction in America.

Connected with the reform of the revenue laws was the design to keep a standing army in America, partly at the expense of the colonies. The great Indian war of 1763, and the prospect of a French attempt to recover Canada in the future, made it reasonable, but it was objected to in the colonies. The principal Acts are 4 Geo. III. cc. 15, 26, 27, 29.

1765. The Stamp Act was passed, making it obligatory that Bills, Bonds, Leases, Policies of Insurance, Newspapers, Broadsides, and Legal Documents of all kinds should be written or printed on Stamped Paper, to be sold by public officers at varying prices according to the Act. It was expected to produce about £100,000, to be expended in America upon the defence of the country. Overtures were made to several colonies for suggestions of some alternative way of raising the money by colonial action, but they were not responded to. The Act was accompanied by another modifying the trade restrictions. (5 Geo. III. c. 12 ; and 5 Geo. III. c. 45.)

The Stamp Act was repealed by 6 Geo. III. c. 11.

1767. Charles Townshend passed an Act raising about £40,000 by Customs in America. (7 Geo. III. c. 41.)

The duties, except that on tea, were repealed. (10 Geo. III. c. 17.)

1771. The Reporting of Parliamentary debates practically allowed, after a contest with certain printers and with the Lord Mayor and Aldermen who had refused to commit them "as not guilty of any crime." The House committed the Lord Mayor and one Alderman, who were Members, but on their release the practice was allowed, though still technically a breach of Privilege. (See *Parl. Hist.* xvii. 59-163.)

1773. Lord North's Regulating Act revolutionized the government of India. A Governor-General of Bengal, with a Council of Four, was appointed by the Crown, and the Governor-General was made supreme over the Governors of Madras and Bombay. A High Court was also appointed by the Crown, consisting of a Chief Justice and Three Puisne Judges. Future appointments were to be in the hands of the Company, but subject to the approbation of the Crown. No person in the employ of the Crown or of the Company was to receive presents, and the Governor General, Councillors, and Judges were not to engage in any commercial pursuits. The whole civil and military correspondence of the Company was to be laid before the Government.

The financial difficulties of the Company, who were obliged to resort to Parliament for aid, gave the opportunity for this Act. The blow to the Company was to be softened by allowing them to export to America 17,000,000 lbs. of tea subject only to the 3d. duty in America, which produced the tea riots in Boston. (13 Geo. III. c. 63, 64.)

1774. The Quebec Act was passed, appointing a Legislative Council in Canada, nominated by the Crown, open to men of all religions; preserving the old French law, except in criminal cases where trial by jury was introduced; and virtually establishing the Roman Catholic church among the French Canadians. (14 Geo. III. c. 83.)

This act had much to do with the loyal attitude of Canada during the War of American Independence, but increased the hostile feeling in the Puritan Colonies of New England.

1775. Lord North proposed a conciliatory Resolution towards America, to the effect that if any colony thought fit of its own accord to make such a contribution to the defence of the Empire, and such a fixed provision for the support of the civil government and administration of justice in the colonies as should meet with the approbation of Parliament, such colony should be relieved from all taxation by Parliament for the sake of revenue. (*Annual Register*, xviii. 95.)

1776, July 4th. The American Declaration of Independence voted by the delegates of 12 Colonies, New York at first abstaining. (Bancroft, *Hist. of the United States*, chap. 70.)

1778. North carried a Conciliatory Act, undertaking to impose no taxes for the sake of revenue in America, and while preserving the right of Parliament to regulate commerce undertaking that the customs so raised should be applied in the several colonies according to the vote of the colonial assemblies. The Tea duty and the act which had interfered with the old constitution of Massachusetts were repealed. Free pardons were offered to all persons. (18 Geo. III. cc. 11, 12, 13.)

These measures were rendered futile by the American alliance with France, by distrust in America of the source whence they came, and by the feebleness of the military operations of England. Congress was committed to the French alliance, which meant Independence, but a really vigorous English commander with a real army in America would probably have caused a separation from the Congress of many persons or even states when the original grievances of the colonists were so fully redressed.

1778. The Catholic Relief Act was passed, repealing the Act of William III. which imposed perpetual imprisonment upon Roman Catholic Bishops, Priests, Jesuits, and Schoolmasters, and which disabled all Roman Catholics from inheriting or purchasing land. The benefits of the law were extended to all who by oath abjured the Pretender, the temporal Jurisdiction and Deposing Power of the Pope. It applied only to England. (18 Geo. III. c. 60.)

The proposal next year to pass a similar measure for Scotland led to great riots in that country, and the excitement spread to England, culminating in the great "Gordon Riots" of May 29th to June 7th, 1780. The agitation had passed from the control of mere fanatics, and had resulted in a temporary triumph of anarchic and criminal violence, which was not without serious effect upon the subsequent attitude of the Government of Pitt towards the members of Revolutionary Societies, and more moderate sympathisers with the principles of the French Revolution. (See *Annual Register*, xxiii. 254.)

1779. The conditions in the Toleration Act of William III. by which Dissenting Ministers and Schoolmasters had to subscribe to 35 of the Articles were relaxed by the Toleration Act. (19 Geo. III. c. 44.)

1782. The Irish Parliament made Independent of Great Britain.

The war with France and Spain in 1778-79 found Ireland almost denuded of troops, with a large Catholic population vehemently hostile to the ruling Protestant minority, and Catholics and Protestants alike suffering under trade restrictions similar to those which had been at the bottom of the American troubles.

A large Protestant Volunteer force was raised, nominally against invasion, but was used as a lever for demands which it was impossible to refuse.

In 1778 some of the restrictions upon Irish trade were modified. (18 Geo. III. cc. 55, 56.)

In Feb., 1782, the delegates of 143 Volunteer corps, assembled at Dungannon, demanded independence and free trade.

The Act of 6 Geo. I. c. 5, making Ireland dependant upon the English Parliament and Poynings' Law, were repealed in consequence by 22 Geo. III. c. 53.

Henceforward the Crown was the only link between Great Britain and Ireland till the Union. The danger of the severing of that link at the time of the Regency Bill of 1788-89, the unrepresentative and corrupt character of the Irish Parliament, the religious hostility, and the progress of the principles of the Revolution led to the failure of the "Dual Monarchy," and after the rebellion of 1798 to the Union 1800. (39 & 40 George III. c. 67.)

The student should consult, above all other works, the *History of England and Ireland in the Eighteenth Century*, by Mr. Lecky. *The History of Ireland*, by Mr. Lecky, has also been published as a separate work.

1780. Burke brought forward a Bill for Economical Reform, intended to cut down expenses and also to abolish many of the means of corruption enjoyed by the Government. It was defeated in Committee. A *résumé* of it is printed in the *Annual Register*, vol. xxiii. p. 300.

1782. Burke, in office under the Marquis of Rockingham, carried a very much modified Act of Economical Reform. (22 Geo. III. c. 82.)

1783. The Peace of Versailles concluded the American War. The separate treaties with Holland, France, Spain, and the United States are printed in the *Annual Register*, xxvi. 319, 322, 331, 339; and see *Koch et Schoell*, iii. 401, &c.

1784. Pitt carried the India Bill. By it the chartered rights of the Company and their patronage were left intact, but the superintendence of all political affairs was transferred to a Board of Control nominated by the Crown and forming a Ministerial Department, going out with the Ministry. The authority of the Governor-General over the subordinate Governors was increased. The Governor-General, Governors, Council, and Commander-in-Chief, were to be nominated by the Directors subject to the approval of the Crown. (24 Geo. III. c. 25.)

This Act, slightly modified, formed the basis of the system of Dual Government in India up to 1858, when after the Mutiny the direct control of the Government was assumed by the English Crown.

In Fox's Bill, which was thrown out in 1783, all power was given to a Board of Seven nominated in the Bill, the mercantile affairs of the Company were put under their control, and the whole of the patronage was taken from the Company also. (See *Annual Register*, xxvii. 58, &c.)

1785. Pitt proposed measures for Free Trade between England and Ireland. Commercial jealousy in England led to their modification, and they were rejected in Ireland as interfering with the freedom of commercial legislation by the Irish Parliament. It was pointed out at the time that similar commercial equality had only been granted to Scotland on the condition of complete Parliamentary Union. The Resolutions are printed in the *Annual Register*, xxvii. 359.

1785. Pitt introduced a Bill for Parliamentary Reform. Its distinguishing feature was that it provided not only for the immediate or not distant transfer of 72 seats from decayed places to large towns and counties, but provided means for the future spontaneous transference of members as need arose. It also enfranchised copyholders in the counties. It was thrown out by 248 to 174. (See *Parl. Hist.* xxv. 445.)

1786. Pitt negotiated a Commercial Treaty with France, which but for the Revolution might have been the beginning of a new era of friendship between the nations. (Printed in the *Annual Register*, xxviii. 266.)

1787. Pitt carried an Act consolidating the different branches of Customs and Excise, and establishing the "Consolidated Fund." (27 Geo. III. c. 13.)

1791. The Canada Act introduced Representative Government into Canada, and divided it into two Provinces, Upper and Lower Canada, corresponding roughly to the English and French population. A Council nominated by the Governor for life, and an Assembly elected for seven years, was established in each province. Canada was governed under this Constitution till 1840. (31 Geo. III. c. 31.)

The debate upon the Bill was the occasion for the political severance between Burke and Fox, who had taken different views of the French Revolution.

1792, Nov. 19th and Dec. 15th. Declarations published by the French Convention against all existing Governments. The aristocratic republics of Holland, Venice, and the Swiss Cantons, the Constitutional Monarchy of England, were threatened equally with despotic monarchies. "All people who wish to recover their liberty" are to be assisted. In "all countries which are or shall be occupied by the French armies," "all existing imposts and contributions" are to be abolished. (*Annual Register*, xxxiv. 153, 155.)

The occupation of the Austrian Netherlands, followed by the invasion of Holland and the throwing open of the Scheldt, in addition to the above encouragement to Secret Societies in Great Britain and Ireland, gave the English Government what would at any time have been regarded as a *casus belli ;* but the actual declaration of war came from France.

The course of the war that ensued depended so much upon the action of Continental powers that the treaties by which they in turn terminated their stages of hostility with France belong almost equally to English History.

1794. By the Treaty at Bâle Prussia retired from the contest.

1796. Spain joined France against England.

1797. By the treaty of Campo Formio Austria agreed to exchange the Netherlands and other territories for the Venetian provinces.

1800. Russia withdrew from the war against France and entered into the "Armed Neutrality" with Sweden, Denmark, and Prussia against England. (*Annual Register,* xlii. 266.)

1801. By the Treaty of Luneville Austria terminated her second war with France, the Empire being included in the pacification.

1802. The Treaty of Amiens between England and France. (See *Koch et Schoell,* vi. 145, &c., and *Annual Register,* xliii. 277.) The words of the clause concerning Malta, the dispute about which was the pretext for the rupture of the Treaty, were as follows in the preliminary treaty : "The island of Malta, with its dependencies, shall be evacuated by the English troops, and restored to the Order of St. John of Jerusalem. To secure the absolute independence of that isle from both the contracting parties, it shall be placed under the guarantee of a third power, to be named in the definitive treaty." By the definitive treaty the King of Sicily, Ferdinand I., was invited to occupy Malta with 2000 men. These were actually landed; but the action of Napoleon in Holland, Switzerland, and Italy, and the military mission of General

George III.

Sebastiani to the Levant, caused us to refrain from the evacuation of Malta, without further guarantees which Napoleon refused to give.

1805. Austria made the Treaty of Pressburg with Napoleon, by which the Holy Roman Empire was dissolved.

1806. The Berlin Decree—extended by the Milan Decree of 1807—by which the British Islands were declared in a state of blockade, and all intercourse forbidden between them and the territories subject to or in alliance with the French Empire. (*Annual Register*, xlviii. 201.)

1807. In answer to the Berlin Decree, and before the Milan Decree, the British "Orders in Council" were issued, declaring all the ports of France and her allies, and ports from which the British flag was excluded, to be in a state of blockade, so that vessels trading to them were lawful prize. Also vessels carrying "certificates of origin" to avoid the Berlin Decree were lawful prize. (*Annual Register*, xlix. 779.)

The Berlin and Milan Decrees were intended to annihilate English commerce. They were in fact systematically evaded, even by Napoleon's own officials. The pressure of them alienated Russia from Napoleon in 1812. The Orders in Council and the Decrees between them did nearly annihilate the European mercantile marine in all the countries subject to or allied with Napoleon.

The Right of Search claimed in pursuance of the Orders in Council was the cause of the war of 1812 with the United States.

1807. Prussia and Russia made the Peace of Tilsit with Napoleon, whereby Russia acceded to the Continental System against England. (See *Koch et Schoell*, viii. 434, &c.)

1807. The Slave Trade was finally abolished. (47 Geo. III. c. 36.)

An Act of 1806 had prohibited British subjects trading in slaves to the colonies captured during the war, or to foreign countries.

1809. Austria concluded her fourth disastrous war with France by the Peace of Vienna.

1814. The Treaty of Ghent concluded the war with the United States. The questions raised by the Orders in Council were passed over, and certain boundary disputes referred to arbitration. The Slave Trade was formally condemned by both Governments. (See *Koch et Schoell*, vol. ix. chap. 40; and *Annual Register*, lvii. 352, 358.)

1814. The Preliminaries of peace were concluded at Paris; but the settlement of Europe was still under discussion at Vienna when Napoleon left Elba. (See *Koch et Schoell*, vol. x. chap. 41, sec. 4.)

1815, Nov. 20th. The Treaty of Paris concluded the war.

The efforts of England and Russia prevented a dismemberment of France, which must have been more immediately fatal to the restored dynasty than the actual circumstances of their return were, and would probably have precipitated another European war before long. The frontiers of France, though slightly curtailed of the proposed limits of 1814, were wider than they had been before the Revolution. England restored several of her colonial conquests, Java to the Dutch, Guadaloupe and Martinique to the French, but retained Malta, Heligoland, the Ionian Islands, Cape Colony, Ceylon, Mauritius, Trinidad, and some smaller islands, and Malacca.

In Europe, a Germanic Confederation replaced the Holy Roman Empire; the Austrian Netherlands were united to Holland, Norway to Sweden, Lombardy and Venetia to Austria, half Saxony and part of Westphalia and the electorate of Cologne to Prussia; the partition of Poland was confirmed, Russia taking the largest share. (See *Koch et Schoell*, vol. x. chap. 41, sec. 6.)

1815. The Corn Laws passed. The sudden throwing open of foreign corn supplies by the peace, and bad seasons in England, produced a violent fluctuation in the price of corn. With the idea of steadying the price of corn, to the supposed advantage of both farmers and consumers, importation was forbidden from foreign countries unless wheat stood at an average price of 80s. a quarter; rye, peas, and beans at 53s.; barley at 40s.; oats at 26s. Importation from the British North American Colonies was allowed when prices stood at 67s., 44s., 33s., 22s. respectively. (55 Geo. III. c. 26.)

The Act was of course inoperative to stop fluctuation of prices, though it ensured high prices generally; and later the principle of admitting imported corn with a high duty was adopted, with equally bad results. (Students may consult McCulloch's *Commercial Dictionary*, art. *Corn Laws*.)

1815–18. The Holy Alliance was formed between Russia, Prussia, and Austria, nominally binding the powers to govern and conduct themselves towards each other on purely Christian principles. France acceded to the Alliance in 1818. Practically it was a compact to combat the principles of the Revolution. (*Koch et Schoell*, vol. xi. chap. 41, sec. 6.)

1819. The Six Acts were passed against riot and sedition, seditious libels and assemblies, against training persons in the use of arms, and also imposing restrictions on the press. They were passed in consequence of the troubles arising from distress in the country after the war, and mark the acmé of the Tory reaction from the Revolution. (60 Geo. III. cc. 1, 2, 4, 6, 8, 9.)

In the subsequent reign the Tory party began gradually to revert to the more liberal policy of Pitt, Canning and Huskisson taking the lead, and Sir Robert Peel and the Duke of Wellington bowing by degrees to the teaching of facts. The Whig party at the same time, released from the suspicion of anti-patriotic aims, which had hampered them during the French war, were enabled to embark upon the course of Constitutional Reform which they pursued for the next fifty years.

AUTHORS

Lord Stanhope's *History of England down to* 1783, mentioned above (George I. and George II.) is not quite so good as it is for the earlier part of the century.

Mr. Lecky's *History of England and Ireland in the* 18*th Century*, is unrivalled for its philosophic completeness of treatment of the social forces at work in moulding events, and is the one great history of the important Irish affairs of the last 20 years of the century.

Bancroft's *History of the United States* gives the American view of the War of Independence and of the events which led to it; but it is to be usefully checked by the more impartial and comprehensive views of Mr. Lecky.

Stanhope's *Life of Pitt;* Sir G. O. Trevelyan's *Early History of Charles James Fox;* Mr. Morley's *Edmund Burke, a Historical Study;* Earl Russell's *Life and Times of Fox;* Lord E. Fitzmaurice's *Life of the Earl of Shelburne;* Lord Campbell's *Life of Lord Mansfield;* Sir Archibald Alison's *Life of Lord Castlereagh*, are the leading lives of leading statesmen in the period.

Alison's *History of Europe*, though distorted by the violent Tory prejudices of the writer, is the most complete survey in English of the events which centred round the history of France from 1789 to 1815.

Napier's *History of the War in the Peninsula* is the great and trustworthy military history of the revival of English military reputation.

James' *Naval History* is the most complete account of the services of the English fleet in detail; but *The Influence of Sea Power upon the French Revolution and Empire*, by Captain Mahan of the U.S.A. Navy, gives a view of the real bearings and importance of the Naval War such as has been never before attempted. *The Influence of Sea Power upon History*, by the same author, is no less valuable in itself, but is of less special importance in the study of English History.

Southey's *Life of Nelson* is not always accurate. Clarke and McArthur's *Life of Nelson* is better, but larger and not so well written.

Of the many lives of the Duke of Wellington, Brialmont's, translated by Gleig, is the best.

Ropes' *Campaign of Waterloo* is the last contribution to the military history of 1815.

In *Constitutional History* Sir Erskine May's *Constitutional History* stands alone.

The *Annual Register*, beginning in 1758, contains contemporary chronicles of events, and gives many important treaties and acts in full or in substance.

Mr. Spencer Walpole's *History of England* since 1815 is the best for the period after the war.

The mass of contemporary letters, papers, and memoirs is too great for special mention. Horace Walpole's *Memoirs of the Early Reign of George III.*, the *Auckland Correspondence*, the *Cornwallis Correspondence*, dealing with events in America, Ireland, and India, the *Malmesbury Correspondence*, the *Bedford Correspondence*, the *Memoirs of the Marquis of Rockingham*, the *Letters and Despatches of the Duke of Wellington*, are among the more important.

Burke's *Political Pamphlets* are valuable as contributions to Political Philosophy, apart from the light which they throw on the party feeling of the first thirty years of George III.

The *Letters of Junius* are valuable as party pamphlets only.

On Indian affairs Sir John Malcolm's *Life of Lord Clive*, the *Cornwallis Correspondence* and *Wellington Despatches* as above, Mill's *History of British India*, *Despatches of the Marquis Wellesley* (not exclusively Indian), are all most useful.

Among smaller works on India Lord Macaulay's *Essays* on *Clive* and *Warren Hastings* are brilliant, but the latter must be carefully corrected, and is shown in parts to be entirely erroneous, as are also some views of Mill's, by Impey's *Life of Sir Elijah Impey*, and by Strachey's *Hastings and the Rohilla War*.

The best short History of India is the *Student's Manual of the History of India* by Colonel Meadows Taylor.

Among short works on the general history, or on special parts of it, the Earl of Rosebery's *Life of Pitt* (English Statesmen Series), Professor Seeley's *Expansion of England* (see above), putting the wars with France of 1778, 1793, and 1803 in the proper relation to the earlier wars with France and Spain, Professor Seeley's *Napoleon*, are all good. Mr. Ludlow's *War of American Independence* (Epochs Series) is fair. None of the short general histories are first-rate upon this period, which is too full of known details and too much concerned with matters touching modern party divisions to be adequately treated briefly. Dr. Gardiner's *Student's History* and Dr. Bright's are perhaps the best.

POSSESSIONS ACQUIRED SINCE 1820

1825. Tennasserim, Arracan, and Assam.   Fernando Po.
1838. Aden.   Natal.
1841. Hongkong.
1843. Scinde.
1846. Labuan.   Part of the Seikh territory.
1849. Sattara.   The Punjaub and Peshawur.
1852. Pegu and Lower Burmah.
1853. Jhansi, Nagpore and Berar.   Kaffraria.
1856. Oude.
1858. Various territories in Central and North-west India, before ruled by the supporters of the Mutiny.
1861. Lagos.
1864. (Ionian Islands given to Greece.)
1868. Gold Coast.   Basutoland.
1874. Fiji.

1877. North Borneo Protectorate.
1878. Cyprus.
1880. Quetta and Pisheen.
1882. Egypt occupied.
1884. New Guinea. Niger Protectorate. Bechuanaland.
1886. Upper Burma.
1887. Zululand.
1888. South African Company incorporated, with powers in Mashonaland, &c.
1889. Nyassaland, &c.
1890. Zanzibar Protectorate, Uganda, and Central African "sphere of influence," under the British East African Company, incorporated 1888.
(Heligoland given to Germany.)

POPULATION OF ENGLAND

The exact numbers of the population were never attempted to be ascertained with accuracy till 1801. Even the improved methods of the modern census do not produce an exact return, though one near enough to the truth for all useful purposes. In the Mediæval period, however, the estimates of population are extremely vague. The following estimates have been made.

1086, from the Domesday Survey, 1,500,000. But this depends upon disputed interpretations of some of the returns in Domesday, and the returns are incomplete at any rate.

1377, from the Poll Tax returns, 2,250,000. But this rests largely upon conjecture.

1528, from the assumption that the population of the whole country would correspond in proportion to area with that of Wilts, Kent, and Essex, 4,356,000. But the assumption is unsound, these counties were more thickly inhabited, or two of them were, than many others, and it is not clear that their population was correctly ascertained.

1696, calculated from the Hearth Tax, 5,500,000.

1700, it was calculated at 5,000,000, or rather more.

1760, at 6,500,000.

1780, as differently as 4,800,000 and 7,800,000. That the former figures were much too low appears from the first census of 1801.

   1801. 16,237,300.
   1811. 18,500,116.
   1821. 21,272,187.
   1881. 35,246,633.
   1891. 37,740,283.

The growth of manufacturing towns dating from the earlier part of George III.'s reign led to a great increase; but the figures of 1801 shew that probably all the estimates of the latter part of the eighteenth century were too low.

In 1881 the population of the British Empire was 315,885,000.

PUBLIC REVENUE

William I., in money of the time, said to be £60,000.

Henry I., £66,000.

Henry III., £50,000.

Edward I., £65,000.

Henry VIII., £300,000. In the two years 1545-7 Henry spent £1,300,000.

Elizabeth, £460,000. In time of war.

James I., £560,000. In time of peace.

Commonwealth, £2,200,000.

Charles II., nominally fixed at £1,200,000.

William III., £3,900,000. Exclusive of extraordinary taxation.

Anne, £5,700,000.

George I., £6,760,000.

George II., £8,520,000.

George III., £15,570,000.

Since the revolution of 1688, however, the revenue in fact varied very largely from war taxes, and no fair average can be taken for a whole reign.

1880–1. The Revenue was £81,265,055.
1891–2. The Revenue was £90,994,786.

NATIONAL DEBT

1688. £664,263.

1702. £16,394,702. Additions owing to the French war.

1714. £54,145,363. Owing to the War of the Spanish Succession.

1727. £52,092,238.

1739. £46,000,000. The decrease owing to the peace policy and management of Sir Robert Walpole.

1763. £138,865,430. After the War of the Austrian Succession and the Seven Years' War.

1775. £128,583,635.

1784. £249,851,628. After the American War.

1793. £239,350,248.

1817. £840,850,591. After the Revolutionary and Napoleonic Wars.

1820. £794,980,481.

1837. £761,422,570.

1890. £689,944,027.

1892. £677,679,571.

HISTORICAL GEOGRAPHY

The best general Historical Atlas is Dr. Karl von Spruner's. It includes maps of England, India, and America.

Mr. Pearson's *Historical Maps of England during the First Thirteen Centuries* is useful; but the best Atlas on a small scale is the one published with Dr. Gardiner's *Student's History*, though the map of England after the Peace of Wedmore needs correction. (See page 9, *supra*.) Freeman's *Historical Geography of Europe*, with an Atlas, explains the varying frontiers of the possessions of the English kings in France.

PLYMOUTH
WILLIAM BRENDON AND SON
PRINTERS

A CATALOGUE OF BOOKS AND ANNOUNCEMENTS OF METHUEN AND COMPANY PUBLISHERS : LONDON 36 ESSEX STREET W.C.

CONTENTS

	PAGE
FORTHCOMING BOOKS,	2
POETRY,	12
BELLES LETTRES, ANTHOLOGIES, ETC.	12
ILLUSTRATED AND GIFT BOOKS,	16
HISTORY,	17
BIOGRAPHY,	19
TRAVEL, ADVENTURE AND TOPOGRAPHY,	21
NAVAL AND MILITARY,	23
GENERAL LITERATURE,	24
PHILOSOPHY,	26
SCIENCE,	27
THEOLOGY,	27
FICTION,	32
BOOKS FOR BOYS AND GIRLS,	42
THE PEACOCK LIBRARY,	42
UNIVERSITY EXTENSION SERIES,	42
SOCIAL QUESTIONS OF TO-DAY	43
CLASSICAL TRANSLATIONS,	44
EDUCATIONAL BOOKS,	44

JULY 1901

JULY 1901.

MESSRS. METHUEN'S ANNOUNCEMENTS

Belles Lettres

STUDIES IN DANTE. By PAGET TOYNBEE. *Crown 8vo. 6s.*
Among the subjects dealt with are 'Dante's Latin Dictionary,' 'Dante and the Lancelot Romance,' Dante's references to Pythagoras, Dante's obligations to Alfraganus, to Orosius, to Albertus Magnus; Dante's theories as to the spots on the moon, the seven examples of munificence in the Convivio, the Commentary of Benvenuto da Imola on the *Divina Commedia*, etc., etc.

Methuen's Standard Library

THE FRENCH REVOLUTION. By THOMAS CARLYLE. Edited by C. R. L. FLETCHER, Fellow of Magdalen College, Oxford. *Three Volumes. Crown 8vo. 6s. each.*
This edition is magnificently equipped with notes by a scholar who has given three years to its preparation.

THE LIFE AND LETTERS OF OLIVER CROMWELL. By THOMAS CARLYLE. With an Introduction by C. H. FIRTH, M.A., and Notes and Appendices by Mrs. LOMAS. *Three Volumes. 6s. each.*
This edition is brought up to the standard of modern scholarship by the addition of numerous new letters of Cromwell, and by the correction of many errors which recent research has discovered.

CRITICAL AND HISTORICAL ESSAYS. By LORD MACAULAY. Edited by F. C. MONTAGUE, M.A. *Three Volumes. Crown 8vo. 6s. each.*
The only edition of this book completely annotated.

Little Biographies

Fcap. 8vo. Each Volume, cloth, 3s. 6d.; leather, 4s. net.

Messrs. METHUEN are publishing a new series bearing the above title. Each book contains the biography of a character famous in war, art, literature or science, and is written by an acknowledged expert. The books are charmingly produced and well illustrated. They form delightful gift books.

THE LIFE OF JOHN HOWARD. By E. C. S. GIBSON, D.D., Vicar of Leeds. With 12 Illustrations.

The Works of Shakespeare

General Editor, EDWARD DOWDEN, Litt. D.

Messrs. METHUEN are publishing an Edition of Shakespeare in single Plays. Each play is edited with a full Introduction, Textual Notes, and a Commentary at the foot of the page.

KING LEAR. Edited by W. J. CRAIG. *Demy 8vo.* 3s. 6d.

The Little Library

'The volumes are compact in size, printed on thin but good paper in clear type, prettily and at the same time strongly bound, and altogether good to look upon and handle.'—*Outlook.*

Pott 8vo. Each Volume, cloth, 1s. 6d. *net; leather,* 2s. 6d. *net.*

Messrs. METHUEN are producing a series of small books under the above title, containing some of the famous books in English and other literatures, in the domains of fiction, poetry, and belles lettres. The series contains several volumes of selections in prose and verse.

The books are edited with the most sympathetic and scholarly care. Each one contains an Introduction which gives (1) a short biography of the author, (2) a critical estimate of the book. Where they are necessary, short notes are added at the foot of the page.

Each book has a portrait or frontispiece in photogravure, and the volumes are produced with great care in a style uniform with that of 'The Library of Devotion.'

CHRISTMAS BOOKS. By W. M. THACKERAY. Edited by S. GWYNN.

ESMOND. By W. M. THACKERAY. Edited by S. GWYNN.

CHRISTMAS BOOKS. By CHARLES DICKENS. Edited by GEORGE GISSING.

THE EARLY POEMS OF ROBERT BROWNING. Edited by W. H. GRIFFIN.

OUR VILLAGE. By Miss MITFORD. (First Series.) Edited by E. V. LUCAS.

THE COMPLEAT ANGLER. By ISAAC WALTON. Edited by J. BUCHAN.

THE ESSAYS OF ELIA; First and Second Series. By CHARLES LAMB. Edited by E. V. LUCAS.

STEPS TO THE TEMPLE, AND OTHER POEMS. By ROBERT CRASHAW. Edited by EDWARD HUTTON.

A SENTIMENTAL JOURNEY. By LAURENCE STERNE. Edited by H. W. PAUL.

Illustrated Books and Books for Children

THE ESSAYS OF ELIA. By CHARLES LAMB. With 70 Illustrations by A. GARTH JONES, and an Introduction by E. V. LUCAS. *Demy 8vo.* 10s. 6d.

This is probably the most beautiful edition of Lamb's Essays that has ever been published. The illustrations display the most remarkable sympathy, insight, and skill, and the introduction is by a critic whose knowledge of Lamb is unrivalled.

THE VISIT TO LONDON. Described in verse by E. V. LUCAS, and in coloured pictures by F. D. BEDFORD. *Small 4to.* 6s.

This charming book describes the introduction of a country child to the delights and sights of London. It is the result of a well-known partnership between author and artist.

A GALLANT QUAKER. By Mrs. MARGARET H. ROBERTSON. Illustrated by F. BUCKLAND. *Crown 8vo.* 6s.

The Little Blue Books for Children.
Edited by E. V. LUCAS.
Illustrated. Square Fcap, 8vo. 2s. 6d.

Messrs. METHUEN have in preparation a series of children's books under the above general title. The aim of the editor is to get entertaining or exciting stories about normal children, the moral of which is implied rather than expressed. The books will be reproduced in a somewhat unusual form, which will have a certain charm of its own. The first three volumes arranged are:

1. THE CASTAWAYS OF MEADOW BANK. By T. COBB.

2. THE BEECHNUT BOOK. By JACOB ABBOTT. Edited by E. V. LUCAS.

3. THE AIR GUN : or, How the Mastermans and Dobson Major nearly lost their Holidays. By T. HILBERT.

History

CROMWELL'S ARMY : A History of the English Soldier during the Civil Wars, the Commonwealth, and the Protectorate. By C. H. FIRTH, M.A. *Crown 8vo.* 7s. 6d.

An elaborate study and description of Cromwell's army by which the victory of the Parliament was secured. The 'New Model' is described in minute detail, and the author, who is one of the most distinguished historians of the day, has made great use of unpublished MSS.

A HISTORY OF RUSSIA FROM PETER THE GREAT TO ALEXANDER II. By W. R. MORFILL, Jesus College, Oxford. *Crown 8vo.* 7s. 6d.

This history, by the most distinguished authority in England, is founded on a study of original documents, and though necessarily brief, is the most comprehensive narrative in existence. Considerable attention has been paid to the social and literary development of the country, and the recent expansion of Russia in Asia.

A HISTORY OF THE POLICE IN ENGLAND. By Captain MELVILLE LEE. *Crown 8vo.* 7s. 6d.

This highly interesting book is the first history of the police force from its first beginning to its present development. Written as it is by an author of competent historical and legal qualifications, it will be indispensable to every magistrate and to all who are indirectly interested in the police force.

ECTHESIS CHRONICA. Edited by Professor LAMBROS. *Demy 8vo.* net. [*Byzantine Texts.*

A HISTORY OF ENGLISH LITERATURE: From its Beginning to Tennyson. By L. ENGEL. Translated from the German by J. H. FREESE. *Demy 8vo.* 7s. 6d.

This is a very complete and convenient sketch of the evolution of our literature from early days. The treatment is biographical as well as critical, and is rendered more interesting by the quotation of characteristic passages from the chief authors.

A HISTORY OF THE BRITISH IN INDIA. By A. D. INNES, M.A. With Maps and Plans. *Crown 8vo.* 7s. 6d.

Biography

THE LIFE OF ROBERT LOUIS STEVENSON. By GRAHAM BALFOUR. *Two Volumes. Demy 8vo.* 25s. net.

This highly interesting biography has been entrusted by Mr. Stevenson's family to his cousin, Mr. Balfour, and all available materials have been placed at his disposal. The book is rich in unpublished MSS. and letters, diaries of travel, reminiscences of friends, and a valuable fragment of autobiography. It also contains a complete bibliography of all Stevenson's work. This biography of one of the most attractive and sympathetic personalities in English literature should possess a most fascinating interest. The book will be uniform with The Edinburgh Edition.

THE LIFE OF FRANÇOIS DE FENELON. By VISCOUNT ST. CYRES. *Demy 8vo.* 10s. 6d.

This biography has engaged the author for many years, and the book is not only the study of an interesting personality, but an important contribution to the history of the period

THE CONVERSATIONS OF JAMES NORTHCOTE, R.A. AND JAMES WARD. Edited by ERNEST FLETCHER. With many Portraits. *Demy 8vo.* 10s. 6d.

This highly interesting, racy, and stimulating book, contains hitherto unpublished utterances of Northcote during a period of twenty-one years. There are many reminiscences of Sir Joshua Reynolds, much advice to young painters, and many references to the great artists and great figures of the day.

Travel, Adventure and Topography

HEAD-HUNTERS, BLACK, WHITE, AND BROWN. By A. C. HADDON, SC.D., F.R.S. With many Illustrations and a Map. *Demy 8vo.* 15s.

> A narrative of adventure and exploration in Northern Borneo. It contains much matter of the highest scientific interest.

A BOOK OF BRITTANY. By S. BARING GOULD. With numerous Illustrations. *Crown 8vo.* 6s.

> Uniform in scope and size with Mr. Baring Gould's well-known books on Devon, Cornwall, and Dartmoor.

General Literature

WOMEN AND THEIR WORK. By the Hon. Mrs. LYTTELTON. *Crown 8vo.* 2s. 6d.

> A discussion of the present position of women in view of the various occupations and interests which are or may be open to them. There will be an introduction dealing with the general question, followed by chapters on the family, the household, philanthropic work, professions, recreation, and friendship.

ENGLISH VILLAGES. By P. H. DITCHFIELD, M.A., F.S.A. Illustrated. *Crown 8vo.* 6s.

> A popular and interesting account of the history of a typical village, and of village life in general in England.

SPORTING MEMORIES. By J. OTHO PAGET. *Demy 8vo.* 12s. 6d.

> This volume of reminiscences by a well-known sportsman and Master of Hounds deals chiefly with fox-hunting experiences.

Science

DRAGONS OF THE AIR. By H. G. SEELEY, F.R.S., With many Illustrations. *Crown 8vo.* 6s.

> A popular history of the most remarkable flying animals which ever lived. Their relations to mammals, birds, and reptiles, living and extinct, are shown by an original series of illustrations. The scattered remains preserved in Europe and the United States have been put together accurately to show the varied forms of the animals. The book is a natural history of these extinct animals, which flew by means of a single finger.

Theology

REGNUM DEI. THE BAMPTON LECTURES OF 1901. By A. ROBERTSON, D.D., Principal of King's College, London. *Demy 8vo.* 12s. 6d. *net.*

> This book is an endeavour to ascertain the meaning of the 'Kingdom of God' in its original prominence in the teaching of Christ. It reviews historically the main interpretations of this central idea in the successive phases of Christian tradition and life. Special attention is given to the sense in which St. Augustine identified the Church with the Kingdom of God. The later lectures follow out the alternative ideas of the Church, and of its relation to civil society which the Middle Ages and more recent types of Christian thought have founded upon alternative conceptions of the Kingdom of God.

A HISTORY OF THE OLD TESTAMENT. By G. W. WADE. With Maps. *Crown 8vo.* 6s.

> This book presents a connected account of the Hebrew people during the period covered by the Old Testament; and has been drawn up from the Scripture records in accordance with the methods of historical criticism. The text of the Bible has been studied in the light thrown upon it by the best modern commentators; but the reasons for the conclusions stated are not left to be sought for in the commentaries, but are discussed in the course of the narrative. Much attention has been devoted to tracing the progress of religion amongst the Hebrews, and the book, which is furnished with maps, is further adapted to the needs of theological students by the addition of geographical notes, tables, and a full index.

THE AGAPE AND THE EUCHARIST. By J. F. KEATING, D.D. *Crown 8vo.* 3s. 6d.

THE IMITATION OF CHRIST. A Revised Translation, with an Introduction, by C. BIGG, D.D., Canon of Christ Church. *Crown 8vo.* 3s. 6d.

> A new edition, carefully revised and set in large type, of Dr. Bigg's well-known version.

Oxford Commentaries

General Editor, WALTER LOCK, D.D., Warden of Keble College, Dean Ireland's Professor of Exegesis in the University of Oxford.

THE ACTS OF THE APOSTLES: With Introduction and Notes by R. B. RACKHAM, M.A. *Demy 8vo.* 10s. 6d.

The Churchman's Library

General Editor, J. H. BURN, B.D., Examining Chaplain to the Bishop of Aberdeen.

THE OLD TESTAMENT AND THE NEW SCHOLARSHIP. By J. W. PETERS, D.D. *Crown 8vo.* 6s.

COMPARATIVE RELIGION. By J. A. MACCULLOCK. *Crown 8vo.*

THE CHURCH OF CHRIST. By E. T. GREEN. *Crown 8vo.*

A POPULAR INTRODUCTION TO THE OLD TESTAMENT. Edited by A. M. MACKAY. *Crown 8vo.*

The Churchman's Bible

General Editor, J. H. BURN, B.D.

Messrs. METHUEN are issuing a series of expositions upon most of the books of the Bible. The volumes will be practical and devotional, and the text of the authorised version is explained in sections, which will correspond as far as possible with the Church Lectionary.

ISAIAH. Edited by W. E. BARNES, D.D., Fellow of Queen's College, Cambridge. *Two Volumes. 2s. net each.*

THE EPISTLE OF ST. PAUL THE APOSTLE TO THE EPHESIANS. Edited by G. H. WHITAKER. *1s. 6d. net.*

The Library of Devotion

Pott 8vo, cloth, 2s.; leather, 2s. 6d. net.

'This series is excellent.'—THE BISHOP OF LONDON.
'Very delightful.'—THE BISHOP OF BATH AND WELLS.
'Well worth the attention of the Clergy.'—THE BISHOP OF LICHFIELD.
'The new "Library of Devotion" is excellent.'—THE BISHOP OF PETERBOROUGH.
'Charming.'—*Record.* 'Delightful.'—*Church Bells.*

THE THOUGHTS OF PASCAL. Edited with an Introduction and Notes by C. S. JERRAM, M.A.

ON THE LOVE OF GOD. By ST. FRANCIS DE SALES. Edited by W. J. KNOX-LITTLE, M.A.

A MANUAL OF CONSOLATION FROM THE SAINTS AND FATHERS. Edited by J. H. BURN, B.D.

THE SONG OF SONGS. Being Selections from ST. BERNARD. Edited by B. BLAXLAND, M.A.

Leaders of Religion

Edited by H. C. BEECHING, M.A. *With Portraits, Crown 8vo. 3s 6d.*

A series of short biographies of the most prominent leaders of religious life and thought of all ages and countries.

BISHOP BUTLER. By W. A. SPOONER, M.A., Fellow of New College, Oxford.

Educational Books

COMMERCIAL EDUCATION IN THEORY AND PRACTICE. By E. E. WHITFIELD, M.A. *Crown 8vo. 5s.*

An introduction to Methuen's Commercial Series treating the question of Commercial Education fully from both the point of view of the teacher and of the parent.

EASY GREEK EXERCISES. By C. G. BOTTING, M.A. *Crown 8vo. 2s.*

DEMOSTHENES: The Olynthiacs and Philippics. Translated upon a new principle by OTHO HOLLAND. *Crown 8vo. 2s. 6d.*

A SOUTH AFRICAN ARITHMETIC. By HENRY HILL, B.A., Assistant Master at Worcester School, Cape Colony. *Crown 8vo.* 3s. 6d.

This book has been specially written for use in South African schools.

JUNIOR EXAMINATION SERIES. Edited by A. M. M. STEDMAN, M.A. *Fcap. 8vo.* 1s.

FRENCH EXAMINATION PAPERS. By F. JACOB, B.A.

LATIN EXAMINATION PAPERS. By C. G. BOTTING, M.A.

ALGEBRA EXAMINATION PAPERS. By AUSTEN S. LESTER, M.A.

ENGLISH GRAMMAR EXAMINATION PAPERS. By W. WILLIAMSON, B.A.

Fiction

THE HISTORY OF SIR RICHARD CALMADY: A Romance. By LUCAS MALET, Author of 'The Wages of Sin.' *Crown 8vo.* 6s.

This is the first long and elaborate book by Lucas Malet since 'The Wages of Sin.' It is a romance on realistic lines, and will certainly be one of the most important novels of the last ten years.

This novel, the scene of which is laid in the moorland country of the northern part of Hampshire, in London, and in Naples, opens in the year of grace 1842. The action covers a period of about three and thirty years; and deals with the experiences and adventures of an English country gentleman of an essentially normal type of character, subjected—owing to somewhat distressing antecedent circumstances—to very abnormal conditions of life. The book is frankly a romance; but it is also frankly a realistic and modern one.

THE SERIOUS WOOING: A Heart's History. By Mrs. CRAIGIE (JOHN OLIVER HOBBES), Author of 'Robert Orange.' *Crown 8vo.* 6s.

LIGHT FREIGHTS. By W. W. JACOBS, Author of 'Many Cargoes.' Illustrated. *Crown 8vo.* 3s. 6d.

A volume of stories by Mr. Jacobs uniform in character and appearance with 'Many Cargoes.'

CLEMENTINA. By A. E. W. MASON, Author of 'The Courtship of Morrice Buckler,' 'Miranda of the Balcony,' etc. Illustrated. *Crown 8vo* 6s.

A spirited romance of the Jacobites somewhat after the manner of 'Morrice Buckler.' The Old Pretender is introduced as one of the chief characters.

A WOMAN ALONE. By Mrs. W. K. CLIFFORD, Author of 'Aunt Anne.' *Crown 8vo.* 3s. 6d.

A volume of stories.

THE STRIKING HOURS. By EDEN PHILLPOTTS, Author of 'Children of the Mist,' 'Sons of the Morning,' etc. *Crown 8vo.* 6s.

The annals of a Devon village, containing much matter of humorous and pathetic interest.

FANCY FREE. By EDEN PHILLPOTTS, Author of 'Children of the Mist.' Illustrated. *Crown 8vo.* 6s.
A humorous book. Uniform with 'The Human Boy.'

TALES OF DUNSTABLE WEIR. By GWENDOLINE KEATS (ZACK). Author of 'Life is Life.' *Crown 8vo.* 6s.
A volume of stories after the style of 'Zack's' well-known first book 'Life is Life.'

WITH ESSEX IN IRELAND. By the Hon. EMILY LAWLESS. Cheaper Edition. *Crown 8vo.* 6s.
A cheaper edition of a book which won considerable popularity in a more expensive form some years ago.

A NEW NOVEL. By Mrs. B. M. CROKER. *Crown 8vo.* 6s.

THE PROPHET OF BERKELEY SQUARE. By ROBERT HICHENS, Author of 'Flames,' 'Tongues of Conscience,' etc. *Crown 8vo.* 6s.
A new long novel.

THE ALIEN. By F. F. MONTRESOR, Author of 'Into the Highways and Hedges.' *Crown 8vo.* 6s.

THE EMBARRASSING ORPHAN. By W. E. NORRIS. *Crown 8vo.* 6s.

ROYAL GEORGIE. By S. BARING GOULD, Author of 'Mehalah.' With eight Illustrations by D. MURRAY SMITH. *Crown 8vo.* 6s.

FORTUNE'S DARLING. By WALTER RAYMOND, Author of 'Love and Quiet Life.' *Crown 8vo.* 6s.

THE MILLION. By DOROTHEA GERARD, Author of 'Lady Baby.' *Crown 8vo.* 6s.

FROM THE LAND OF THE SHAMROCK. By JANE BARLOW, Author of 'Irish Idylls.' *Crown 8vo.* 6s.

THE WOOING OF SHEILA. By GRACE RHYS. *Crown 8vo.* 6s.

RICKERBY'S FOLLY. By TOM GALLON, Author of 'Kiddy.' *Crown 8vo.* 6s.

A GREAT LADY. By ADELINE SERGEANT, Author of 'The Story of a Penitent Soul.' *Crown 8vo.* 6s.

MARY HAMILTON. By LORD ERNEST HAMILTON. *Crown 8vo.* 6s.

MASTER OF MEN. By E. PHILLIPS OPPENHEIM. *Crown 8vo.* 6s.

BOTH SIDES OF THE VEIL. By RICHARD MARSH, Author of 'The Seen and the Unseen.' *Crown 8vo.* 6s.

THE THIRTEEN EVENINGS. By GEORGE BARTRAM, Author of 'The People of Clopton.' *Crown 8vo.* 6s.

THE SKIRTS OF HAPPY CHANCE. By H. B. MARRIOTT WATSON. Illustrated. *Crown 8vo.* 6s.

A NEW NOVEL. By E. H. COOPER, Author of 'Mr. Blake of Newmarket.' *Crown 8vo.* 6s.

This book, like most of Mr. Cooper's novels, is chiefly concerned with sport and racing.

THE YEAR ONE : A Page of the French Revolution. By J. BLOUNDELLE BURTON, Author of 'The Clash of Arms.' *Crown 8vo.* 6s.

A vivid story of the Reign of Terror in France in 1792, when the year 1 of the Republic calendar commenced.

THE DEVASTATORS. By ADA CAMBRIDGE, Author of 'Path and Goal.' *Crown 8vo.* 6s.

JOHN TOPP : Pirate. By WEATHERBY CHESNEY. *Crown 8vo.* 6s.

A book of breathless adventure.

The Novelist

Messrs. METHUEN are issuing under the above general title a Monthly Series of Novels by popular authors at the price of Sixpence. Each Number is as long as the average Six Shilling Novel.

XXIII. THE HUMAN BOY. EDEN PHILLPOTTS.
[*July.*
XXIV. THE CHRONICLES OF COUNT ANTONIO. ANTHONY HOPE.
[*August.*
XXV. BY STROKE OF SWORD. ANDREW BALFOUR.
[*September.*

Methuen's Sixpenny Library

A New Series of Copyright Books.
NEW VOLUMES

THE CONQUEST OF LONDON. DOROTHEA GERARD. [*July.*

THE MUTABLE MANY. ROBERT BARR. [*August.*

A VOYAGE OF CONSOLATION. SARA J. DUNCAN.
[*September.*

THE WAR WITH THE BOERS : A Sketch of the Boer War of 1899-1901. With Maps and Plans. By H. SIDEBOTHAM. (Double number. 1s.) [*October.*

A CATALOGUE OF

MESSRS. METHUEN'S
PUBLICATIONS

◆

Poetry

Rudyard Kipling. BARRACK-ROOM BALLADS. By RUDYARD KIPLING. *68th Thousand. Crown 8vo.* 6s. *Leather*, 6s. net.

'Mr. Kipling's verse is strong, vivid, full of character.... Unmistakeable genius rings in every line.'—*Times.*

'The ballads teem with imagination, they palpitate with emotion. We read them with laughter and tears; the metres throb in our pulses, the cunningly ordered words tingle with life; and if this be not poetry, what is?'—*Pall Mall Gazette.*

Rudyard Kipling. THE SEVEN SEAS. By RUDYARD KIPLING. *57th Thousand. Cr. 8vo. Buckram, gilt top.* 6s. *Leather*, 6s. net.

'The Empire has found a singer; it is no depreciation of the songs to say that statesmen may have, one way or other, to take account of them.'—*Manchester Guardian.*

'Animated through and through with indubitable genius.'—*Daily Telegraph.*

"Q." POEMS AND BALLADS. By "Q." *Crown 8vo.* 3s. 6d.

"Q." GREEN BAYS: Verses and Parodies. By "Q." *Second Edition. Crown 8vo.* 3s. 6d.

H. Ibsen. BRAND. A Drama by HENRIK IBSEN. Translated by WILLIAM WILSON. *Third Edition. Crown 8vo.* 3s. 6d.

A. D. Godley. LYRA FRIVOLA. By A. D. GODLEY, M.A., Fellow of Magdalen College, Oxford. *Third Edition. Pott 8vo.* 2s. 6d.

'Combines a pretty wit with remarkably neat versification.... Every one will wish there was more of it.'—*Times.*

A. D. Godley. VERSES TO ORDER. By A. D. GODLEY. *Crown 8vo.* 2s. 6d. net.

J. G. Cordery. THE ODYSSEY OF HOMER. A Translation by J. G. CORDERY. *Crown 8vo.* 7s. 6d.

Herbert Trench. DEIRDRE WED: and Other Poems. By HERBERT TRENCH. *Crown 8vo.* 5s.

Edgar Wallace. WRIT IN BARRACKS. By EDGAR WALLACE. *Crown 8vo.* 3s. 6d.

Belles Lettres, Anthologies, etc.

R. L. Stevenson. VAILIMA LETTERS. By ROBERT LOUIS STEVENSON. With an Etched Portrait by WILLIAM STRANG. *Third Edition. Crown 8vo. Buckram.* 6s.

'A fascinating book.'—*Standard.*
'Unique in Literature.'—*Daily Chronicle.*

G. Wyndham. THE POEMS OF WILLIAM SHAKESPEARE. Edited with an Introduction and Notes by GEORGE WYNDHAM, M.P. *Demy 8vo. Buckram, gilt top.* 10s. 6d.

This edition contains the 'Venus,' 'Lucrece,' and Sonnets, and is prefaced with an elaborate introduction of over 140 pp.

'We have no hesitation in describing Mr. George Wyndham's introduction as a masterly piece of criticism, and all who love our Elizabethan literature will find a very garden of delight in it.'—*Spectator.*

Edward FitzGerald. THE RUBAIYAT OF OMAR KHAYYAM. Translated by EDWARD FITZGERALD. With a Commentary by H. M. BATSON, and a Biography of Omar by E. D. ROSS. 6s. Also an Edition on large paper limited to 50 copies.

'One of the most desirable of the many reprints of Omar.'—*Glasgow Herald.*

W. E. Henley. ENGLISH LYRICS. Selected and Edited by W. E. HENLEY. *Crown 8vo. Gilt top.* 3s. 6d.

'It is a body of choice and lovely poetry.'—*Birmingham Gazette.*

Henley and Whibley. A BOOK OF ENGLISH PROSE. Collected by W. E. HENLEY and CHARLES WHIBLEY. *Crown 8vo. Buckram, gilt top.* 6s.

H. C. Beeching. LYRA SACRA: An Anthology of Sacred Verse. Edited by H. C. BEECHING, M.A. *Crown 8vo. Buckram.* 6s.

'A charming selection, which maintains a lofty standard of excellence.'—*Times.*

"Q." THE GOLDEN POMP. A Procession of English Lyrics. Arranged by A. T. QUILLER COUCH. *Crown 8vo. Buckram.* 6s.

W. B. Yeats. AN ANTHOLOGY OF IRISH VERSE. Edited by W. B. YEATS. *Revised and Enlarged Edition. Crown 8vo.* 3s. 6d.

W. M. Dixon. A PRIMER OF TENNYSON. By W. M. DIXON, M.A. *Cr. 8vo.* 2s. 6d.

'Much sound and well-expressed criticism. The bibliography is a boon.'—*Speaker.*

W. A. Craigie. A PRIMER OF BURNS. By W. A. CRAIGIE. *Crown 8vo.* 2s. 6d.

'A valuable addition to the literature of the poet.'—*Times.*

Gibbon. MEMOIRS OF MY LIFE AND WRITINGS. By EDWARD GIBBON. Edited, with an Introduction and Notes, by G. BIRKBECK HILL, LL.D. *Crown 8vo.* 6s.

G. W. Steevens. MONOLOGUES OF THE DEAD. By G. W. STEEVENS. *Foolscap 8vo.* 3s. 6d.

L. Magnus. A PRIMER OF WORDSWORTH. By LAURIE MAGNUS. *Crown 8vo.* 2s. 6d.

'A valuable contribution to Wordsworthian literature.'—*Literature.*

Sterne. THE LIFE AND OPINIONS OF TRISTRAM SHANDY. By LAWRENCE STERNE. With an Introduction by CHARLES WHIBLEY, and a Portrait. 2 vols. 7s.

Congreve. THE COMEDIES OF WILLIAM CONGREVE. With an Introduction by G. S. STREET, and a Portrait. 2 vols. 7s.

Morier. THE ADVENTURES OF HAJJI BABA OF ISPAHAN. By JAMES MORIER. With an Introduction by E. G. BROWNE, M.A. and a Portrait. 2 vols. 7s.

Walton. THE LIVES OF DONNE, WOTTON, HOOKER, HERBERT AND SANDERSON. By IZAAK WALTON. With an Introduction by VERNON BLACKBURN, and a Portrait. 3s. 6d.

Johnson. THE LIVES OF THE ENGLISH POETS. By SAMUEL JOHNSON, LL.D. With an Introduction by J. H. MILLAR, and a Portrait. 3 vols. 10s. 6d.

Burns. THE POEMS OF ROBERT BURNS. Edited by ANDREW LANG and W. A. CRAIGIE. With Portrait. *Second Edition. Demy 8vo, gilt top.* 6s.

F. Langbridge. BALLADS OF THE BRAVE; Poems of Chivalry, Enterprise, Courage, and Constancy. Edited by Rev. F. LANGBRIDGE. *Second Edition. Cr. 8vo.* 3s. 6d. *School Edition.* 2s. 6d.

'The book is full of splendid things.'—*World.*

Methuen's Standard Library

'An admirable edition of one of the most interesting personal records of a literary life. Its notes and its numerous appendices are a repertory of almost all that can be known about Gibbon.'—*Manchester Guardian.*

Gibbon. THE DECLINE AND FALL OF THE ROMAN EMPIRE. By EDWARD GIBBON. A New Edition, Edited with Notes, Appendices, and Maps, by J. B. BURY, LL.D., Fellow of Trinity College, Dublin. *In Seven Volumes. Demy 8vo. Gilt top. 8s. 6d. each. Also Cr. 8vo. 6s. each.*

'At last there is an adequate modern edition of Gibbon. . . . The best edition the nineteenth century could produce.'—*Manchester Guardian.*

'A great piece of editing.'—*Academy.*

Gilbert White. THE NATURAL HISTORY OF SELBORNE. By GILBERT WHITE. Edited by L. C. MIALL, F.R.S., assisted by W. WARDE FOWLER, M.A. *Crown 8vo. 6s.*

C. G. Crump. THE HISTORY OF THE LIFE OF THOMAS ELLWOOD. Edited by C. G. CRUMP, M.A. *Crown 8vo. 6s.*

This edition is the only one which contains the complete book as originally published. It contains a long Introduction and many Footnotes.

Dante. LA COMMEDIA DI DANTE ALIGHIERI. The Italian Text edited by PAGET TOYNBEE, M.A. *Demy 8vo. Gilt top. 8s. 6d. Also Crown 8vo. 6s.*

Tennyson. THE EARLY POEMS OF ALFRED, LORD TENNYSON, Edited, with Notes and an Introduction by J. CHURTON COLLINS, M.A. *Crown 8vo. 6s.*

An elaborate edition of the celebrated volume which was published in its final and definitive form in 1853. This edition contains a long Introduction and copious Notes, textual and explanatory. It also contains in an Appendix all the Poems which Tennyson afterwards omitted.

Jonathan Swift. THE JOURNAL TO STELLA. By JONATHAN SWIFT. Edited by G. A. AITKEN. *Crown 8vo. 6s.*

Chesterfield. THE LETTERS OF LORD CHESTERFIELD TO HIS SON. Edited, with an Introduction by C. STRACHEY, and Notes by A. CALTHROP. *Two Volumes. Crown 8vo. 6s. each.*

The Works of Shakespeare
General Editor, EDWARD DOWDEN, Litt.D.

Messrs. METHUEN have in preparation an Edition of Shakespeare in single Plays. Each play will be edited with a full Introduction, Textual Notes, and a Commentary at the foot of the page.

The first volumes are:

HAMLET. Edited by EDWARD DOWDEN. *Demy 8vo. 3s. 6d.*

'Fully up to the level of recent scholarship, both English and German.'—*Academy.*

ROMEO AND JULIET. Edited by EDWARD DOWDEN, Litt.D. *Demy 8vo. 3s. 6d.*

'No edition of Shakespeare is likely to prove more attractive and satisfactory than this one. It is beautifully printed and paged and handsomely and simply bound.'—*St. James's Gazette.*

The Novels of Charles Dickens

Crown 8vo. Each Volume, cloth 3s. net; leather 4s. 6d. net.

With Introductions by Mr. GEORGE GISSING, Notes by Mr. F. G. KITTON, and Topographical Illustrations.

THE PICKWICK PAPERS. With Illustrations by E. H. NEW. *Two Volumes.*

'As pleasant a copy as any one could desire. The notes add much to the value of the edition, and Mr. New's illustrations are also historical. The volumes promise well for the success of the edition.'—*Scotsman.*

NICHOLAS NICKLEBY. With Illustrations by R. J. WILLIAMS. *Two Volumes.*

BLEAK HOUSE. With Illustrations by BEATRICE ALCOCK. *Two Volumes.*
OLIVER TWIST. With Illustrations by G. H. NEW.
THE OLD CURIOSITY SHOP. With Illustrations by G. M. BRIMELOW. *Two Volumes.*
BARNABY RUDGE. With Illustrations by BEATRICE ALCOCK. *Two Volumes.*

Little Biographies

Fcap. 8vo. Each volume, cloth, 3s. 6d.

THE LIFE OF DANTE ALIGHIERI. By PAGET TOYNBEE. With 12 Illustrations.

'This excellent little volume is a clear, compact, and convenient summary of the whole subject.'—*Academy.*

THE LIFE OF SAVONAROLA. By E. L. S. HORSBURGH, M.A. With Portraits and Illustrations.

The Little Library

With Introductions, Notes, and Photogravure Frontispieces.

Pott 8vo. Each Volume, cloth 1s. 6d. net, leather 2s. 6d. net.

'Altogether good to look upon, and to handle.'—*Outlook.*
'In printing, binding, lightness, etc., this is a perfect series.'—*Pilot.*
'It is difficult to conceive more attractive volumes.'—*St. James's Gazette.*
'Very delicious little books.'—*Literature.*
'Delightful editions.'—*Record.*
'Exceedingly tastefully produced.'—*Morning Leader.*

VANITY FAIR. By W. M. THACKERAY. With an Introduction by S. GWYNN. *Three Volumes.*

THE PRINCESS. By ALFRED, LORD TENNYSON. Edited by ELIZABETH WORDSWORTH.

IN MEMORIAM. By ALFRED, LORD TENNYSON. Edited, with an Introduction and Notes, by H. C. BEECHING, M.A.

THE EARLY POEMS OF ALFRED, LORD TENNYSON. Edited by J. C. COLLINS, M.A.

MAUD. By ALFRED, LORD TENNYSON. Edited by ELIZABETH WORDSWORTH.

A LITTLE BOOK OF ENGLISH LYRICS. With Notes.

EOTHEN. By A. W. KINGLAKE. With an Introduction and Notes.

CRANFORD. By Mrs. GASKELL. Edited by E. V. LUCAS.

THE INFERNO OF DANTE. Translated by H. F. CARY. Edited by PAGET TOYNBEE.

THE PURGATORIO OF DANTE. Translated by H. F. CARY. Edited by PAGET TOYNBEE, M.A.

JOHN HALIFAX, GENTLEMAN. By Mrs. CRAIK. Edited by ANNIE MATHESON. *Two Volumes.*

A LITTLE BOOK OF SCOTTISH VERSE. Arranged and edited by T. F. HENDERSON.

A LITTLE BOOK OF ENGLISH PROSE. Arranged and edited by Mrs. P. A. BARNETT.

SELECTIONS FROM WORDSWORTH. Edited by NOWELL C. SMITH, Fellow of New College, Oxford.

SELECTIONS FROM WILLIAM BLAKE. Edited by M. PERUGINI.

PRIDE AND PREJUDICE. By JANE AUSTEN. Edited by E. V. LUCAS. *Two Volumes.*

PENDENNIS. By W. M. THACKERAY, Edited by S. GWYNN. *Three Volumes.*

LAVENGRO. By GEORGE BORROW. Edited by F. HINDES GROOME. *Two Volumes.*

The Little Guides

Pott 8vo, cloth 3s.; leather, 3s. 6d. net.

OXFORD AND ITS COLLEGES. By J. WELLS, M.A., Fellow and Tutor of Wadham College. Illustrated by E. H. NEW. *Fourth Edition.*

'An admirable and accurate little treatise, attractively illustrated.'—*World.*

CAMBRIDGE AND ITS COLLEGES. By A. HAMILTON THOMPSON. Illustrated by E. H. NEW.

'It is brightly written and learned, and is just such a book as a cultured visitor needs.'—*Scotsman.*

THE MALVERN COUNTRY. By B. C. A. WINDLE, D.Sc., F.R.S. Illustrated by E. H. NEW.

SHAKESPEARE'S COUNTRY. By B. C. A. WINDLE, F.R.S., M.A. Illustrated by E. H. NEW. *Second Edition.*

'One of the most charming guide books. Both for the library and as a travelling companion the book is equally choice and serviceable.'—*Academy.*

SUSSEX. By F. G. BRABANT, M.A. Illustrated by E. H. NEW.

'A charming little book; as full of sound information as it is practical in conception.'—*Athenæum.*

'Accurate, complete, and agreeably written.' —*Literature.*

WESTMINSTER ABBEY. By G. E. TROUTBECK. Illustrated by F. D. BEDFORD.

'A delightful miniature hand-book.'— *Glasgow Herald.*

'In comeliness, and perhaps in completeness, this work must take the first place.'—*Academy.*

'A really first-rate guide-book.'— *Literature.*

Illustrated and Gift Books

Tennyson. THE EARLY POEMS OF ALFRED, LORD TENNYSON. Edited, with Notes and an Introduction by J. CHURTON COLLINS, M.A. With 10 Illustrations in Photogravure by W. E. F. BRITTEN. *Demy 8vo. 10s. 6d.*

Gelett Burgess. GOOPS AND HOW TO BE THEM. By GELETT BURGESS. With numerous Illustrations. *Small 4to. 6s.*

Gelett Burgess. THE LIVELY CITY OF LIGG. By GELETT BURGESS. With 53 Illustrations, 8 of which are coloured. *Small 4to. 6s.*

Phil May. THE PHIL MAY ALBUM. *4to. 6s.*

'There is a laugh in each drawing.'— *Standard.*

A. H. Milne. ULYSSES; OR, DE ROUGEMONT OF TROY. Described and depicted by A. H. MILNE. *Small quarto. 3s. 6d.*

'Clever, droll, smart.'—*Guardian.*

Edmund Selous. TOMMY SMITH'S ANIMALS. By EDMUND SELOUS. Illustrated by G. W. ORD. *Fcap. 8vo. 2s. 6d.*

A little book designed to teach children respect and reverence for animals.

'A quaint, fascinating little book: a nursery classic.'—*Athenæum.*

S. Baring Gould. THE CROCK OF GOLD. Fairy Stories told by S. BARING GOULD. *Crown 8vo. 6s.*

'Twelve delightful fairy tales.'—*Punch.*

M. L. Gwynn. A BIRTHDAY BOOK. Arranged and Edited by M. L. GWYNN. *Demy 8vo. 12s. 6d.*

This is a birthday-book of exceptional dignity, and the extracts have been chosen with particular care.

John Bunyan. THE PILGRIM'S PROGRESS. By JOHN BUNYAN. Edited, with an Introduction, by C. H. FIRTH, M.A. With 39 Illustrations by R. ANNING BELL. *Crown 8vo. 6s.*

'The best "Pilgrim's Progress."'— *Educational Times.*

F. D. Bedford. NURSERY RHYMES. With many Coloured Pictures by F. D. BEDFORD. *Super Royal 8vo.* 2*s.* 6*d.*

S. Baring Gould. A BOOK OF FAIRY TALES retold by S. BARING GOULD. With numerous Illustrations and Initial Letters by ARTHUR J. GASKIN. *Second Edition. Cr. 8vo. Buckram.* 6*s.*

S. Baring Gould. OLD ENGLISH FAIRY TALES. Collected and edited by S. BARING GOULD. With Numerous Illustrations by F. D. BEDFORD. *Second Edition. Cr. 8vo. Buckram.* 6*s.*
'A charming volume.'—*Guardian.*

S. Baring Gould. A BOOK OF NURSERY SONGS AND RHYMES. Edited by S. BARING GOULD, and Illustrated by the Birmingham Art School. *Buckram, gilt top. Crown 8vo.* 6*s.*

H. C. Beeching. A BOOK OF CHRISTMAS VERSE. Edited by H. C. BEECHING, M.A., and Illustrated by WALTER CRANE. *Cr. 8vo, gilt top.* 3*s.* 6*d.*

History

Flinders Petrie. A HISTORY OF EGYPT, FROM THE EARLIEST TIMES TO THE PRESENT DAY. Edited by W. M. FLINDERS PETRIE, D.C.L., LL.D., Professor of Egyptology at University College. *Fully Illustrated. In Six Volumes. Cr. 8vo.* 6*s. each.*

  VOL. I. PREHISTORIC TIMES TO XVITH DYNASTY. W. M. F. Petrie. *Fourth Edition.*
  VOL. II. THE XVIITH AND XVIIITH DYNASTIES. W. M. F. Petrie. *Third Edition.*
  VOL. IV. THE EGYPT OF THE PTOLEMIES. J. P. Mahaffy.
  VOL. V. ROMAN EGYPT. J. G. Milne.
  VOL. VI. EGYPT IN THE MIDDLE AGES. STANLEY LANE-POOLE.

'A history written in the spirit of scientific precision so worthily represented by Dr. Petrie and his school cannot but promote sound and accurate study, and supply a vacant place in the English literature of Egyptology.'—*Times.*

Flinders Petrie. RELIGION AND CONSCIENCE IN ANCIENT EGYPT. By W. M. FLINDERS PETRIE, D.C.L., LL.D. Fully Illustrated. *Crown 8vo.* 2*s.* 6*d.*
'The lectures will afford a fund of valuable information for students of ancient ethics.'—*Manchester Guardian.*

Flinders Petrie. SYRIA AND EGYPT, FROM THE TELL EL AMARNA TABLETS. By W. M. FLINDERS PETRIE, D.C.L., LL.D. *Crown 8vo.* 2*s.* 6*d.*
'A marvellous record. The addition made to our knowledge is nothing short of amazing.'—*Times.*

Flinders Petrie. EGYPTIAN TALES. Edited by W. M. FLINDERS PETRIE. Illustrated by TRISTRAM ELLIS. *In Two Volumes. Cr. 8vo.* 3*s.* 6*d. each.*
'Invaluable as a picture of life in Palestine and Egypt.'—*Daily News.*

Flinders Petrie. EGYPTIAN DECORATIVE ART. By W. M. FLINDERS PETRIE. With 120 Illustrations. *Cr. 8vo.* 3*s.* 6*d.*
'In these lectures he displays rare skill in elucidating the development of decorative art in Egypt.'—*Times.*

C. W. Oman. A HISTORY OF THE ART OF WAR. Vol. II.: The Middle Ages, from the Fourth to the Fourteenth Century. By C. W. OMAN, M.A., Fellow of All Souls', Oxford. Illustrated. *Demy 8vo.* 21*s.*
'The whole art of war in its historic evolution has never been treated on such an ample and comprehensive scale, and we question if any recent contribution to the exact history of the world has possessed more enduring value.'—*Daily Chronicle.*

S. Baring Gould. THE TRAGEDY OF THE CÆSARS. With numerous Illustrations from Busts, Gems, Cameos, etc. By S. BARING GOULD. *Fifth Edition. Royal 8vo.* 15s.

'A most splendid and fascinating book on a subject of undying interest. The great feature of the book is the use the author has made of the existing portraits of the Caesars and the admirable critical subtlety he has exhibited in dealing with this line of research. It is brilliantly written, and the illustrations are supplied on a scale of profuse magnificence.'—*Daily Chronicle.*

F. W. Maitland. CANON LAW IN ENGLAND. By F. W. MAITLAND, LL.D., Downing Professor of the Laws of England in the University of Cambridge. *Royal 8vo.* 7s. 6d.

'Professor Maitland has put students of English law under a fresh debt. These essays are landmarks in the study of the history of Canon Law.'—*Times.*

John Hackett. A HISTORY OF THE CHURCH OF CYPRUS. By JOHN HACKETT, M.A. With Maps and Illustrations. *Demy 8vo.* 15s. *net.*

A work which brings together all that is known on the subject from the introduction of Christianity to the commencement of the British occupation. A separate division deals with the local Latin Church during the period of the Western Supremacy.

E. L. Taunton. A HISTORY OF THE JESUITS IN ENGLAND. By E. L. TAUNTON. With Illustrations. *Demy 8vo.* 21s. *net.*

'A history of permanent value, which covers ground never properly investigated before, and is replete with the results of original research. A most interesting and careful book.'—*Literature.*

'A volume which will attract considerable attention.'—*Athenæum.*

H. de B. Gibbins. INDUSTRY IN ENGLAND: HISTORICAL OUTLINES. By H. DE B. GIBBINS, Litt.D., M.A. With 5 Maps. *Second Edition. Demy 8vo.* 10s. 6d.

H. E. Egerton. A HISTORY OF BRITISH COLONIAL POLICY. By H. E. EGERTON, M.A. *Demy 8vo.* 12s. 6d.

'It is a good book, distinguished by accuracy in detail, clear arrangement of facts, and a broad grasp of principles.'—*Manchester Guardian.*

Albert Sorel. THE EASTERN QUESTION IN THE EIGHTEENTH CENTURY. By ALBERT SOREL. Translated by F. C. BRAMWELL, M.A. *Cr. 8vo.* 3s. 6d.

C. H. Grinling. A HISTORY OF THE GREAT NORTHERN RAILWAY, 1845-95. By C. H. GRINLING. With Illustrations. *Demy 8vo.* 10s. 6d.

'Mr. Grinling has done for a Railway what Macaulay did for English History.'—*The Engineer.*

Clement Stretton. A HISTORY OF THE MIDLAND RAILWAY. By CLEMENT STRETTON. With numerous Illustrations. *Demy 8vo.* 12s. 6d.

'A fine record of railway development.'—*Outlook.*

'The volume is as exhaustive as it is comprehensive, and is made especially attractive by its pictures.'—*Globe.*

W. Sterry. ANNALS OF ETON COLLEGE. By W. STERRY, M.A. With numerous Illustrations. *Demy 8vo.* 7s. 6d.

'A treasury of quaint and interesting reading. Mr. Sterry has by his skill and vivacity given these records new life.'—*Academy.*

G. W. Fisher. ANNALS OF SHREWSBURY SCHOOL. By G. W. FISHER, M.A. With numerous Illustrations. *Demy 8vo.* 10s. 6d.

'This careful, erudite book.'—*Daily Chronicle.*

'A book of which Old Salopians are sure to be proud.'—*Globe.*

J. Sargeaunt. ANNALS OF WESTMINSTER SCHOOL. By J. SARGEAUNT, M.A. With numerous Illustrations. *Demy 8vo.* 7s. 6d.

A. Clark. THE COLLEGES OF OXFORD: Their History and their Traditions. Edited by A. CLARK, M.A., Fellow of Lincoln College. *8vo.* 12s. 6d.

'A work which will be appealed to for many years as the standard book.'—*Athenæum.*

T. M. Taylor. A CONSTITUTIONAL AND POLITICAL HISTORY OF ROME. By T. M. TAYLOR, M.A., Fellow of Gonville and Caius College, Cambridge. *Crown 8vo. 7s. 6d.*

'We fully recognise the value of this carefully written work, and admire especially the fairness and sobriety of his judgment and the human interest with which he has inspired a subject which in some hands becomes a mere series of cold abstractions. It is a work that will be stimulating to the student of Roman history.'—*Athenæum.*

J. Wells. A SHORT HISTORY OF ROME. By J. WELLS, M.A., Fellow and Tutor of Wadham Coll., Oxford. *Third Edition.* With 3 Maps. *Crown 8vo. 3s. 6d.*

This book is intended for the Middle and Upper Forms of Public Schools and for Pass Students at the Universities. It contains copious Tables, etc.

'An original work written on an original plan, and with uncommon freshness and vigour.'—*Speaker.*

O. Browning. A SHORT HISTORY OF MEDIÆVAL ITALY, A.D. 1250-1530. By OSCAR BROWNING, Fellow and Tutor of King's College, Cambridge. *In Two Volumes. Cr. 8vo. 5s. each.*

VOL. I. 1250-1409.—Guelphs and Ghibellines.

VOL. II. 1409-1530.—The Age of the Condottieri.

O'Grady. THE STORY OF IRELAND. By STANDISH O'GRADY, Author of 'Finn and his Companions.' *Crown 8vo. 2s. 6d.*

Byzantine Texts
Edited by J. B. BURY, M.A., Litt.D.

ZACHARIAH OF MITYLENE. Translated into English by F. J. HAMILTON, D.D., and E. W. BROOKS. *Demy 8vo. 12s. 6d. net.*

EVAGRIUS. Edited by Professor LÉON PARMENTIER and M. BIDEZ. *Demy 8vo. 10s. 6d. net.*

THE HISTORY OF PSELLUS By C. SATHAS. *Demy 8vo. 15s. net.*

Biography

R. L. Stevenson. THE LETTERS OF ROBERT LOUIS STEVENSON TO HIS FAMILY AND FRIENDS. Selected and Edited, with Notes and Introductions, by SIDNEY COLVIN. *Fourth and Cheaper Edition. Crown 8vo. 12s.*
LIBRARY EDITION. *Demy 8vo.* 2 vols. 25s. net.

'Irresistible in their raciness, their variety, their animation . . . of extraordinary fascination. A delightful inheritance, the truest record of a "richly compounded spirit" that the literature of our time has preserved.'—*Times.*

J. G. Millais. THE LIFE AND LETTERS OF SIR JOHN EVERETT MILLAIS, President of the Royal Academy. By his Son, J. G. MILLAIS. With 319 Illustrations, of which 9 are in Photogravure. *Second Edition.* 2 vols. *Royal 8vo.* 32s. net.

'This splendid work.'—*World.*
'Of such absorbing interest is it, of such completeness in scope and beauty. Special tribute must be paid to the extraordinary completeness of the illustrations.'—*Graphic.*

S. Baring Gould. THE LIFE OF NAPOLEON BONAPARTE. By S. BARING GOULD. With over 450 Illustrations in the Text and 12 Photogravure Plates. *Large quarto. Gilt top.* 36s.

'The main feature of this gorgeous volume is its great wealth of beautiful photogravures and finely-executed wood engravings, constituting a complete pictorial chronicle of Napoleon I.'s personal history from the days of his early childhood at Ajaccio to the date of his second interment.'—*Daily Telegraph.*

W. A. Bettesworth. THE WALKERS OF SOUTHGATE: Being the Chronicles of a Cricketing Family. By W. A. BETTESWORTH. Illustrated. *Demy 8vo.* 7s. 6d.

'A most engaging contribution to cricket literature ... a lasting joy.'—*Vanity Fair.*

G. S. Layard. THE LIFE OF MRS. LYNN LINTON. By G. S. LAYARD. With Portraits. *Demy 8vo.* 12s. 6d.

'Mrs. Lynn Linton is here presented to us in all her moods. She lives in the book; she is presented to us so that we really know her.'—*Literature.*

'A thoroughly good book, very interesting, and at the same time in very good taste.'—*Daily Graphic.*

'Mr. Layard may be congratulated on having produced an honest and interesting record of a notable woman.'—*Athenæum.*

Stanley Lane-Poole. THE LIFE OF SIR HARRY PARKES. By STANLEY LANE-POOLE. *A New and Cheaper Edition. Crown 8vo.* 6s.

Helen C. Wetmore. THE LAST OF THE GREAT SCOUTS ('Buffalo Bill'). By his Sister, HELEN C. WETMORE. With Illustrations. *Demy 8vo.* 6s.

'The stirring adventures of Buffalo Bill's career are described vigorously and picturesquely, and with a directness that inspires the fullest confidence.'—*Glasgow Herald.*

'A narrative of one of the most attractive figures in the public eye.'—*Daily Chronicle.*

Constance Bache. BROTHER MUSICIANS. Reminiscences of Edward and Walter Bache. By CONSTANCE BACHE. With Sixteen Illustrations. *Crown 8vo.* 6s. net.

P. H. Colomb. MEMOIRS OF ADMIRAL SIR A. COOPER KEY. By Admiral P. H. COLOMB. With a Portrait. *Demy 8vo.* 16s.

C. Cooper King. THE STORY OF THE BRITISH ARMY. By Colonel COOPER KING. Illustrated. *Demy 8vo.* 7s. 6d.

'An authoritative and accurate story of England's military progress.'—*Daily Mail.*

R. Southey. ENGLISH SEAMEN (Howard, Clifford, Hawkins, Drake, Cavendish). By ROBERT SOUTHEY. Edited, with an Introduction, by DAVID HANNAY. *Second Edition. Crown 8vo.* 6s.

'A brave, inspiriting book.'—*Black and White.*

W. Clark Russell. THE LIFE OF ADMIRAL LORD COLLINGWOOD. By W. CLARK RUSSELL. With Illustrations by F. BRANGWYN. *Fourth Edition. Crown 8vo.* 6s.

'A book which we should like to see in the hands of every boy in the country.'—*St. James's Gazette.*

Morris Fuller. THE LIFE AND WRITINGS OF JOHN DAVENANT, D.D. (1571-1641), Bishop of Salisbury. By MORRIS FULLER, B.D. *Demy 8vo.* 10s. 6d.

J. M. Rigg. ST. ANSELM OF CANTERBURY: A CHAPTER IN THE HISTORY OF RELIGION. By J. M. RIGG. *Demy 8vo.* 7s. 6d.

F. W. Joyce. THE LIFE OF SIR FREDERICK GORE OUSELEY. By F. W. JOYCE, M.A. 7s. 6d.

W. G. Collingwood. THE LIFE OF JOHN RUSKIN. By W. G. COLLINGWOOD, M.A. With Portraits, and 13 Drawings by Mr. Ruskin. *Second Edition.* 2 vols. *8vo.* 32s. *Cheap Edition. Crown 8vo.* 6s.

C. Waldstein. JOHN RUSKIN. By CHARLES WALDSTEIN, M.A. With a Photogravure Portrait, *Post 8vo.* 5s.

A. M. F. Darmesteter. THE LIFE OF ERNEST RENAN. By MADAME DARMESTETER. With Portrait. *Second Edition. Cr. 8vo.* 6s.

W. H. Hutton. THE LIFE OF SIR THOMAS MORE. By W. H. HUTTON, M.A. With Portraits. *Second Edition. Cr. 8vo.* 5s.

'The book lays good claim to high rank among our biographies. It is excellently, even lovingly, written.'—*Scotsman.*

S. Baring Gould. THE VICAR OF MORWENSTOW: A Biography. By S. BARING GOULD, M.A. A new and Revised Edition. With Portrait. *Crown 8vo.* 3s. 6d.

A completely new edition of the well known biography of R. S. Hawker.

Travel, Adventure and Topography

Sven Hedin. THROUGH ASIA. By SVEN HEDIN, Gold Medallist of the Royal Geographical Society. With 300 Illustrations from Sketches and Photographs by the Author, and Maps. 2 *vols. Royal* 8*vo.* 20*s. net.*

'One of the greatest books of the kind issued during the century. It is impossible to give an adequate idea of the richness of the contents of this book, nor of its abounding attractions as a story of travel unsurpassed in geographical and human interest. Much of it is a revelation. Altogether the work is one which in solidity, novelty, and interest must take a first rank among publications of its class.'—*Times.*

F. H. Skrine and E. D. Ross. THE HEART OF ASIA. By F. H. SKRINE and E. D. ROSS. With Maps and many Illustrations by VERESTCHAGIN. *Large Crown* 8*vo.* 10*s.* 6*d. net.*

'This volume will form a landmark in our knowledge of Central Asia. . . . Illuminating and convincing.'—*Times.*

R. E. Peary. NORTHWARD OVER THE GREAT ICE. By R. E. PEARY, Gold Medallist of the Royal Geographical Society. With over 800 Illustrations. 2 *vols. Royal* 8*vo.* 32*s. net.*

'His book will take its place among the permanent literature of Arctic exploration.' —*Times.*

T. H. Holdich. THE INDIAN BORDERLAND: being a Personal Record of Twenty Years. By Sir T. H. Holdich, K.C.I.E. Illustrated. *Demy* 8*vo.* 15*s. net.*

'Probably the most important work on frontier topography that has lately been presented to the general public.'—*Literature.*

'Interesting and inspiriting from cover to cover, it will assuredly take its place as the classical on the history of the Indian frontier.'—*Pilot.*

'A work that should long remain the standard authority.'—*Daily Chronicle.*

A. B. Wylde. MODERN ABYSSINIA. By A. B. WYLDE. With a Map and a Portrait. *Demy* 8*vo.* 15*s. net.*

'The most valuable contribution that has yet been made to our knowledge of Abyssinia.'—*Manchester Guardian.*

'A book which will rank among the very best of African works.'—*Daily Chronicle.*

'A repertory of information on every branch of the subject.'—*Literature.*

Alex. Hosie. MANCHURIA. By ALEXANDER HOSIE. With Illustrations and a Map. *Demy* 8*vo.* 10*s.* 6*d. net.*

A complete account of this important province by the highest living authority on the subject.

'This book is especially useful at the present moment when the future of the country appears uncertain.'—*Times.*

E. A. FitzGerald. THE HIGHEST ANDES. By E. A. FITZGERALD. With 2 Maps, 51 Illustrations, 13 of which are in Photogravure, and a Panorama. *Royal* 8*vo,* 30*s. net.* Also a Small Edition on Hand-made Paper, limited to 50 Copies, 4*to,* £5, 5*s.*

'The record of the first ascent of the highest mountain yet conquered by mortal man. A volume which will continue to be the classic book of travel on this region of the Andes.'—*Daily Chronicle.*

F. W. Christian. THE CAROLINE ISLANDS. By F. W. CHRISTIAN. With many Illustrations and Maps. *Demy* 8*vo.* 12*s.* 6*d. net.*

'A real contribution to our knowledge of the peoples and islands of Micronesia, as well as fascinating as a narrative of travels and adventure.'—*Scotsman.*

H. H. Johnston. BRITISH CENTRAL AFRICA. By Sir H. H. JOHNSTON, K.C.B. With nearly Two Hundred Illustrations, and Six Maps. *Second Edition. Crown* 4*to.* 18*s. net.*

'A fascinating book, written with equal skill and charm—the work at once of a literary artist and of a man of action who is singularly wise, brave, and experienced. It abounds in admirable sketches.'—*Westminster Gazette.*

L. Decle. THREE YEARS IN SAVAGE AFRICA. By LIONEL DECLE. With 100 Illustrations and 5 Maps. *Second Edition. Demy* 8*vo.* 10*s.* 6*d. net.*

A. Hulme Beaman. TWENTY YEARS IN THE NEAR EAST. By A. HULME BEAMAN. *Demy 8vo.* With Portrait. 10s. 6d.

Henri of Orleans. FROM TONKIN TO INDIA. By PRINCE HENRI OF ORLEANS. Translated by HAMLEY BENT, M.A. With 100 Illustrations and a Map. *Cr. 4to, gilt top.* 25s.

Chester Holcombe. THE REAL CHINESE QUESTION. By CHESTER HOLCOMBE. *Crown 8vo.* 6s.

'It is an important addition to the materials before the public for forming an opinion on a most difficult and pressing problem.'—*Times.*

'It is this practical "note" in the book, coupled with the fairness, moderation, and sincerity of the author, that gives it, in our opinion, the highest place among books published in recent years on the Chinese question.'—*Manchester Guardian.*

J. W. Robertson-Scott. THE PEOPLE OF CHINA. By J. W. ROBERTSON-SCOTT. With a Map. *Crown 8vo.* 3s. 6d.

'A vivid impression . . . This excellent, brightly written epitome.'—*Daily News.*
'Excellently well done. . . . Enthralling.'—*Weekly Dispatch.*

S. L. Hinde. THE FALL OF THE CONGO ARABS. By S. L. HINDE. With Plans, etc. *Demy 8vo.* 12s. 6d.

A. St. H. Gibbons. EXPLORATION AND HUNTING IN CENTRAL AFRICA. By Major A. ST. H. GIBBONS. With full-page Illustrations by C. WHYMPER, and Maps. *Demy 8vo.* 15s.

A. H. Norway. NAPLES: PAST AND PRESENT. By A. H. NORWAY, Author of 'Highways and Byways in Devon and Cornwall.' With 40 Illustrations by A. G. FERARD. *Crown 8vo.* 6s.

In this book Mr. Norway gives not only a highly interesting description of modern Naples, but a historical account of its antiquities and traditions.

S. Baring Gould. DARTMOOR: A Descriptive and Historical Sketch. By S. BARING GOULD. With Plans and Numerous Illustrations. *Crown 8vo.* 6s.

'A most delightful guide, companion, and instructor.'—*Scotsman.*
'Informed with close personal knowledge.'—*Saturday Review.*

S. Baring Gould. THE BOOK OF THE WEST. By S. BARING GOULD. With numerous Illustrations. *Two volumes.* Vol. I. Devon. Second Edition. Vol. II. Cornwall. *Crown 8vo.* 6s. *each.*

'Bracing as the air of Dartmoor, the legend weird as twilight over Dozmare Pool, they give us a very good idea of this enchanting and beautiful district.'—*Guardian.*

S. Baring Gould. A BOOK OF BRITTANY. By S. BARING GOULD. With numerous Illustrations. *Crown 8vo.* 6s.

Uniform in scope and size with Mr. Baring Gould's well-known books on Devon, Cornwall, and Dartmoor.

S. Baring Gould. THE DESERTS OF SOUTHERN FRANCE. By S. BARING GOULD. 2 *vols. Demy 8vo.* 32s.

J. F. Fraser. ROUND THE WORLD ON A WHEEL. By JOHN FOSTER FRASER. With 100 Illustrations. *Crown 8vo.* 6s.

'A classic of cycling, graphic and witty.'—*Yorkshire Post.*

R. L. Jefferson. A NEW RIDE TO KHIVA. By R. L. JEFFERSON. Illustrated. *Crown 8vo.* 6s.

J. K. Trotter. THE NIGER SOURCES. By Colonel J. K. TROTTER, R.A. With a Map and Illustrations. *Crown 8vo.* 5s.

W. Crooke. THE NORTH-WESTERN PROVINCES OF INDIA: THEIR ETHNOLOGY AND ADMINISTRATION. By W. CROOKE. With Maps and Illustrations. *Demy 8vo.* 10s. 6d.

A. Boisragon. THE BENIN MASSACRE. By CAPTAIN BOISRAGON. Second Edition. *Cr. 8vo.* 3s. 6d.

H. S. Cowper. THE HILL OF THE GRACES: OR, THE GREAT STONE TEMPLES OF TRIPOLI. By H. S. COWPER, F.S.A. With Maps, Plans, and 75 Illustrations. *Demy 8vo.* 10s. 6d.

W. B. Worsfold. SOUTH AFRICA. By W. B. WORSFOLD, M.A. With a Map. *Second Edition*. *Cr. 8vo.* 6s.
'A monumental work compressed into a very moderate compass.'—*World.*

Katherine and Gilbert Macquoid. IN PARIS. By KATHERINE and GILBERT MACQUOID. Illustrated by THOMAS R. MACQUOID, R.I. With 2 maps. *Crown 8vo.* 1s.
'A useful little guide, judiciously supplied with information.'—*Athenæum.*

A. H. Keane. THE BOER STATES: A History and Description of the Transvaal and the Orange Free State. By A. H. KEANE, M.A. With Map. *Crown 8vo.* 6s.

Naval and Military

F. H. E. Cunliffe. THE HISTORY OF THE BOER WAR. By F. H. E. CUNLIFFE, Fellow of All Souls' College, Oxford. With many Illustrations, Plans, and Portraits. *In 2 vols. Vol. I.*, 15s.
'The excellence of the work is double ; for the narrative is vivid and temperate, and the illustrations form a picture gallery of the war which is not likely to be rivalled. ... An ideal gift book.'—*Academy.*

G. S. Robertson. CHITRAL: The Story of a Minor Siege. By Sir G. S. ROBERTSON, K.C.S.I. With numerous Illustrations, Map and Plans. *Second Edition. Demy 8vo.* 10s. 6d.
'A book which the Elizabethans would have thought wonderful. More thrilling, more piquant, and more human than any novel.'—*Newcastle Chronicle.*
'As fascinating as Sir Walter Scott's best fiction.'—*Daily Telegraph.*

R. S. S. Baden-Powell. THE DOWNFALL OF PREMPEH. A Diary of Life in Ashanti, 1895. By Maj.-Gen. BADEN-POWELL. With 21 Illustrations and a Map. *Third Edition. Large Crown 8vo.* 6s.

R. S. S. Baden-Powell. THE MATABELE CAMPAIGN, 1896. By Maj.-Gen. BADEN-POWELL. With nearly 100 Illustrations. *Fourth and Cheaper Edition. Large Crown 8vo.* 6s.

J. B. Atkins. THE RELIEF OF LADYSMITH. By JOHN BLACK ATKINS. With 16 Plans and Illustrations. *Third Edition. Crown 8vo.* 6s.

H. W. Nevinson. LADYSMITH: The Diary of a Siege. By H. W. NEVINSON. With 16 Illustrations and a Plan. *Second Edition. Crown 8vo.* 6s.

Barclay Lloyd. A THOUSAND MILES WITH THE C.I.V. By Captain BARCLAY LLOYD. With an Introduction by Colonel MACKINNON, and a Portrait and Map. *Crown 8vo.* 6s.

Filson Young. THE RELIEF OF MAFEKING. By FILSON YOUNG. With Maps and Illustrations. *Crown 8vo.* 6s.

J. Angus Hamilton. THE SIEGE OF MAFEKING. By J. ANGUS HAMILTON. With many Illustrations. *Crown 8vo.* 6s.
'A thrilling story.'—*Observer.*

H. F. Prevost Battersby. IN THE WEB OF A WAR. By H. F. PREVOST BATTERSBY. With Plans, and Portrait of the Author. *Crown 8vo.* 6s.
'The pathos, the comedy, the majesty of war are all in these pages.'—*Daily Mail.*

Howard C. Hillegas. WITH THE BOER FORCES. By HOWARD C. HILLEGAS. With 24 Illustrations. *Second Edition. Crown 8vo.* 6s.
'A most interesting book. It has many and great merits.'—*Athenæum.*
'Has extreme interest and scarcely less value.'—*Pall Mall Gazette.*

H. C. J. Biss. THE RELIEF OF KUMASI. By Captain H. C. J. BISS. With Maps and Illustrations. *Second Edition. Crown 8vo.* 6s.
'Pleasantly written and highly interesting. The illustrations are admirable.'—*Queen.*
'We should say it will remain the standard work on its very interesting subject.'—*Globe.*

E. H. Alderson. WITH THE MOUNTED INFANTRY AND THE MASHONALAND FIELD FORCE, 1896. By Lieut.-Colonel ALDERSON. With numerous Illustrations and Plans. *Demy 8vo.* 10s. 6d.

Seymour Vandeleur. CAMPAIGNING ON THE UPPER NILE AND NIGER. By Lieut. SEYMOUR VANDELEUR. With an Introduction by Sir G. GOLDIE, K.C.M.G. With 4 Maps, Illustrations, and Plans. *Large Crown 8vo.* 10s. 6d.

Lord Fincastle. A FRONTIER CAMPAIGN. By Viscount FINCASTLE, V.C., and Lieut. P. C. ELLIOTT-LOCKHART. With a Map and 16 Illustrations. *Second Edition. Crown 8vo.* 6s.

E. N. Bennett. THE DOWNFALL OF THE DERVISHES: A Sketch of the Sudan Campaign of 1898. By E. N. BENNETT, Fellow of Hertford College. With a Photogravure Portrait of Lord Kitchener. *Third Edition. Crown 8vo.* 3s. 6d.

W. Kinnaird Rose. WITH THE GREEKS IN THESSALY. By W. KINNAIRD ROSE. With Illustrations. *Crown 8vo.* 6s.

G. W. Steevens. NAVAL POLICY: By G. W. STEEVENS. *Demy 8vo.* 6s.

D. Hannay. A SHORT HISTORY OF THE ROYAL NAVY, FROM EARLY TIMES TO THE PRESENT DAY. By DAVID HANNAY. Illustrated. 2 *Vols. Demy 8vo.* 7s. 6d. *each.* Vol. I., 1200-1688.
'We read it from cover to cover at a sitting, and those who go to it for a lively and brisk picture of the past, with all its faults and its grandeur, will not be disappointed. The historian is endowed with literary skill and style.'—*Standard.*

E. L. S. Horsburgh. WATERLOO: A Narrative and Criticism. By E. L. S. HORSBURGH, M.A. With Plans. *Second Edition. Crown 8vo.* 5s.
'A brilliant essay—simple, sound, and thorough.'—*Daily Chronicle.*

H. B. George. BATTLES OF ENGLISH HISTORY By H. B. GEORGE, M.A., Fellow of New College, Oxford. With numerous Plans. *Third Edition. Cr. 8vo.* 6s.
'Mr. George has undertaken a very useful task—that of making military affairs intelligible and instructive to non-military readers—and has executed it with a large measure of success.'—*Times.*

General Literature

S. Baring Gould. OLD COUNTRY LIFE. By S. BARING GOULD. With Sixty-seven Illustrations. *Large Cr. 8vo. Fifth Edition.* 6s.
'"Old Country Life," as healthy wholesome reading, full of breezy life and movement, full of quaint stories vigorously told, will not be excelled by any book to be published throughout the year. Sound, hearty, and English to the core.' —*World.*

S. Baring Gould. AN OLD ENGLISH HOME. By S. BARING GOULD. With numerous Plans and Illustrations. *Crown 8vo.* 6s.
'The chapters are delightfully fresh, very informing, and lightened by many a good story. A delightful fireside companion.' —*St. James's Gazette.*

S. Baring Gould. HISTORIC ODDITIES AND STRANGE EVENTS. By S. BARING GOULD. *Fifth Edition. Crown 8vo.* 6s.

S. Baring Gould. FREAKS OF FANATICISM. By S. BARING GOULD. *Third Edition. Cr. 8vo.* 6s.

S. Baring Gould. A GARLAND OF COUNTRY SONG: English Folk Songs with their Traditional Melodies. Collected and arranged by S. BARING GOULD and H. F. SHEPPARD. *Demy 4to.* 6s.

S. Baring Gould. SONGS OF THE WEST: Traditional Ballads and Songs of the West of England, with their Melodies. Collected by S.

Baring Gould, M.A., and H. F. Sheppard, M.A. In 4 Parts. *Parts I., II., III.,* 3s. *each. Part IV.,* 5s. *In one Vol., French morocco,* 15s.

'A rich collection of humour, pathos, grace, and poetic fancy.'—*Saturday Review.*

S. Baring Gould. YORKSHIRE ODDITIES AND STRANGE EVENTS. By S. BARING GOULD. *Fifth Edition. Crown 8vo.* 6s.

S. Baring Gould. STRANGE SURVIVALS AND SUPERSTITIONS. By S. BARING GOULD. *Cr. 8vo. Second Edition.* 6s.

Marie Corelli. THE PASSING OF THE GREAT QUEEN: A Tribute to the Noble Life of Victoria Regina. By MARIE CORELLI. *Small 4to.* 1s.

Cotton Minchin. OLD HARROW DAYS. By J. G. COTTON MINCHIN. *Cr. 8vo. Second Edition.* 5s.

W. E. Gladstone. THE SPEECHES OF THE RT. HON. W. E. GLADSTONE, M.P. Edited by A. W. HUTTON, M.A., and H. J. COHEN, M.A. With Portraits. *Demy 8vo. Vols. IX. and X.,* 12s. 6d. *each.*

M. N. Oxford. A HANDBOOK OF NURSING. By M. N. OXFORD, of Guy's Hospital. *Crown 8vo.* 3s. 6d.

'The most useful work of the kind that we have seen. A most valuable and practical manual.'—*Manchester Guardian.*

E. V. Zenker. ANARCHISM. By E. V. ZENKER. *Demy 8vo.* 7s. 6d.

Emily Lawless. A GARDEN DIARY. By the Hon. EMILY LAWLESS. *Demy 8vo.* 7s. 6d. *net.*

S. J. Duncan. ON THE OTHER SIDE OF THE LATCH. By SARA JEANNETTE DUNCAN (Mrs. COTES), Author of 'A Voyage of Consolation.' *Crown 8vo.* 6s

W. Williamson. THE BRITISH GARDENER. By W. WILLIAMSON. Illustrated. *Demy 8vo.* 10s. 6d.

Arnold White. EFFICIENCY AND EMPIRE. By ARNOLD WHITE. *Crown 8vo.* 6s.

'Stimulating and entertaining throughout, it deserves the attention of every patriotic Englishman.'—*Daily Mail.*

'A notable book.'—*Literature.*

'A book of sound work, deep thought, and a sincere endeavour to rouse the British to a knowledge of the value of their Empire.'—*Bookman.*

'A more vigorous work has not been written for many years.'—*Review of the Week.*

A. Silva White. THE EXPANSION OF EGYPT: A Political and Historical Survey. By A. SILVA WHITE. With four Special Maps. *Demy 8vo.* 15s. *net.*

'This is emphatically the best account of Egypt as it is under English control that has been published for many years.'—*Spectator.*

Chas. Richardson. THE ENGLISH TURF. By CHARLES RICHARDSON. With numerous Illustrations and Plans. *Demy 8vo.* 15s.

'As a record of horses and courses, this work is a valuable addition to the literature of the Turf. It is crammed with sound information, and with reflections and suggestions that are born of a thorough knowledge of the subject.'—*Scotsman.*

'A book which is sure to find many readers; written with consummate knowledge and in an easy, agreeable style.'—*Daily Chronicle.*

'From its sensible introduction to its very complex index, this is about the best book that we are likely for some time to see upon the subject with which it deals.'—*Athenæum.*

Philip Trevor. THE LIGHTER SIDE OF CRICKET. By Captain PHILIP TREVOR (DUX). *Crown 8vo.* 6s.

A highly interesting volume, dealing with such subjects as county cricket, village cricket, cricket for boys and girls, literary cricket, and various other subjects which do not require a severe and technical treatment.

'A wholly entertaining book.'—*Glasgow Herald.*

'The most welcome book on our national game published for years.'—*County Gentleman.*

Peter Beckford. THOUGHTS ON HUNTING. By PETER BECKFORD. Edited by J. OTHO PAGET, and Illustrated by G. H. JALLAND. *Demy 8vo.* 10s. 6d.

'Beckford's "Thoughts on Hunting" has

long been a classic with sportsmen, and the present edition will go far to make it a favourite with lovers of literature.'—*Speaker.*

E. B. Michell. THE ART AND PRACTICE OF HAWKING. By E. B. MICHELL. With 3 Photogravures by G. E. LODGE, and other Illustrations. *Demy 8vo.* 10*s.* 6*d.*
'No book is more full and authoritative than this handsome treatise.'
—*Morning Leader.*

H. G. Hutchinson. THE GOLFING PILGRIM. By HORACE G. HUTCHINSON. *Crown 8vo.* 6*s.*
'Without this book the golfer's library will be incomplete.'—*Pall Mall Gazette.*

J. Wells. OXFORD AND OXFORD LIFE. By Members of the University. Edited by J. WELLS, M.A., Fellow and Tutor of Wadham College. *Third Edition. Cr. 8vo.* 3*s.* 6*d.*

C. G. Robertson. VOCES ACADEMICÆ. By C. GRANT ROBERTSON, M.A., Fellow of All Souls', Oxford. With a Frontispiece. *Pott 8vo.* 3*s.* 6*d.*
'Decidedly clever and amusing.'—*Athenæum.*

Rosemary Cotes. DANTE'S GARDEN. By ROSEMARY COTES. With a Frontispiece. *Second Edition. Fcp. 8vo.* 2*s.* 6*d. Leather,* 3*s.* 6*d. net.*
'A charming collection of legends of the flowers mentioned by Dante.'—*Academy.*

Clifford Harrison. READING AND READERS. By CLIFFORD HARRISON. *Fcp. 8vo.* 2*s.* 6*d.*
'An extremely sensible little book.'—*Manchester Guardian.*

L. Whibley. GREEK OLIGARCHIES: THEIR ORGANISATION AND CHARACTER. By L. WHIBLEY, M.A., Fellow of Pembroke College, Cambridge. *Crown 8vo.* 6*s.*

L. L. Price. ECONOMIC SCIENCE AND PRACTICE. By L. L. PRICE, M.A., Fellow of Oriel College, Oxford. *Crown 8vo.* 6*s.*

J. S. Shedlock. THE PIANOFORTE SONATA: Its Origin and Development. By J. S. SHEDLOCK. *Crown 8vo.* 5*s.*
'This work should be in the possession of every musician and amateur. A concise and lucid history and a very valuable work for reference.'—*Athenæum.*

A. Hulme Beaman. PONS ASINORUM; OR, A GUIDE TO BRIDGE. By A. HULME BEAMAN. *Fcap 8vo.* 2*s.*
A practical guide, with many specimen games, to the new game of Bridge.

E. M. Bowden. THE EXAMPLE OF BUDDHA: Being Quotations from Buddhist Literature for each Day in the Year. Compiled by E. M. BOWDEN. *Third Edition.* 16*mo.* 2*s.* 6*d.*

F. Ware. EDUCATIONAL REFORM. By FABIAN WARE, M.A. *Crown 8vo.* 2*s.* 6*d.*

Sidney Peel. PRACTICAL LICENSING REFORM. By the Hon SIDNEY PEEL, late Fellow of Trinity College, Oxford, and Secretary to the Royal Commission on the Licensing Laws. *Crown 8vo.* 1*s.* 6*d.*

Philosophy

L. T. Hobhouse. THE THEORY OF KNOWLEDGE. By L. T. HOBHOUSE, Fellow of C.C.C., Oxford. *Demy 8vo.* 21*s.*
'The most important contribution to English philosophy since the publication of Mr. Bradley's "Appearance and Reality."'—*Glasgow Herald.*

W. H. Fairbrother. THE PHILOSOPHY OF T. H. GREEN. By W. H. FAIRBROTHER, M.A. *Second Edition. Cr. 8vo.* 3*s.* 6*d.*

'In every way an admirable book.'—*Glasgow Herald.*

F. W. Bussell. THE SCHOOL OF PLATO. By F. W. BUSSELL, D.D., Fellow of Brasenose College, Oxford. *Demy 8vo.* 10*s.* 6*d.*

F. S. Granger. THE WORSHIP OF THE ROMANS. By F. S. GRANGER, M.A., Litt.D. *Crown 8vo.* 6*s.*

Science

E. H. Colbeck. DISEASES OF THE HEART. By E. H. COLBECK, M.D. With numerous Illustrations. *Demy 8vo.* 12s.

W. C. C. Pakes. THE SCIENCE OF HYGIENE. By W. C. C. PAKES. With numerous Illustrations. *Demy 8vo.* 15s.

'A thoroughgoing working text-book of its subject, practical and well-stocked.' —*Scotsman.*

A. T. Hare. THE CONSTRUCTION OF LARGE INDUCTION COILS. By A. T. HARE, M.A. With numerous Diagrams. *Demy 8vo.* 6s.

J. E. Marr. THE SCIENTIFIC STUDY OF SCENERY. By J. E. MARR, F.R.S., Fellow of St. John's College, Cambridge. Illustrated. *Crown 8vo.* 6s.

'A volume, moderate in size and readable in style, which will be acceptable alike to the student of geology and geography, and to the tourist.'—*Athenæum.*

J. Ritzema Bos. AGRICULTURAL ZOOLOGY. By Dr. J. RITZEMA BOS. Translated by J. R. AINSWORTH DAVIS, M.A. With an Introduction by ELEANOR A. ORMEROD, F.E.S. With 155 Illustrations. *Crown 8vo.* 3s. 6d.

'The illustrations are exceedingly good, whilst the information conveyed is invaluable.'—*Country Gentleman.*

Ed. von Freudenreich. DAIRY BACTERIOLOGY. A Short Manual for the Use of Students. By Dr. ED. VON FREUDENREICH, Translated by J. R. AINSWORTH DAVIS, M.A. *Second Edition, Revised. Crown 8vo.* 2s. 6d.

Chalmers Mitchell. OUTLINES OF BIOLOGY. By P. CHALMERS MITCHELL, M.A. *Illustrated. Cr. 8vo.* 6s.

A text-book designed to cover the new Schedule issued by the Royal College of Physicians and Surgeons.

George Massee. A MONOGRAPH OF THE MYXOGASTRES. By GEORGE MASSEE. With 12 Coloured Plates. *Royal 8vo.* 18s. net.

'A work much in advance of any book in the language treating of this group of organisms. Indispensable to every student of the Myxogastres.'—*Nature.*

C. Stephenson and F. Suddards. ORNAMENTAL DESIGN FOR WOVEN FABRICS. By C. STEPHENSON, of the Technical College, Bradford, and F. SUDDARDS, of the Yorkshire College, Leeds. With 65 full-page plates. *Demy 8vo. Second Edition.* 7s. 6d.

'The book is very ably done, displaying an intimate knowledge of principles, good taste, and the faculty of clear exposition.'—*Yorkshire Post.*

C. C. Channer and M. E. Roberts. LACE-MAKING IN THE MIDLANDS, PAST AND PRESENT. By C. C. CHANNER and M. E. ROBERTS. With 16 full-page Illustrations. *Crown 8vo.* 2s. 6d.

'An interesting book, illustrated by fascinating photographs.'—*Speaker.*

Theology

W. R. Inge. CHRISTIAN MYSTICISM. The Bampton Lectures for 1899. By W. R. INGE, M.A., Fellow and Tutor of Hertford College, Oxford. *Demy 8vo.* 12s. 6d. net.

'It is fully worthy of the best traditions connected with the Bampton Lectureship.'—*Record.*

Lady Julian of Norwich. REVELATIONS OF DIVINE LOVE. By the LADY JULIAN of Norwich. Edited by GRACE WARRACK. *Crown 8vo.* 6s.

A partially modernised version, from the MS. in the British Museum of a book which Dr. Dalgairns terms 'One of the most remarkable books of the Middle Ages.' Mr. Inge in his Bampton Lectures on Christian Mysticism calls it 'The beautiful but little known *Revelations*.'

R. M. Benson. THE WAY OF HOLINESS: a Devotional Commentary on the 119th Psalm. By R. M. BENSON, M.A., of the Cowley Mission, Oxford. *Crown 8vo.* 5s.

'His facility is delightful, and his very sound and accurate theological sense saves him from many of the obvious dangers of such a gift. Give him a word or a number and at once there springs fort · a fertile stream of thought, never commonplace, usually both deep and fresh. For devotional purposes we think this book most valuable. Readers will find a great wealth of thought if they use the book simply as a help to meditation.'—*Guardian*.

Jacob Behmen. THE SUPERSENSUAL LIFE. By JACOB BEHMEN. Edited by BERNARD HOLLAND. *Fcap 8vo.* 3s. 6d.

S. R. Driver. SERMONS ON SUBJECTS CONNECTED WITH THE OLD TESTAMENT. By S. R. DRIVER, D.D., Canon of Christ Church, Regius Professor of Hebrew in the University of Oxford. *Cr. 8vo.* 6s.

'A welcome companion to the author's famous "Introduction."'—*Guardian*.

T. K. Cheyne. FOUNDERS OF OLD TESTAMENT CRITICISM. By T. K. CHEYNE, D.D., Oriel Professor at Oxford. *Large Crown 8vo.* 7s. 6d.

A historical sketch of O. T. Criticism.

Walter Lock. ST. PAUL, THE MASTER-BUILDER. By WALTER LOCK, D.D., Warden of Keble College. *Crown 8vo.* 3s. 6d.

'The essence of the Pauline teaching is condensed into little more than a hundred pages, yet no point of importance is overlooked.'—*Guardian*.

F. S. Granger. THE SOUL OF A CHRISTIAN. By F. S. GRANGER, M.A., Litt.D. *Crown 8vo.* 6s.

A book dealing with the evolution of the religious life and experiences.

'A remarkable book.'—*Glasgow Herald*.
'Both a scholarly and thoughtful book.'—*Scotsman*.

H. Rashdall. DOCTRINE AND DEVELOPMENT. By HASTINGS RASHDALL, M.A., Fellow and Tutor of New College, Oxford. *Cr. 8vo.* 6s.

H. H. Henson. APOSTOLIC CHRISTIANITY: As Illustrated by the Epistles of St. Paul to the Corinthians. By H. H. HENSON, M.A., Fellow of All Souls', Oxford, Canon of Westminster. *Cr. 8vo.* 6s.

H. H. Henson. DISCIPLINE AND LAW. By H. HENSLEY HENSON, M.A., Fellow of All Souls', Oxford. *Fcap. 8vo.* 2s. 6d.

H. H. Henson. LIGHT AND LEAVEN : HISTORICAL AND SOCIAL SERMONS. By H. H. HENSON, M.A. *Crown 8vo.* 6s.

J. Houghton Kennedy. ST. PAUL'S SECOND AND THIRD EPISTLES TO THE CORINTHIANS. With Introduction, Dissertations, and Notes, by JAMES HOUGHTON KENNEDY, D.D., Assistant Lecturer in Divinity in the University of Dublin. *Crown 8vo.* 6s.

Bennett and Adeney. A BIBLICAL INTRODUCTION. By W. H. BENNETT, M.A., and W. F. ADENEY, M.A. *Crown 8vo.* 7s. 6d.

'It makes available to the ordinary reader the best scholarship of the day in the field of Biblical introduction. We know of no book which comes into competition with it.'—*Manchester Guardian*.

W. H. Bennett. A PRIMER OF THE BIBLE. By W. H. BENNETT. *Second Edition. Cr. 8vo.* 2s. 6d.

'The work of an honest, fearless, and sound critic, and an excellent guide in a small compass to the books of the Bible.'—*Manchester Guardian*.

C. F. G. Masterman. TENNYSON AS A RELIGIOUS TEACHER. By C. F. G. MASTERMAN. *Crown 8vo.* 6s.

'A thoughtful and penetrating appreciation, full of interest and suggestion.'—*World*.

Messrs. Methuen's Catalogue 29

William Harrison. CLOVELLY SERMONS. By WILLIAM HARRISON, M.A., late Rector of Clovelly. With a Preface by 'LUCAS MALET.' *Cr. 8vo.* 3*s.* 6*d.*

Cecilia Robinson. THE MINISTRY OF DEACONESSES. By Deaconess CECILIA ROBINSON. With an Introduction by the Lord Bishop of Winchester. *Cr. 8vo.* 3*s.* 6*d.*

'A learned and interesting book.'—*Scotsman.*

E. B. Layard. RELIGION IN BOYHOOD. Notes on the Religious Training of Boys. By E. B. LAYARD, M.A. 18*mo.* 1*s.*

T. Herbert Bindley. THE OECUMENICAL DOCUMENTS OF THE FAITH. Edited with Introductions and Notes by T. HERBERT BINDLEY, B.D., Merton College, Oxford. *Crown 8vo.* 6*s.*

A historical account of the Creeds.

H. M. Barron. TEXTS FOR SERMONS ON VARIOUS OCCASIONS AND SUBJECTS. Compiled and Arranged by H. M. BARRON, B.A., of Wadham College, Oxford, with a Preface by Canon SCOTT HOLLAND. *Crown 8vo.* 3*s.* 6*d.*

W. Yorke Fausset. THE *DE CATECHIZANDIS RUDIBUS* OF ST. AUGUSTINE. Edited, with Introduction, Notes, etc., by W. YORKE FAUSSET, M.A. *Cr. 8vo.* 3*s.* 6*d.*

J. H. Burn. THE SOUL'S PILGRIMAGE: Devotional Readings from the published and unpublished writings of GEORGE BODY, D.D. Selected and arranged by J. H. BURN, B.D. *Pott 8vo.* 2*s.* 6*d.*

F. Weston. THE HOLY SACRIFICE. By F. WESTON, M.A., Curate of St. Matthew's, Westminster. *Pott 8vo.* 6*d. net.*

À Kempis. THE IMITATION OF CHRIST. By THOMAS À KEMPIS. With an Introduction by DEAN FARRAR. Illustrated by C. M. GERE. *Second Edition. Fcap. 8vo.* 3*s.* 6*d. Padded morocco,* 5*s.*

'Amongst all the innumerable English editions of the "Imitation," there can have been few which were prettier than this one, printed in strong and handsome type, with all the glory of red initials.'—*Glasgow Herald.*

J. Keble. THE CHRISTIAN YEAR. By JOHN KEBLE. With an Introduction and Notes by W. LOCK, D.D., Warden of Keble College. Illustrated by R. ANNING BELL. *Second Edition. Fcap. 8vo.* 3*s.* 6*d. Padded morocco,* 5*s.*

'The present edition is annotated with all the care and insight to be expected from Mr. Lock.'—*Guardian.*

Oxford Commentaries

General Editor, WALTER LOCK, D.D., Warden of Keble College, Dean Ireland's Professor of Exegesis in the University of Oxford.

THE BOOK OF JOB. Edited, with Introduction and Notes, by E. C. S. GIBSON, D.D., Vicar of Leeds. *Demy 8vo.* 6*s.*

'The publishers are to be congratulated on the start the series has made.'—*Times.*

'Dr. Gibson's work is worthy of a high degree of appreciation. To the busy worker and the intelligent student the commentary will be a real boon; and it will, if we are not mistaken, be much in demand. The Introduction is almost a model of concise, straightforward, prefatory remarks on the subject treated.'—*Athenæum.*

Handbooks of Theology

General Editor, A. ROBERTSON, D.D., Principal of King's College, London.

THE XXXIX. ARTICLES OF THE CHURCH OF ENGLAND. Edited with an Introduction by E. C. S. GIBSON, D.D., Vicar of Leeds, late Principal of Wells Theological College. *Second and Cheaper Edition in One Volume. Demy 8vo.* 12*s.* 6*d.*

'We welcome with the utmost satisfaction

a new, cheaper, and more convenient edition of Dr. Gibson's book. It was greatly wanted. Dr. Gibson has given theological students just what they want, and we should like to think that it was in the hands of every candidate for orders.'—*Guardian.*

AN INTRODUCTION TO THE HISTORY OF RELIGION. By F. B. JEVONS, M.A., Litt.D., Principal of Bishop Hatfield's Hall. *Demy 8vo.* 10s. 6d.

'The merit of this book lies in the penetration, the singular acuteness and force of the author's judgment. He is at once critical and luminous, at once just and suggestive. A comprehensive and thorough book.'—*Birmingham Post.*

THE DOCTRINE OF THE INCARNATION. By R. L. OTTLEY, M.A., late fellow of Magdalen College, Oxon., and Principal of Pusey House. *In Two Volumes. Demy 8vo.* 15s.

'A clear and remarkably full account of the main currents of speculation. Scholarly precision . . . genuine tolerance . . . intense interest in his subject—are Mr. Ottley's merits.'—*Guardian.*

AN INTRODUCTION TO THE HISTORY OF THE CREEDS. By A. E. BURN, B.D., Examining Chaplain to the Bishop of Lichfield. *Demy 8vo.* 10s. 6d.

'This book may be expected to hold its place as an authority on its subject.'—*Spectator.*

THE PHILOSOPHY OF RELIGION IN ENGLAND AND AMERICA. By ALFRED CALDECOTT, D.D., *Demy 8vo.* 10s. 6d.

'Singularly well-informed, comprehensive, and fair.'—*Glasgow Herald.*

'A lucid and informative account, which certainly deserves a place in every philosophical library.'—*Scotsman.*

The Churchman's Library

General Editor, J. H. BURN, B.D., Examining Chaplain to the Bishop of Aberdeen.

THE BEGINNINGS OF ENGLISH CHRISTIANITY. By W. E. COLLINS, M.A. With Map. *Cr. 8vo.* 3s. 6d.

'An excellent example of thorough and fresh historical work.'—*Guardian.*

SOME NEW TESTAMENT PROBLEMS. By ARTHUR WRIGHT, M.A., Fellow of Queen's College, Cambridge. *Crown 8vo.* 6s.

'Real students will revel in these reverent, acute, and pregnant essays in Biblical scholarship.'—*Great Thoughts.*

THE KINGDOM OF HEAVEN HERE AND HEREAFTER. By CANON WINTERBOTHAM, M.A., B.Sc., LL.B. *Cr. 8vo.* 3s. 6d.

'A most able book at once exceedingly thoughtful and richly suggestive.'—*Glasgow Herald.*

THE WORKMANSHIP OF THE PRAYER BOOK: Its Literary and Liturgical Aspects. By J. DOWDEN, D.D., Lord Bishop of Edinburgh. *Crown 8vo.* 3s. 6d.

'Scholarly and interesting.'—*Manchester Guardian.*

EVOLUTION. By F. B. JEVONS, M.A., Litt.D., Principal of Hatfield Hall, Durham. *Crown 8vo.* 3s. 6d.

'A well-written book, full of sound thinking happily expressed.'—*Manchester Guardian.*

The Churchman's Bible

General Editor, J. H. BURN, B.D.

Messrs. METHUEN are issuing a series of expositions upon most of the books of the Bible. The volumes will be practical and devotional, and the text of the authorised version is explained in sections, which will correspond as far as possible with the Church Lectionary.

THE EPISTLE OF ST. PAUL TO THE GALATIANS. Explained by A. W. ROBINSON, Vicar of All Hallows, Barking. *Fcap. 8vo.* 1s. 6d. net.

'The most attractive, sensible, and instructive manual for people at large, which we have ever seen.'—*Church Gazette.*

ECCLESIASTES. Explained by A. W. STREANE, D.D. *Fcap. 8vo.* 1s. 6d. net.

'Scholarly suggestive, and particularly interesting.'—*Bookman.*

THE EPISTLE OF PAUL THE APOSTLE TO THE PHILIPPIANS. Explained by C. R. D. BIGGS, B.D. *Fcap. 8vo.* 1s. 6d. net.

'Mr. Biggs' work is very thorough, and he has managed to compress a good deal of information into a limited space.'
—*Guardian.*

THE EPISTLE OF ST. JAMES. Edited by H. W. FULFORD, M.A. *Fcap. 8vo.* 1s. 6d. net.

The Library of Devotion

Pott 8vo, cloth, 2s.; leather, 2s. 6d. net.

'This series is excellent.'—THE BISHOP OF LONDON.
'Very delightful.'—THE BISHOP OF BATH AND WELLS.
'Well worth the attention of the Clergy.'—THE BISHOP OF LICHFIELD.
'The new "Library of Devotion" is excellent.'—THE BISHOP OF PETERBOROUGH.
'Charming.'—*Record.* 'Delightful.'—*Church Bells.*

THE CONFESSIONS OF ST. AUGUSTINE. Newly Translated, with an Introduction and Notes, by C. BIGG, D.D., late Student of Christ Church. *Third Edition.*
'The translation is an excellent piece of English, and the introduction is a masterly exposition. We augur well of a series which begins so satisfactorily.'—*Times.*

THE CHRISTIAN YEAR. By JOHN KEBLE. With Introduction and Notes by WALTER LOCK, D.D., Warden of Keble College, Ireland Professor at Oxford.

THE IMITATION OF CHRIST. A Revised Translation, with an Introduction, by C. BIGG, D.D., late Student of Christ Church. *Second Edition.*
A practically new translation of this book, which the reader has, almost for the first time, exactly in the shape in which it left the hands of the author.

A BOOK OF DEVOTIONS. By J. W. STANBRIDGE, B.D., Rector of Bainton, Canon of York, and sometime Fellow of St. John's College, Oxford.
'It is probably the best book of its kind. It deserves high commendation.'—*Church Gazette.*

LYRA INNOCENTIUM. By JOHN KEBLE. Edited, with Introduction and Notes, by WALTER LOCK, D.D., Warden of Keble College, Oxford.
'This sweet and fragrant book has never been published more attractively.'—*Academy.*

A SERIOUS CALL TO A DEVOUT AND HOLY LIFE. By WILLIAM LAW. Edited, with an Introduction, by C. BIGG, D.D., late Student of Christ Church.
This is a reprint, word for word and line for line, of the *Editio Princeps.*

THE TEMPLE. By GEORGE HERBERT. Edited, with an Introduction and Notes, by E. C. S. GIBSON, D.D., Vicar of Leeds.
This edition contains Walton's Life of Herbert, and the text is that of the first edition.

A GUIDE TO ETERNITY. By Cardinal BONA. Edited, with an Introduction and Notes, by J. W. STANBRIDGE, B.D., late Fellow of St. John's College, Oxford.

THE PSALMS OF DAVID. With an Introduction and Notes by B. W. RANDOLPH, D.D., Principal of the Theological College, Ely.
A devotional and practical edition of the Prayer Book version of the Psalms.

LYRA APOSTOLICA. With an Introduction by Canon SCOTT HOLLAND, and Notes by H. C. BEECHING, M.A.

THE INNER WAY. Being Thirty-six Sermons for Festivals by JOHN TAULER. Edited, with an Introduction, by A. W. HUTTON, M.A.

Leaders of Religion

Edited by H. C. BEECHING, M.A. With Portraits, *Crown 8vo.* 3s. 6d.

A series of short biographies of the most prominent leaders of religious life and thought of all ages and countries.

The following are ready—

CARDINAL NEWMAN. By R. H. HUTTON.
JOHN WESLEY. By J. H. OVERTON, M.A.
BISHOP WILBERFORCE. By G. W. DANIELL, M.A.
CARDINAL MANNING. By A. W. HUTTON, M.A.
CHARLES SIMEON. By H. C. G. MOULE, D.D.
JOHN KEBLE. By WALTER LOCK, D.D.
THOMAS CHALMERS. By Mrs. OLIPHANT.
LANCELOT ANDREWES. By R. L. OTTLEY, M.A.
AUGUSTINE OF CANTERBURY. By E. L. CUTTS, D.D.
WILLIAM LAUD. By W. H. HUTTON, M.A.
JOHN KNOX. By F. MACCUNN.
JOHN HOWE. By R. F. HORTON, D.D.
BISHOP KEN. By F. A. CLARKE, M.A.
GEORGE FOX, THE QUAKER. By T. HODGKIN, D.C.L.
JOHN DONNE. By AUGUSTUS JESSOPP, D.D.
THOMAS CRANMER. By. A. J. MASON.
BISHOP LATIMER. By R. M. CARLYLE and A. J. CARLYLE, M.A.

Other volumes will be announced in due course.

Fiction

Marie Corelli's Novels
Crown 8vo. 6s. *each.*

A ROMANCE OF TWO WORLDS. *Twenty-Second Edition.*
VENDETTA. *Sixteenth Edition.*
THELMA. *Twenty-Fifth Edition.*
ARDATH: THE STORY OF A DEAD SELF. *Thirteenth Edition.*
THE SOUL OF LILITH. *Tenth Edition.*
WORMWOOD. *Eleventh Edition.*
BARABBAS: A DREAM OF THE WORLD'S TRAGEDY. *Thirty-sixth Edition.*

'The tender reverence of the treatment and the imaginative beauty of the writing have reconciled us to the daring of the conception, and the conviction is forced on us that even so exalted a subject cannot be made too familiar to us, provided it be presented in the true spirit of Christian faith. The amplifications of the Scripture narrative are often conceived with high poetic insight, and this "Dream of the World's Tragedy" is a lofty and not inadequate paraphrase of the supreme climax of the inspired narrative.'—*Dublin Review.*

THE SORROWS OF SATAN. *Forty-Fourth Edition.*

'A very powerful piece of work. ... The conception is magnificent, and is likely to win an abiding place within the memory of man. ... The author has immense command of language, and a limitless audacity. ... This interesting and remarkable romance will live long after much of the ephemeral literature of the day is forgotten. ... A literary phenomenon ... novel, and even sublime.'—W. T. STEAD in the *Review of Reviews.*

THE MASTER CHRISTIAN.

[160*th Thousand.*

'It cannot be denied that "The Master Christian" is a powerful book; that it is one likely to raise uncomfortable questions in all but the most self-satisfied readers, and that it strikes at the root of the failure of the Churches—the decay of faith—in a manner which shows the inevitable disaster heaping up ... The good Cardinal Bonpré is a beautiful figure, fit to stand beside the good Bishop in "Les Misérables" ... The chapter in which the Cardinal appears with Manuel before Leo XIII. is characterised by extraordinary realism and dramatic intensity ... It is a book with a serious purpose expressed with absolute unconventionality and passion ... And this is to say it is a book worth reading.'—*Examiner.*

Anthony Hope's Novels

Crown 8vo. 6s. each.

THE GOD IN THE CAR. *Ninth Edition.*

'A very remarkable book, deserving of critical analysis impossible within our limit; brilliant, but not superficial; well considered, but not elaborated; constructed with the proverbial art that conceals, but yet allows itself to be enjoyed by readers to whom fine literary method is a keen pleasure.'—*The World.*

A CHANGE OF AIR. *Sixth Edition.*

'A graceful, vivacious comedy, true to human nature. The characters are traced with a masterly hand.'—*Times.*

A MAN OF MARK. *Fifth Edition.*

'Of all Mr. Hope's books, "A Man of Mark" is the one which best compares with "The Prisoner of Zenda."'—*National Observer.*

THE CHRONICLES OF COUNT ANTONIO. *Fourth Edition.*

'It is a perfectly enchanting story of love and chivalry, and pure romance. The Count is the most constant, desperate, and modest and tender of lovers, a peerless gentleman, an intrepid fighter, a faithful friend, and a magnanimous foe.'—*Guardian.*

PHROSO. Illustrated by H. R. MILLAR. *Fifth Edition.*

'The tale is thoroughly fresh, quick with vitality, stirring the blood.'—*St. James's Gazette.*

SIMON DALE. Illustrated. *Fifth Edition.*

'There is searching analysis of human nature, with a most ingeniously constructed plot. Mr. Hope has drawn the contrasts of his women with marvellous subtlety and delicacy.'—*Times.*

THE KING'S MIRROR. *Third Edition.*

'In elegance, delicacy, and tact it ranks with the best of his novels, while in the wide range of its portraiture and the subtilty of its analysis it surpasses all his earlier ventures.'—*Spectator.*

QUISANTE. *Third Edition.*

'The book is notable for a very high literary quality, and an impress of power and mastery on every page.'—*Daily Chronicle.*

Gilbert Parker's Novels

Crown 8vo. 6s. each.

PIERRE AND HIS PEOPLE. *Fifth Edition.*

'Stories happily conceived and finely executed. There is strength and genius in Mr. Parker's style.'—*Daily Telegraph.*

MRS. FALCHION. *Fourth Edition.*

'A splendid study of character.'—*Athenæum.*

THE TRANSLATION OF A SAVAGE.

'The plot is original and one difficult to work out; but Mr. Parker has done it with great skill and delicacy.'—*Daily Chronicle.*

THE TRAIL OF THE SWORD. Illustrated. *Seventh Edition.*

'A rousing and dramatic tale. A book like this, in which swords flash, great surprises are undertaken, and daring deeds done, in which men and women live and love in the old passionate way, is a joy inexpressible.'—*Daily Chronicle.*

WHEN VALMOND CAME TO PONTIAC: The Story of a Lost Napoleon. *Fifth Edition.*

'Here we find romance—real, breathing, living romance. The character of Valmond is drawn unerringly.'—*Pall Mall Gazette.*

AN ADVENTURER OF THE NORTH: The Last Adventures of 'Pretty Pierre.' *Second Edition.*

'The present book is full of fine and moving stories of the great North, and it will add to Mr. Parker's already high reputation.'—*Glasgow Herald.*

THE SEATS OF THE MIGHTY. Illustrated. *Eleventh Edition.*

'Mr. Parker has produced a really fine historical novel.'—*Athenæum.*

'A great book.'—*Black and White.*

THE BATTLE OF THE STRONG: a Romance of Two Kingdoms. Illustrated. *Fourth Edition.*

'Nothing more vigorous or more human has come from Mr. Gilbert Parker than this novel. It has all the graphic power of his last book, with truer feeling for the romance, both of human life and wild nature.'—*Literature.*

THE POMP OF THE LAVILETTES. *Second Edition.* 3s. 6d.

'Unforced pathos, and a deeper knowledge of human nature than Mr. Parker has ever displayed before.'—*Pall Mall Gazette.*

S. Baring Gould's Novels

Crown 8vo. 6s. each.

ARMINELL. *Fifth Edition.*
URITH. *Fifth Edition.*
IN THE ROAR OF THE SEA. *Seventh Edition.*
MRS. CURGENVEN OF CURGENVEN. *Fourth Edition.*
CHEAP JACK ZITA. *Fourth Edition.*
THE QUEEN OF LOVE. *Fifth Edition.*
MARGERY OF QUETHER. *Third Edition.*
JACQUETTA. *Third Edition.*
KITTY ALONE. *Fifth Edition.*
NOÉMI. Illustrated. *Fourth Edition.*
THE BROOM-SQUIRE. Illustrated. *Fourth Edition.*
THE PENNYCOMEQUICKS. *Third Edition.*
DARTMOOR IDYLLS.
GUAVAS THE TINNER. Illustrated. *Second Edition.*
BLADYS. Illustrated. *Second Edition.*
DOMITIA. Illustrated. *Second Edition.*
PABO THE PRIEST.
WINEFRED. Illustrated. *Second Edition.*
THE FROBISHERS.

Conan Doyle. ROUND THE RED LAMP. By A. CONAN DOYLE. *Seventh Edition. Crown 8vo. 6s.*

'The book is far and away the best view that has been vouchsafed us behind the scenes of the consulting-room.'—*Illustrated London News.*

Stanley Weyman. UNDER THE RED ROBE. By STANLEY WEYMAN, Author of 'A Gentleman of France.' With Illustrations by R. C. WOODVILLE. *Sixteenth Edition. Crown 8vo. 6s.*

'Every one who reads books at all must read this thrilling romance, from the first page of which to the last the breathless reader is haled along. An inspiration of manliness and courage.'—*Daily Chronicle.*

Lucas Malet. THE WAGES OF SIN. By LUCAS MALET. *Thirteenth Edition. Crown 8vo. 6s.*

Lucas Malet. THE CARISSIMA. By LUCAS MALET, Author of 'The Wages of Sin,' etc. *Fourth Edition. Crown 8vo. 6s.*

Lucas Malet. THE GATELESS BARRIER. By LUCAS MALET, Author of 'The Wages of Sin.' *Third Edition. Crown 8vo. 6s.*

'The story is told with a sense of style and a dramatic vigour that makes it a pleasure to read. The workmanship arouses enthusiasm.'—*Times.*

W. W. Jacobs. A MASTER OF CRAFT. By W. W. JACOBS, Author of 'Many Cargoes.' Illustrated. *Fourth Edition. Crown 8vo. 3s. 6d.*

'Can be unreservedly recommended to all who have not lost their appetite for wholesome laughter.'—*Spectator.*

'The best humorous book published for many a day.'—*Black and White.*

W. W. Jacobs. MANY CARGOES. By W. W. JACOBS. *Twenty-fifth Edition. Crown 8vo. 3s. 6d.*

W. W. Jacobs. SEA URCHINS. By W. W. JACOBS. *Crown 8vo. 3s. 6d.*

Edna Lyall. DERRICK VAUGHAN, NOVELIST. *42nd thousand.* By EDNA LYALL. *Crown 8vo. 3s. 6d.*

George Gissing. THE TOWN TRAVELLER. By GEORGE GISSING, Author of 'Demos,' 'In the Year of Jubilee,' etc. *Second Edition. Cr. 8vo. 6s.*

'It is a bright and witty book above all things. Polly Sparkes is a splendid bit of work.'—*Pall Mall Gazette.*

'The spirit of Dickens is in it.'—*Bookman.*

George Gissing. THE CROWN OF LIFE. By GEORGE GISSING, Author of 'Demos,' 'The Town Traveller,' etc. *Crown 8vo. 6s.*

Henry James. THE SOFT SIDE. By HENRY JAMES, Author of 'What Maisie Knew.' *Second Edition. Crown 8vo. 6s.*

'The amazing cleverness marks the great worker.'—*Speaker.*

H. James. THE SACRED FOUNT. By HENRY JAMES, Author of ' What Maisie Knew.' *Crown 8vo.* 6s.

'"The Sacred Fount" is only for the few, but they will prize it highly, for it is worthy of its illustrious author.'—*Pall Mall Gazette.*

S. R. Crockett. LOCHINVAR. By S. R. CROCKETT, Author of 'The Raiders,' etc. Illustrated. *Second Edition. Crown 8vo.* 6s.

'Full of gallantry and pathos, of the clash of arms, and brightened by episodes of humour and love.'—*Westminster Gazette.*

S. R. Crockett. THE STANDARD BEARER. By S. R. CROCKETT. *Crown 8vo.* 6s.

'A delightful tale.'—*Speaker.*
'Mr. Crockett at his best.'—*Literature.*

Arthur Morrison. TALES OF MEAN STREETS. By ARTHUR MORRISON. *Fifth Edition. Cr. 8vo.* 6s.

Told with consummate art and extraordinary detail. In the true humanity of the book lies its justification, the permanence of its interest, and its indubitable triumph.'—*Athenæum.*
'A great book. The author's method is amazingly effective, and produces a thrilling sense of reality. The writer lays upon us a master hand. The book is simply appalling and irresistible in its interest. It is humorous also; without humour it would not make the mark it is certain to make.'—*World.*

Arthur Morrison. A CHILD OF THE JAGO. By ARTHUR MORRISON. *Third Edition. Cr. 8vo.* 6s.

'The book is a masterpiece.'—*Pall Mall Gazette.*
'Told with great vigour and powerful simplicity.'—*Athenæum.*

Arthur Morrison. TO LONDON TOWN. By ARTHUR MORRISON, Author of 'Tales of Mean Streets,' etc. *Second Edition. Crown 8vo.* 6s.

'We have idyllic pictures, woodland scenes full of tenderness and grace. . . . This is the new Mr. Arthur Morrison gracious and tender, sympathetic and human.'—*Daily Telegraph.*

Arthur Morrison. CUNNING MURRELL. By ARTHUR MORRISON, Author of 'A Child of the Jago,' etc. *Crown 8vo.* 6s.

'The plot hangs admirably. The dialogue is perfect.'—*Daily Mail.*
'Admirable. . . . Delightful humorous relief . . . a most artistic and satisfactory achievement.'—*Spectator.*

Max Pemberton. THE FOOTSTEPS OF A THRONE. By MAX PEMBERTON. Illustrated. *Second Edition. Crown 8vo.* 6s.

'A story of pure adventure, with a sensation on every page.'—*Daily Mail.*

M. Sutherland. ONE HOUR AND THE NEXT. By THE DUCHESS OF SUTHERLAND. *Third Edition. Crown 8vo.* 6s.

'Passionate, vivid, dramatic.'—*Literature.*

Mrs. Clifford. A FLASH OF SUMMER. By Mrs. W. K. CLIFFORD, Author of 'Aunt Anne,' etc. *Second Edition. Crown 8vo.* 6s.

'The story is a very beautiful one, exquisitely told.'—*Speaker.*

Emily Lawless. HURRISH. By the Honble. EMILY LAWLESS, Author of 'Maelcho,' etc. *Fifth Edition. Cr. 8vo.* 6s.

Emily Lawless. MAELCHO: a Sixteenth Century Romance. By the Honble. EMILY LAWLESS. *Second Edition. Crown 8vo.* 6s.

'A really great book.'—*Spectator.*

Emily Lawless. TRAITS AND CONFIDENCES. By the Honble. EMILY LAWLESS. *Crown 8vo.* 6s.

Eden Phillpotts. LYING PROPHETS. By EDEN PHILLPOTTS. *Crown 8vo.* 6s.

Eden Phillpotts. CHILDREN OF THE MIST. By EDEN PHILLPOTTS. *Crown 8vo.* 6s.

Eden Phillpotts. THE HUMAN BOY. By EDEN PHILLPOTTS, Author of 'Children of the Mist.' With a Frontispiece. *Fourth Edition. Crown 8vo.* 6s.

'Mr. Phillpotts knows exactly what schoolboys do, and can lay bare their inmost thoughts; likewise he shows an all-pervading sense of humour.'—*Academy.*

Eden Phillpotts. SONS OF THE MORNING. By EDEN PHILLPOTTS, Author of 'The Children of the Mist.' *Second Edition. Crown 8vo.* 6s.

'A book of strange power and fascination.'—*Morning Post.*
'Inimitable humour.'—*Daily Graphic.*

Jane Barlow. A CREEL OF IRISH STORIES. By JANE BARLOW, Author of 'Irish Idylls.' *Second Edition. Crown 8vo. 6s.*
'Vivid and singularly real.'—*Scotsman.*

Jane Barlow. FROM THE EAST UNTO THE WEST. By JANE BARLOW. *Crown 8vo. 6s.*

J. H. Findlater. THE GREEN GRAVES OF BALGOWRIE. By JANE H. FINDLATER. *Fourth Edition. Crown 8vo. 6s.*
'A powerful and vivid story.'—*Standard.*
'A beautiful story, sad and strange as truth itself.'—*Vanity Fair.*
'A singularly original, clever, and beautiful story.'—*Guardian.*
'Reveals to us a new writer of undoubted faculty and reserve force.'—*Spectator.*
'An exquisite idyll, delicate, affecting, and beautiful.'—*Black and White.*

J. H. Findlater. A DAUGHTER OF STRIFE. By JANE H. FINDLATER. *Crown 8vo. 6s.*

J. H. Findlater. RACHEL. By JANE H. FINDLATER. *Second Edition. Crown 8vo. 6s.*
'A not unworthy successor to "The Green Graves of Balgowrie."'—*Critic.*

J. H. and Mary Findlater. TALES THAT ARE TOLD. By JANE H. FINDLATER, and MARY FINDLATER. *Crown 8vo. 6s.*
'Delightful and graceful stories for which we have the warmest welcome.'—*Literature.*

Mary Findlater. A NARROW WAY. By MARY FINDLATER, Author of 'Over the Hills.' *Third Edition. Crown 8vo. 6s.*
'A wholesome, thoughtful, and interesting novel.'—*Morning Post.*
'Singularly pleasant, full of quiet humour and tender sympathy.'—*Manchester Guardian.*

Mary Findlater. OVER THE HILLS. By MARY FINDLATER. *Second Edition. Cr. 8vo. 6s.*
'A strong and wise book of deep insight and unflinching truth.'—*Birmingham Post.*

Mary Findlater. BETTY MUSGRAVE. By MARY FINDLATER. *Second Edition. Crown 8vo. 6s.*
'Handled with dignity and delicacy. . . . A most touching story.'—*Spectator.*

Alfred Ollivant. OWD BOB, THE GREY DOG OF KENMUIR. By ALFRED OLLIVANT. *Fourth Edition. Cr. 8vo. 6s.*
'Weird, thrilling, strikingly graphic.'—*Punch.*
'We admire this book. . . . It is one to read with admiration and to praise with enthusiasm.'—*Bookman.*
'It is a fine, open-air, blood-stirring book, to be enjoyed by every man and woman to whom a dog is dear.'—*Literature.*

B. M. Croker. PEGGY OF THE BARTONS. By B. M. CROKER, Author of 'Diana Barrington.' *Fifth Edition. Crown 8vo. 6s.*
'Mrs. Croker excels in the admirably simple, easy, and direct flow of her narrative, the briskness of her dialogue, and the geniality of her portraiture.'—*Spectator.*

B. M. Croker. A STATE SECRET. By B. M. CROKER, Author of 'Peggy of the Bartons,' etc. *Second Edition. Crown 8vo. 3s. 6d.*
'Full of humour, and always fresh and pleasing.'—*Daily Express.*
'Ingenious, humorous, pretty, pathetic.'—*World.*

H. G. Wells. THE STOLEN BACILLUS, and other Stories. By H. G. WELLS. *Second Edition. Crown 8vo. 6s.*
'The impressions of a very striking imagination.'—*Saturday Review.*

H. G. Wells. THE PLATTNER STORY AND OTHERS. By H. G. WELLS. *Second Edition. Cr. 8vo. 6s.*
'Weird and mysterious, they seem to hold the reader as by a magic spell.'—*Scotsman.*

Sara Jeannette Duncan. A VOYAGE OF CONSOLATION. By SARA JEANNETTE DUNCAN, Author of 'An American Girl in London.' Illustrated. *Third Edition. Cr. 8vo. 6s.*
'The dialogue is full of wit.'—*Globe.*

Sara Jeannette Duncan. THE PATH OF A STAR. By SARA JEANNETTE DUNCAN, Author of 'A Voyage of Consolation.' Illustrated. *Second Edition. Crown 8vo. 6s.*

C. F. Keary. THE JOURNALIST. By C. F. KEARY. *Cr. 8vo. 6s.*

W. E. Norris. MATTHEW AUSTIN. By W. E. NORRIS, Author of 'Mademoiselle de Mersac,' etc. *Fourth Edition. Crown 8vo. 6s.*
'An intellectually satisfactory and morally bracing novel.'—*Daily Telegraph.*

W. E. Norris. HIS GRACE. By W. E. NORRIS. *Third Edition. Cr. 8vo. 6s.*

W. E. Norris. THE DESPOTIC LADY AND OTHERS. By W. E. NORRIS. *Crown 8vo. 6s.*

W. E. Norris. CLARISSA FURIOSA. By W. E. NORRIS. *Cr. 8vo. 6s.*
'As a story it is admirable, as a *jeu d'esprit* it is capital, as a lay sermon studded with gems of wit and wisdom it is a model.'—*The World.*

W. E. Norris. GILES INGILBY. By W. E. NORRIS. Illustrated. *Second Edition. Crown 8vo. 6s.*
'Interesting, wholesome, and charmingly written.'—*Glasgow Herald.*

W. E. Norris. AN OCTAVE. By W. E. NORRIS. *Second Edition. Crown 8vo. 6s.*

W. Clark Russell. MY DANISH SWEETHEART. By W. CLARK RUSSELL. Illustrated. *Fourth Edition. Crown 8vo. 6s.*

Robert Barr. IN THE MIDST OF ALARMS. By ROBERT BARR. *Third Edition. Cr. 8vo. 6s.*
'A book which has abundantly satisfied us by its capital humour.'—*Daily Chronicle.*

Robert Barr. THE MUTABLE MANY. By ROBERT BARR. *Second Edition. Crown 8vo. 6s.*
'Very much the best novel that Mr. Barr has yet given us. There is much insight in it, and much excellent humour.'—*Daily Chronicle.*

Robert Barr. THE COUNTESS TEKLA. By ROBERT BARR. *Third Edition. Crown 8vo. 6s.*
'Of these mediæval romances, which are now gaining ground, "The Countess Tekla" is the very best we have seen. The story is written in clear English, and a picturesque, moving style.'—*Pall Mall Gazette.*

Robert Barr. THE STRONG ARM. By ROBERT BARR, Author of 'The Countess Tekla.' Illustrated. *Second Edition. 8vo. 6s.*

C. J. Cutcliffe Hyne. PRINCE RUPERT THE BUCCANEER. By C. J. CUTCLIFFE HYNE, Author of 'Captain Kettle.' With 8 Illustrations by G. GRENVILLE MANTON. *Second Edition. Crown 8vo. 6s.*
A narrative of the romantic adventures of the famous Prince Rupert, and of his exploits in the Spanish Indies after the Cromwellian wars.

Mrs. Dudeney. THE THIRD FLOOR. By Mrs. DUDENEY, Author of 'Folly Corner.' *Second Edition. Crown 8vo. 6s.*
'One of the brightest, wittiest, and most entertaining novels published this spring.'—*Sketch.*

Andrew Balfour. BY STROKE OF SWORD. By A. BALFOUR. Illustrated. *Fourth Edition. Cr. 8vo. 6s.*
'A recital of thrilling interest, told with unflagging vigour.'—*Globe.*

Andrew Balfour. TO ARMS! By ANDREW BALFOUR. Illustrated. *Second Edition. Crown 8vo. 6s.*
'The marvellous perils through which Allan passes are told in powerful and lively fashion.'—*Pall Mall Gazette.*

Andrew Balfour. VENGEANCE IS MINE. By ANDREW BALFOUR, Author of 'By Stroke of Sword.' Illustrated. *Crown 8vo. 6s.*
'A vigorous piece of work, well written, and abounding in stirring incidents.'—*Glasgow Herald.*

R. Hichens. BYEWAYS. By ROBERT HICHENS. Author of 'Flames,' etc. *Second Edition. Cr. 8vo. 6s.*
'The work is undeniably that of a man of striking imagination.'—*Daily News.*

R. Hichens. TONGUES OF CONSCIENCE. By ROBERT HICHENS, Author of 'Flames.' *Second Edition. Crown 8vo. 6s.*
'Of a strange, haunting quality.'—*Glasgow Herald.*

Stephen Crane. WOUNDS IN THE RAIN. WAR STORIES. By STEPHEN CRANE, Author of 'The Red Badge of Courage.' *Second Edition. Crown 8vo. 6s.*
'A fascinating volume.'—*Spectator.*

Dorothea Gerard. THE CONQUEST OF LONDON. By DOROTHEA GERARD, Author of 'Lady Baby.' *Second Edition. Crown 8vo.* 6s.

'Bright and entertaining.'—*Spectator.*
'Highly entertaining and enjoyable.'—*Scotsman.*

Dorothea Gerard. THE SUPREME CRIME. By DOROTHEA GERARD. *Crown 8vo.* 6s.

'One of the very best plots we have met with in recent fiction, and handled with that quiet unerring realism which always distinguishes the author's best work.'—*Academy.*

C. F. Goss. THE REDEMPTION OF DAVID CORSON. By C. F. GOSS. *Third Edition. Crown 8vo.* 6s.

'Dramatic instinct and a vigorous imagination mark this soul history of a Quaker mystic.'—*Athenæum.*
'A really fine book.'—*Public Opinion.*
'A powerful and original book, and unusually striking.'—*Pilot.*
'Worthy to stand high in the ranks of modern fiction.'—*Literature.*

OTHER SIX-SHILLING NOVELS

Crown 8vo.

A SECRETARY OF LEGATION. By HOPE DAWLISH.

THE SALVATION SEEKERS. By NOEL AINSLIE.

STRANGE HAPPENINGS. By W. CLARK RUSSELL and other Authors.

THE BLACK WOLF'S BREED. By HARRIS DICKSON. Illustrated. *Second Edition.*

BELINDA FITZWARREN. By the EARL OF IDDESLEIGH.

DERWENT'S HORSE. By VICTOR ROUSSEAU.

ANNE MAULEVERER. By Mrs. CAFFYN (Iota).

SIREN CITY. By BENJAMIN SWIFT.

AN ENGLISHMAN. By MARY L. PENDERED.

THE PLUNDERERS. By MORLEY ROBERTS.

THE HUMAN INTEREST. By VIOLET HUNT.

THE KING OF ANDAMAN: A Saviour of Society. By J. MACLAREN COBBAN.

THE ANGEL OF THE COVENANT. By J. MACLAREN COBBAN.

IN THE DAY OF ADVERSITY. By J. BLOUNDELLE-BURTON.

DENOUNCED. By J. BLOUNDELLE-BURTON.

THE CLASH OF ARMS. By J. BLOUNDELLE-BURTON.

ACROSS THE SALT SEAS. By J. BLOUNDELLE-BURTON.

SERVANTS OF SIN. By J. BLOUNDELLE-BURTON.

PATH AND GOAL. *Second Edition.* By ADA CAMBRIDGE.

THE SEEN AND THE UNSEEN. By RICHARD MARSH.

MARVELS AND MYSTERIES. By RICHARD MARSH.

ELMSLIE'S DRAG-NET. By E. H. STRAIN.

A FOREST OFFICER. By Mrs. PENNY.

THE WHITE HECATOMB. By W. C. SCULLY.

BETWEEN SUN AND SAND. By W. C. SCULLY.

SIR ROBERT'S FORTUNE. By Mrs. OLIPHANT.

THE TWO MARYS. By Mrs. OLIPHANT.

THE LADY'S WALK. By Mrs. OLIPHANT.

MIRRY-ANN. By NORMA LORIMER.

JOSIAH'S WIFE. By NORMA LORIMER.

THE STRONG GOD CIRCUMSTANCE. By HELEN SHIPTON.

CHRISTALLA. By ESMÉ STUART.

THE DESPATCH RIDER. By ERNEST GLANVILLE

AN ENEMY TO THE KING. By R. N. STEPHENS.

A GENTLEMAN PLAYER. By R. N. STEPHENS.

THE PATHS OF THE PRUDENT. By J. S. Fletcher.
THE BUILDERS. By J. S. Fletcher.
DANIEL WHYTE. By A. J. Dawson.
THE CAPSINA. By E. F. Benson.
DODO: A DETAIL OF THE DAY. By E. F. Benson.
THE VINTAGE. By E. F. Benson. Illustrated by G. P. Jacomb-Hood.
ROSE À CHARLITTE. By Marshall Saunders.
WILLOWBRAKE. By R. Murray Gilchrist.
THINGS THAT HAVE HAPPENED. By Dorothea Gerard.
LONE PINE: A ROMANCE OF MEXICAN LIFE. By R. B. Townshend.
WILT THOU HAVE THIS WOMAN? By J. Maclaren Cobban.
A PASSIONATE PILGRIM. By Percy White.
SECRETARY TO BAYNE, M.P. By W. Pett Ridge.
ADRIAN ROME. By E. Dawson and A. Moore.
GALLIA. By Ménie Muriel Dowie.
THE CROOK OF THE BOUGH. By Ménie Muriel Dowie.
A BUSINESS IN GREAT WATERS. By Julian Corbett.
MISS ERIN. By M. E. Francis.
ANANIAS. By the Hon. Mrs. Alan Brodrick.
CORRAGEEN IN '98. By Mrs. Orpen.
THE PLUNDER PIT. By J. Keighley Snowden.
CROSS TRAILS. By Victor Waite.
SUCCESSORS TO THE TITLE. By Mrs. Walford.
KIRKHAM'S FIND. By Mary Gaunt.
DEADMAN'S. By Mary Gaunt.
CAPTAIN JACOBUS: A ROMANCE OF THE ROAD. By L. Cope Cornford.
SONS OF ADVERSITY. By L. Cope Cornford.
THE KING OF ALBERIA. By Laura Daintrey.
THE DAUGHTER OF ALOUETTE. By Mary A. Owen.
CHILDREN OF THIS WORLD. By Ellen F. Pinsent.
AN ELECTRIC SPARK. By G. Manville Fenn.
UNDER SHADOW OF THE MISSION. By L. S. McChesney.
THE SPECULATORS. By J. F. Brewer.
THE SPIRIT OF STORM. By Ronald Ross.
THE QUEENSBERRY CUP. By Clive P. Wolley.
A HOME IN INVERESK. By T. L. Paton.
MISS ARMSTRONG'S AND OTHER CIRCUMSTANCES. By John Davidson.
DR. CONGALTON'S LEGACY. By Henry Johnston.
TIME AND THE WOMAN. By Richard Pryce.
THIS MAN'S DOMINION. By the Author of 'A High Little World.'
DIOGENES OF LONDON. By H. B. Marriott Watson.
THE STONE DRAGON. By R. Murray Gilchrist.
A VICAR'S WIFE. By Evelyn Dickinson.
ELSA. By E. M'Queen Gray.
THE SINGER OF MARLY. By I. Hooper.
THE FALL OF THE SPARROW. By M. C. Balfour.
A SERIOUS COMEDY. By Herbert Morrah.
THE FAITHFUL CITY. By Herbert Morrah.
IN THE GREAT DEEP. By J. A. Barry.
BIJLI, THE DANCER. By James Blythe Patton.
THE PHILANTHROPIST. By Lucy Maynard.
VAUSSORE. By Francis Brune.

THREE-AND-SIXPENNY NOVELS
Crown 8vo.

THE MESS DECK. By W. F. SHANNON.

A SON OF THE STATE. By W. PETT RIDGE.

CEASE FIRE! By J. MACLAREN COBBAN.

THE KLOOF BRIDE. By ERNEST GLANVILLE.

THE LOST REGIMENT. By ERNEST GLANVILLE.

BUNTER'S CRUISE. By CHARLES GLEIG. Illustrated.

THE ADVENTURE OF PRINCESS SYLVIA. By Mrs. C. N. WILLIAMSON.

A VENDETTA OF THE DESERT. By W. C. SCULLY.

SUBJECT TO VANITY. By MARGARET BENSON.

FITZJAMES. By LILIAN STREET.

THE SIGN OF THE SPIDER. *Fifth Edition.* By BERTRAM MITFORD.

THE MOVING FINGER. By MARY GAUNT.

JACO TRELOAR. By J. H. PEARCE.

THE DANCE OF THE HOURS. By 'VERA.'

A WOMAN OF FORTY. By ESMÉ STUART.

A CUMBERER OF THE GROUND. By CONSTANCE SMITH.

THE SIN OF ANGELS. By EVELYN DICKINSON.

AUT DIABOLUS AUT NIHIL. By X. L.

THE COMING OF CUCULAIN. By STANDISH O'GRADY.

THE GODS GIVE MY DONKEY WINGS. By ANGUS EVAN ABBOTT.

THE STAR GAZERS. By G. MANVILLE FENN.

THE POISON OF ASPS. By R. ORTON PROWSE.

THE QUIET MRS. FLEMING. By R. PRYCE.

DISENCHANTMENT. By F. MABEL ROBINSON.

THE SQUIRE OF WANDALES. By A. SHIELD.

A REVEREND GENTLEMAN. By J. M. COBBAN.

A DEPLORABLE AFFAIR. By W. E. NORRIS.

A CAVALIER'S LADYE. By Mrs. DICKER.

THE PRODIGALS. By Mrs. OLIPHANT.

THE SUPPLANTER. By P. NEUMANN.

A MAN WITH BLACK EYELASHES. By H. A. KENNEDY.

A HANDFUL OF EXOTICS. By S. GORDON.

AN ODD EXPERIMENT. By HANNAH LYNCH.

TALES OF NORTHUMBRIA. By HOWARD PEASE.

HALF-CROWN NOVELS
Crown 8vo.

HOVENDEN, V.C. By F. MABEL ROBINSON.

THE PLAN OF CAMPAIGN. By F. MABEL ROBINSON.

MR. BUTLER'S WARD. By F. MABEL ROBINSON.

ELI'S CHILDREN. By G. MANVILLE FENN.

A DOUBLE KNOT. By G. MANVILLE FENN.

DISARMED. By M. BETHAM EDWARDS.

IN TENT AND BUNGALOW. By the Author of 'Indian Idylls.'

MY STEWARDSHIP. By E. M'QUEEN GRAY.

JACK'S FATHER. By W. E. NORRIS.

A LOST ILLUSION. By LESLIE KEITH.

THE TRUE HISTORY OF JOSHUA DAVIDSON, Christian and Communist. By E. LYNN LYNTON. *Eleventh Edition. Post 8vo.* 1s.

The Novelist

MESSRS. METHUEN are making an interesting experiment which constitutes a fresh departure in publishing. They are issuing under the above general title a Monthly Series of Novels by popular authors at the price of Sixpence. Many of these Novels have never been published before. Each Number is as long as the average Six Shilling Novel. The first numbers of 'THE NOVELIST' are as follows:—

I. DEAD MEN TELL NO TALES. E. W. HORNUNG.
II. JENNIE BAXTER, JOURNALIST. ROBERT BARR.
III. THE INCA'S TREASURE. ERNEST GLANVILLE.
IV. *Out of print.*
V. FURZE BLOOM. S. BARING GOULD.
VI. BUNTER'S CRUISE. C. GLEIG.
VII. THE GAY DECEIVERS. ARTHUR MOORE.
VIII. PRISONERS OF WAR. A. BOYSON WEEKES.
IX. *Out of print.*
X. VELDT AND LAAGER: Tales of the Transvaal. E. S. VALENTINE.
XI. THE NIGGER KNIGHTS. F. NORREYS CONNELL.
XII. A MARRIAGE AT SEA. W. CLARK RUSSELL.
XIII. THE POMP OF THE LAVILETTES. GILBERT PARKER.
XIV. A MAN OF MARK. ANTHONY HOPE.
XV. THE CARISSIMA. LUCAS MALET.
XVI. THE LADY'S WALK. Mrs. OLIPHANT.
XVII. DERRICK VAUGHAN. EDNA LYALL.
XVIII. IN THE MIDST OF ALARMS. ROBERT BARR.
XIX. HIS GRACE. W. E. NORRIS.
XX. DODO. E. F. BENSON.
XXI. CHEAP JACK ZITA. S. BARING GOULD.
XXII. WHEN VALMOND CAME TO PONTIAC. GILBERT PARKER.

Methuen's Sixpenny Library

A New Series of Copyright Books

I. THE MATABELE CAMPAIGN. By Major-General BADEN-POWELL.
II. THE DOWNFALL OF PREMPEH. By Major-General BADEN-POWELL.
III. MY DANISH SWEETHEART. By W. CLARK RUSSELL.
IV. IN THE ROAR OF THE SEA. By S. BARING-GOULD.
V. PEGGY OF THE BARTONS. By B. M. CROKER.
VII. BADEN-POWELL OF MAFEKING: A Biography. By J. S. FLETCHER.
VIII. ROBERTS OF PRETORIA. By J. S. FLETCHER.
IX. THE GREEN GRAVES OF BALGOWRIE. By JANE H. FINDLATER.
X. THE STOLEN BACILLUS. By H. G. WELLS.
XI. MATTHEW AUSTIN. By W. E. NORRIS.

Books for Boys and Girls

A Series of Books by well-known Authors, well illustrated.

THREE-AND-SIXPENCE EACH

THE ICELANDER'S SWORD. By S. BARING GOULD.

TWO LITTLE CHILDREN AND CHING. By EDITH E. CUTHELL.

TODDLEBEN'S HERO. By M. M. BLAKE.

ONLY A GUARD-ROOM DOG. By EDITH E. CUTHELL.

THE DOCTOR OF THE JULIET. By HARRY COLLINGWOOD.

MASTER ROCKAFELLAR'S VOYAGE. By W. CLARK RUSSELL.

SYD BELTON: Or, The Boy who would not go to Sea. By G. MANVILLE FENN.

The Peacock Library

A Series of Books for Girls by well-known Authors, handsomely bound, and well illustrated.

THREE-AND-SIXPENCE EACH

THE RED GRANGE. By Mrs. MOLESWORTH.

THE SECRET OF MADAME DE MONLUC. By the Author of 'Mdle. Mori.'

OUT OF THE FASHION. By L. T. MEADE.

DUMPS. By Mrs. PARR.

A GIRL OF THE PEOPLE. By L. T. MEADE.

HEPSY GIPSY. By L. T. MEADE. 2s. 6d.

THE HONOURABLE MISS. By L. T. MEADE.

University Extension Series

A series of books on historical, literary, and scientific subjects, suitable for extension students and home-reading circles. Each volume is complete in itself, and the subjects are treated by competent writers in a broad and philosophic spirit.

Edited by J. E. SYMES, M.A.,
Principal of University College, Nottingham.
Crown 8vo. Price (with some exceptions) 2s. 6d.

The following volumes are ready:—

THE INDUSTRIAL HISTORY OF ENGLAND. By H. DE B. GIBBINS, Litt.D., M.A., late Scholar of Wadham College, Oxon., Cobden Prizeman. *Seventh Edition*, Revised. With Maps and Plans. 3s.

A HISTORY OF ENGLISH POLITICAL ECONOMY. By L. L. PRICE, M.A., Fellow of Oriel College, Oxon. *Third Edition.*

PROBLEMS OF POVERTY: An Inquiry into the Industrial Conditions of the Poor. By J. A. HOBSON, M.A. *Fourth Edition.*

VICTORIAN POETS. By A. SHARP.

MESSRS. METHUEN'S CATALOGUE 43

THE FRENCH REVOLUTION. By J. E. SYMES, M.A.

PSYCHOLOGY. By F. S. GRANGER, M.A. *Second Edition.*

THE EVOLUTION OF PLANT LIFE: Lower Forms. By G. MASSEE. With Illustrations.

AIR AND WATER. By V. B. LEWES, M.A. Illustrated.

THE CHEMISTRY OF LIFE AND HEALTH. By C. W. KIMMINS, M.A. Illustrated.

THE MECHANICS OF DAILY LIFE. By V. P. SELLS, M.A. Illustrated.

ENGLISH SOCIAL REFORMERS. By H. DE B. GIBBINS, Litt.D., M.A.

ENGLISH TRADE AND FINANCE IN THE SEVENTEENTH CENTURY. By W. A. S. HEWINS, B.A.

THE CHEMISTRY OF FIRE. The Elementary Principles of Chemistry. By M. M. PATTISON MUIR, M.A. Illustrated.

A TEXT-BOOK OF AGRICULTURAL BOTANY. By M. C. POTTER, M.A., F.L.S. Illustrated. 3*s*. 6*d*.

THE VAULT OF HEAVEN. A Popular Introduction to Astronomy. By R. A. GREGORY. With numerous Illustrations.

METEOROLOGY. The Elements of Weather and Climate. By H. N. DICKSON, F.R.S.E., F.R. Met. Soc. Illustrated.

A MANUAL OF ELECTRICAL SCIENCE. By GEORGE J. BURCH, M.A., F.R.S. With numerous Illustrations. 3*s*.

THE EARTH. An Introduction to Physiography. By EVAN SMALL, M.A. Illustrated.

INSECT LIFE. By F. W. THEOBALD, M.A. Illustrated.

ENGLISH POETRY FROM BLAKE TO BROWNING. By W. M. DIXON, M.A.

ENGLISH LOCAL GOVERNMENT. By E. JENKS, M.A., Professor of Law at University College, Liverpool.

THE GREEK VIEW OF LIFE. By G. L. DICKINSON, Fellow of King's College, Cambridge. *Second Edition.*

Social Questions of To-day

Edited by H. DE B. GIBBINS, Litt.D., M.A.

Crown 8vo. 2s. 6d.

The following Volumes of the Series are ready :—

TRADE UNIONISM—NEW AND OLD. By G. HOWELL. *Third Edition.*

THE CO-OPERATIVE MOVEMENT TO-DAY. By G. J. HOLYOAKE. *Second Edition.*

MUTUAL THRIFT. By Rev. J. FROME WILKINSON, M.A.

PROBLEMS OF POVERTY. By J. A. HOBSON, M.A. *Fourth Edition.*

THE COMMERCE OF NATIONS. By C. F. BASTABLE, M.A., Professor of Economics at Trinity College, Dublin. *Second Edition.*

THE ALIEN INVASION. By W. H. WILKINS, B.A.

THE RURAL EXODUS. By P. ANDERSON GRAHAM.

LAND NATIONALIZATION. By HAROLD COX, B.A.

A SHORTER WORKING DAY. By H. DE B. GIBBINS, D.Litt., M.A., and R. A. HADFIELD, of the Hecla Works, Sheffield.

BACK TO THE LAND: An Inquiry into the Cure for Rural Depopulation. By H. E. MOORE.

TRUSTS, POOLS AND CORNERS. By J. STEPHEN JEANS.

THE FACTORY SYSTEM. By R. W. COOKE-TAYLOR.

THE STATE AND ITS CHILDREN. By GERTRUDE TUCKWELL.

WOMEN'S WORK. By LADY DILKE, Miss BULLEY, and Miss WHITLEY.

SOCIALISM AND MODERN THOUGHT. By M. KAUFMANN.

THE HOUSING OF THE WORKING CLASSES. By E. BOWMAKER.

MODERN CIVILIZATION IN SOME OF ITS ECONOMIC ASPECTS. By W. CUNNINGHAM, D.D., Fellow of Trinity College, Cambridge.

THE PROBLEM OF THE UNEMPLOYED. By J. A. HOBSON, B.A.

LIFE IN WEST LONDON. By ARTHUR SHERWELL, M.A. *Third Edition.*

RAILWAY NATIONALIZATION. By CLEMENT EDWARDS.

WORKHOUSES AND PAUPERISM. By LOUISA TWINING.

UNIVERSITY AND SOCIAL SETTLEMENTS. By W. REASON, M.A.

Classical Translations

Edited by H. F. FOX, M.A., Fellow and Tutor of Brasenose College, Oxford.

ÆSCHYLUS — Agamemnon, Choëphoroe, Eumenides. Translated by LEWIS CAMPBELL, LL.D., late Professor of Greek at St. Andrews. 5s.

CICERO—De Oratore I. Translated by E. N. P. MOOR, M.A. 3s. 6d.

CICERO—Select Orations (Pro Milone, Pro Murena, Philippic II., In Catilinam). Translated by H. E. D. BLAKISTON, M.A., Fellow and Tutor of Trinity College, Oxford. 5s.

CICERO—De Natura Deorum. Translated by F. BROOKS, M.A., late Scholar of Balliol College, Oxford. 3s. 6d.

CICERO DE OFFICIIS. Translated by G. B. GARDINER, M.A. *Crown 8vo.* 2s. 6d.

HORACE: THE ODES AND EPODES. Translated by A. GODLEY, M.A., Fellow of Magdalen College, Oxford. 2s.

LUCIAN—Six Dialogues (Nigrinus, Icaro-Menippus, The Cock, The Ship, The Parasite, The Lover of Falsehood). Translated by S. T. IRWIN, M.A., Assistant Master at Clifton; late Scholar of Exeter College, Oxford. 3s. 6d.

SOPHOCLES — Electra and Ajax. Translated by E. D. A. MORSHEAD, M.A., Assistant Master at Winchester. 2s. 6d.

TACITUS—Agricola and Germania. Translated by R. B. TOWNSHEND, late Scholar of Trinity College, Cambridge. 2s. 6d.

Educational Books

CLASSICAL

THE NICOMACHEAN ETHICS OF ARISTOTLE. Edited with an Introduction and Notes by JOHN BURNET, M.A., Professor of Greek at St. Andrews. *Demy 8vo.* 15s. net.

'We must content ourselves with saying, in conclusion, that we have seldom, if ever, seen an edition of any classical author in which what is held in common with other commentators is so clearly and shortly put, and what is original is (with equal brevity) of such value and interest.'
—*Pilot.*

THE CAPTIVI OF PLAUTUS. Edited, with an Introduction, Textual Notes, and a Commentary, by W. M. LINDSAY, Fellow of Jesus College, Oxford. *Demy 8vo.* 10s. 6d. net.

For this edition all the important MSS. have been re-collated. An appendix deals with the accentual element in early Latin verse. The Commentary is very full.

'A work of great erudition and fine scholarship.'—*Scotsman.*

A GREEK ANTHOLOGY. Selected by E. C. MARCHANT, M.A., Fellow of Peterhouse, Cambridge, and Assistant Master at St. Paul's School. *Crown 8vo.* 3*s.* 6*d.*

PASSAGES FOR UNSEEN TRANSLATION. By E. C. MARCHANT, M.A., Fellow of Peterhouse, Cambridge; and A. M. COOK, M.A., late Scholar of Wadham College, Oxford; Assistant Masters at St. Paul's School. *Crown 8vo.* 3*s.* 6*d.*
'We know no book of this class better fitted for use in the higher forms of schools.'—*Guardian.*

TACITI AGRICOLA. With Introduction, Notes, Map, etc. By R. F. DAVIS, M.A., Assistant Master at Weymouth College. *Crown 8vo.* 2*s.*

TACITI GERMANIA. By the same Editor. *Crown 8vo.* 2*s.*

HERODOTUS: EASY SELECTIONS. With Vocabulary. By A. C. LIDDELL, M.A. *Fcap. 8vo.* 1*s.* 6*d.*

SELECTIONS FROM THE ODYSSEY. By E. D. STONE, M.A., late Assistant Master at Eton. *Fcap. 8vo.* 1*s.* 6*d.*

PLAUTUS: THE CAPTIVI. Adapted for Lower Forms by J. H. FREESE, M.A., late Fellow of St. John's, Cambridge. 1*s.* 6*d.*

DEMOSTHENES AGAINST CONON AND CALLICLES. Edited with Notes and Vocabulary, by F. DARWIN SWIFT, M.A. *Fcap. 8vo.* 2*s.*

EXERCISES IN LATIN ACCIDENCE. By S. E. WINBOLT, Assistant Master in Christ's Hospital. *Crown 8vo.* 1*s.* 6*d.*
An elementary book adapted for Lower Forms to accompany the shorter Latin primer.

NOTES ON GREEK AND LATIN SYNTAX. By G. BUCKLAND GREEN, M.A., Assistant Master at Edinburgh Academy, late Fellow of St. John's College, Oxon. *Crown 8vo.* 3*s.* 6*d.*
Notes and explanations on the chief difficulties of Greek and Latin Syntax, with numerous passages for exercise.

NEW TESTAMENT GREEK. A Course for Beginners. By G. RODWELL, B.A. With a Preface by WALTER LOCK, D.D., Warden of Keble College. *Fcap. 8vo.* 3*s.* 6*d.*

THE FROGS OF ARISTOPHANES. Translated by E. W. HUNTINGFORD, M.A., Professor of Classics in Trinity College, Toronto. *Cr. 8vo.* 2*s.* 6*d.*

GERMAN

A COMPANION GERMAN GRAMMAR. By H. DE B. GIBBINS, D. Litt., M.A., Headmaster at Kidderminster Grammar School. *Crown 8vo.* 1*s.* 6*d.*

GERMAN PASSAGES FOR UNSEEN TRANSLATION. By E. M'QUEEN GRAY. *Crown 8vo.* 2*s.* 6*d.*

SCIENCE

GENERAL ELEMENTARY SCIENCE. By J. T. DUNN, D.Sc., and V. A. MUNDELLA. With 114 Illustrations. *Crown 8vo.* 3*s.* 6*d.*
[*Methuen's Science Primers.*

THE WORLD OF SCIENCE. Including Chemistry, Heat, Light, Sound, Magnetism, Electricity, Botany, Zoology, Physiology, Astronomy, and Geology. By R. ELLIOTT STEEL, M.A., F.C.S. 147 Illustrations. *Second Edition. Cr. 8vo.* 2*s.* 6*d.*

THE PRINCIPLES OF MAGNETISM AND ELECTRICITY: an Elementary Text-Book. By P. L. GRAY, B.Sc., formerly Lecturer in Physics in Mason University College, Birmingham. With 181 Diagrams. *Crown 8vo.* 3*s.* 6*d.*

Textbooks of Technology
Edited by PROFESSORS GARNETT and WERTHEIMER.

HOW TO MAKE A DRESS. By J. A. E. WOOD. *Illustrated. Second Edition. Cr. 8vo. 1s. 6d.*

CARPENTRY AND JOINERY. By F. C. WEBBER. With many Illustrations. *Second Edition. Cr. 8vo. 3s. 6d.*
'An admirable elementary text-book on the subject.'—*Builder.*

PRACTICAL MECHANICS. By SIDNEY H. WELLS. With 75 Illustrations and Diagrams. *Cr. 8vo. 3s. 6d.*

PRACTICAL PHYSICS. By H. STROUD, D.Sc., M.A., Professor of Physics in the Durham College of Science, Newcastle-on-Tyne. Fully illustrated. *Crown 8vo. 3s. 6d.*

MILLINERY, THEORETICAL, AND PRACTICAL. By CLARE HILL, Registered Teacher to the City and Guilds of London Institute. With numerous Diagrams. *Crown 8vo. 2s.*

PRACTICAL CHEMISTRY. By W. FRENCH, M.A., Principal of the Storey Institute, Lancaster. Part I. With numerous diagrams. *Crown 8vo. 1s. 6d.*
'An excellent and eminently practical little book.'—*Schoolmaster.*

ENGLISH

ENGLISH RECORDS. A Companion to the History of England. By H. E. MALDEN, M.A. *Crown 8vo. 3s. 6d.*

THE ENGLISH CITIZEN: HIS RIGHTS AND DUTIES. By H. E. MALDEN, M.A. *1s. 6d.*

A DIGEST OF DEDUCTIVE LOGIC. By JOHNSON BARKER, B.A. *Crown 8vo. 2s. 6d.*

A CLASS-BOOK OF DICTATION PASSAGES. By W. WILLIAMSON, B.A. *Fourth Edition. Cr. 8vo. 1s. 6d.*

A SHORT STORY OF ENGLISH LITERATURE. By EMMA S. MELLOWS. *Crown 8vo. 3s. 6d.*
'A lucid and well-arranged account of the growth of English literature.'—*Pall Mall Gazette.*

TEST CARDS IN EUCLID AND ALGEBRA. By D. S. CALDERWOOD, Headmaster of the Normal School, Edinburgh. In three packets of 40, with Answers. 1s. Or in three Books, price 2d., 2d., and 3d.

THE METRIC SYSTEM. By LEON DELBOS. *Crown 8vo. 2s.*
A theoretical and practical guide, for use in elementary schools and by the general reader.

METHUEN'S COMMERCIAL SERIES
Edited by H. DE B. GIBBINS, Litt.D., M.A.

BRITISH COMMERCE AND COLONIES FROM ELIZABETH TO VICTORIA. By H. DE B. GIBBINS, Litt.D., M.A. *Third Edition. 2s.*

COMMERCIAL EXAMINATION PAPERS. By H. DE B. GIBBINS, Litt.D., M.A. *1s. 6d.*

THE ECONOMICS OF COMMERCE. By H. DE B. GIBBINS, Litt.D., M.A. *1s. 6d.*

FRENCH COMMERCIAL CORRESPONDENCE. By S. E. BALLY, Master at the Manchester Grammar School. *Second Edition. 2s.*

GERMAN COMMERCIAL CORRESPONDENCE. By S. E. BALLY. With Vocabulary. *2s. 6d.*

A FRENCH COMMERCIAL READER. By S. E. BALLY. *Second Edition. 2s.*

MESSRS. METHUEN'S CATALOGUE 47

A GERMAN COMMERCIAL READER. By S. E. BALLY. With Vocabulary. 2s.

COMMERCIAL GEOGRAPHY, with special reference to the British Empire. By L. W. LYDE, M.A. *Third Edition.* 2s.

A PRIMER OF BUSINESS. By S. JACKSON, M.A. *Third Ed.* 1s. 6d.

COMMERCIAL ARITHMETIC. By F. G. TAYLOR, M.A. *Third Edition.* 1s. 6d.

PRÉCIS WRITING AND OFFICE CORRESPONDENCE. By E. E. WHITFIELD, M.A. 2s.

A GUIDE TO PROFESSIONS AND BUSINESS. By H. JONES. 1s. 6d.

THE PRINCIPLES OF BOOK-KEEPING BY DOUBLE ENTRY. By J. E. B. M'ALLEN, M.A. *Cr. 8vo.* 2s.

COMMERCIAL LAW. By W. DOUGLAS EDWARDS. 2s.

WORKS BY A. M. M. STEDMAN, M.A.

INITIA LATINA: Easy Lessons on Elementary Accidence. *Fourth Edition. Fcap. 8vo.* 1s.

FIRST LATIN LESSONS. *Sixth Edition. Crown 8vo.* 2s.

FIRST LATIN READER. With Notes adapted to the Shorter Latin Primer and Vocabulary. *Fifth Edition revised.* 18mo. 1s. 6d.

EASY SELECTIONS FROM CÆSAR. Part I. The Helvetian War. *Second Edition.* 18mo. 1s.

EASY SELECTIONS FROM LIVY. Part I. The Kings of Rome. 18mo. *Second Edition.* 1s. 6d.

EASY LATIN PASSAGES FOR UNSEEN TRANSLATION. *Seventh Edition. Fcap. 8vo.* 1s. 6d.

EXEMPLA LATINA. First Lessons in Latin Accidence. With Vocabulary. *Crown 8vo.* 1s.

EASY LATIN EXERCISES ON THE SYNTAX OF THE SHORTER AND REVISED LATIN PRIMER. With Vocabulary. *Eighth and cheaper Edition, re-written. Crown 8vo.* 1s. 6d. Issued with the consent of Dr. Kennedy. KEY 3s. *net.*

THE LATIN COMPOUND SENTENCE: Rules and Exercises. *Second Edition. Cr. 8vo.* 1s. 6d. With Vocabulary. 2s.

NOTANDA QUAEDAM: Miscellaneous Latin Exercises on Common Rules and Idioms. *Fourth Edition. Fcap. 8vo.* 1s. 6d. With Vocabulary. 2s. Key, 2s. *net.*

LATIN VOCABULARIES FOR REPETITION: Arranged according to Subjects. *Ninth Edition. Fcap. 8vo.* 1s. 6d.

A VOCABULARY OF LATIN IDIOMS. 18mo. *Second Edition.* 1s.

STEPS TO GREEK. *Second Edition, Revised.* 18mo. 1s.

A SHORTER GREEK PRIMER. *Crown 8vo.* 1s. 6d.

EASY GREEK PASSAGES FOR UNSEEN TRANSLATION. *Third Edition Revised. Fcap. 8vo.* 1s. 6d.

GREEK VOCABULARIES FOR REPETITION. Arranged according to Subjects. *Second Edition. Fcap. 8vo.* 1s. 6d.

GREEK TESTAMENT SELECTIONS. For the use of Schools. *Third Edition.* With Introduction, Notes, and Vocabulary. *Fcap. 8vo.* 2s. 6d.

STEPS TO FRENCH. *Fifth Edition.* 18mo. 8d.

FIRST FRENCH LESSONS. *Fifth Edition Revised. Crown 8vo.* 1s.

EASY FRENCH PASSAGES FOR UNSEEN TRANSLATION. *Fourth Edition revised. Fcap. 8vo.* 1s. 6d.

EASY FRENCH EXERCISES ON ELEMENTARY SYNTAX. With Vocabulary. *Second Edition. Crown 8vo.* 2s. 6d. KEY 3s. *net.*

FRENCH VOCABULARIES FOR REPETITION: Arranged according to Subjects. *Ninth Edition. Fcap. 8vo.* 1s.

SCHOOL EXAMINATION SERIES

EDITED BY A. M. M. STEDMAN, M.A. *Crown 8vo.* 2s. 6d.

FRENCH EXAMINATION PAPERS IN MISCELLANEOUS GRAMMAR AND IDIOMS. By A. M. M. STEDMAN, M.A. *Eleventh Edition.*

> A KEY, issued to Tutors and Private Students only, to be had on application to the Publishers. *Fourth Edition. Crown 8vo.* 6s. *net.*

LATIN EXAMINATION PAPERS IN MISCELLANEOUS GRAMMAR AND IDIOMS. By A. M. M. STEDMAN, M.A. *Tenth Edition.*

> KEY (*Fourth Edition*) issued as above. 6s. *net.*

GREEK EXAMINATION PAPERS IN MISCELLANEOUS GRAMMAR AND IDIOMS. By A. M. M. STEDMAN, M.A. *Sixth Edition.*

> KEY (*Second Edition*) issued as above. 6s. *net.*

GERMAN EXAMINATION PAPERS IN MISCELLANEOUS GRAMMAR AND IDIOMS. By R. J MORICH, Clifton College. *Fifth Edition.*

> KEY (*Second Edition*) issued as above. 6s. *net.*

HISTORY AND GEOGRAPHY EXAMINATION PAPERS. By C. H. SPENCE, M.A., Clifton College. *Second Edition.*

PHYSICS EXAMINATION PAPERS. By R. E. STEEL, M.A., F.C.S.

GENERAL KNOWLEDGE EXAMINATION PAPERS. By A. M. M. STEDMAN, M.A. *Third Edition.*

> KEY (*Second Edition*) issued as above. 7s. *net.*

EXAMINATION PAPERS IN ENGLISH HISTORY. By J. TAIT PLOWDEN-WARDLAW, B.A., King's College, Cambridge. *Crown 8vo.* 2s. 6d.

www.ingramcontent.com/pod-product-compliance
Lightning Source LLC
Chambersburg PA
CBHW032049230426
43672CB00009B/1533